SEEING MAHLER: MUSIC AND THE LANGUAGE OF ANTISEMITISM IN FIN-DE-SIÈCLE VIENNA

WITHDRAWN

For Sander and Richard, with Thanks

Seeing Mahler: Music and the Language of Antisemitism in Fin-de-Siècle Vienna

K.M. KNITTEL
The University of Texas at Austin, USA

Routledge
Taylor & Francis Group

LONDON AND NEW YORK

First published 2010 by Ashgate Publishing

2 Park Square, Milton Park, Abingdon, Oxon OX14 4RN
711 Third Avenue, New York, NY 10017, USA

Routledge is an imprint of the Taylor & Francis Group, an informa business

First issued in paperback 2016

British Library Cataloguing in Publication Data
Knittel, K.M.
  Seeing Mahler : music and the language of antisemitism in fin-de-siècle Vienna.
  1. Mahler, Gustav, 1860–1911 – Appreciation – Austria – Vienna. 2. Jewish
  composers – Austria – Vienna – Public opinion. 3. Public opinion – Austria – Vienna
  – History – 20th century. 4. Antisemitism – Austria – Vienna – History – 20th century.
  5. Antisemitism in language – Austria – Vienna – History – 20th century. 6. Music and
  antisemitism – Austria – Vienna – History – 20th century.
  I. Title
  780.9'2–dc22

Library of Congress Cataloging-in-Publication Data
Knittel, K.M.
  Seeing Mahler : music and the language of antisemitism in fin-de-siècle Vienna /
  K.M. Knittel.
    p. cm.
  Includes index.
  ISBN 978–0–7546–6372–0 (hardcover : alk. paper) – ISBN 978–1–4094–1210–6
  (ebook) 1. Mahler, Gustav, 1860–1911. 2. Music and antisemitism. 3. Antisemitism
  – Austria.
  I. Title.
  ML410.M23K65 2010
  780.92–dc22   2010021504

ISBN 978-0-7546-6372-0 (hbk)
ISBN 978-1-138-25361-2 (pbk)

Transferred to Digital Printing in 2012

Contents

List of Figures

List of Tables

Acknowledgments

If all of Gaul can be divided into three parts, then this project can be spread over three laptops, this third one, upon which these words are being written, now on its last legs. Mere years no longer suffice: it was the upgrades that were traumatic. And, like Caesar, for whom the Belgae never would behave, every time I thought I had finally learned all the quirks of a given machine, knew its likes and dislikes, could recover even from the accidental remapping of a keyboard by a wayward cat—the uprising of a new operating system, the storming of the citadel of new software versions, the overthrow of obsolete computers! Now new systems to learn, new software to manage, it always *felt* like war. Unlike Caesar, however, I never sought battle. I held on with gritted teeth until there was no longer any hope: System X had taken over, or some such nonsense. Was there ever a more perfect machine than the first, my PowerBook 190, now in a closet, forgotten by everyone but me? Too heavy, perhaps, but the most exquisite keyboard: I could type German faster than English on that keyboard. Always against my will, it seemed, I was forced to move on—or move up, they said. RIP.

Laptops aside, the research and writing of *Seeing Mahler* was helped enormously by some very generous people. The Vidal Sassoon International Center for the Study of Antisemitism (SICSA) at Hebrew University in Jerusalem provided a Research Grant for travel, copying, and writing time. The National Endowment for the Humanities awarded me a Fellowship for College Teachers and Independent Scholars in 1999, which, because I started the Fellowship in January, allowed a two-year leave of absence and several trips to Vienna. The University of Texas at Austin has been extremely generous: I have been lucky enough to have been the recipient of numerous travel awards, a Summer Research Assignment, and a Dean's Fellow and Walter & Gina Ducloux Fine Arts Fellowship. To everyone, thank you.

I do not think that I was aware of just how many libraries would be involved with this project when I began, but I have been helped by librarians and libraries all across the United States and in Vienna. The Wiener Stadt- und Landesbibliothek, housed in the Rathaus, is Vienna's main depository for newspapers. I want to thank the generous staff for their kindness and patience concerning my many requests for photocopies over my many visits to—and many hours spent in—their reading room. The Österreichische Nationalbibliothek, in particular the purveyors of the Vondenhoff collection, were wonderful correspondents, fulfilling my many requests for materials from their collection. I thank them for their willingness to help me from afar and for the gift of their time.

In the United States, I thank Paula Morgan, former music librarian at Princeton University, with pleasure, and also the Princeton Interlibrary Loan office for their help and patience. I was also greatly assisted by Elizabeth Davis at Columbia University; Majorie Hatten at the University of Pennsylvania Music Library (and particularly her continued help even after she moved on to an administrative position); the staff at the West Point United States Military Academy Library; the Arnold Schoenberg Institute, formerly located at the University of Southern California; the staff in the newspaper collection at the Library of Congress; and, last but in no way least, our own Dr David Hunter and the wonderful staff at both the Fine Arts Library and the Perry-Castañeda Library, here at The University of Texas at Austin. Over the years, I sent many queries to libraries all over the country: if I have forgotten your name, my request, or even your institution, I will never forget the freely offered time and assistance. *Mea culpa.*

The translations in *Seeing Mahler* are a joint effort, to say the least. I cannot commend highly enough the considerable German expertise of Dr Natalka Pavlovsky, Dr Michael C. Tusa, Bjorn Freitag, Patrick Hubenthal, and anonymous readers. Each took great care to turn into English some not always easy German. Michael Tusa also proofread the German without being asked, which stunned me to the point that I have yet to stop thanking him. All errors remaining are my own.

I have managed to make two accidentally brilliant decisions in my life. The first was to attend Carleton College as an undergraduate and major in music. I am reminded every day of the debt I owe to my teachers there. Dr Stephen K. Kelly, my thesis advisor and mentor, not only taught me to think, but also showed me how to think like an historian. Any clarity in my writing, any awareness of my own thought process, is due to his influence and example. Steve was also one of the first to read the manuscript in its entirety, and to offer insights that greatly helped me to focus my argument. Dr Robert Gjerdingen, another role model, helped me to understand what was expected of a young scholar in the field and made me realize exactly what kind of dedication to detail and thoroughness scholarship requires. Dr Larry Archbold introduced me to the writings of Adorno, and I confess that it was the first time that I had read something that I could not understand. That frustration clearly led to a fascination (but not an obsession) with Adorno that I will admit to in public. Finally, Philip Rhodes, my very first teacher of my very first music class: I use what you taught us every single day.

My second brilliant accident was to spend a year at Cornell University and to take a class with Dr Sander L. Gilman. I will never forget looking at the syllabus and realizing that I understood exactly what the class was about and what issues we were going to address and how. To my shame, looking back, I knew Dr Gilman only by reputation, but he quickly became my favorite teacher and the one who saw the potential in the very first iteration of this project. Time and again, he has pointed me in the right direction, often simply by suggesting that I look at a different source. The article "'Polemik im Conzertsaal': Mahler, Beethoven, and the Viennese Critics" came together through his musing on the fact that no one had looked at the reviews of Mahler's repetition of Beethoven's Ninth the very *next* year. I dedicate this book to him in thanks for his unwavering faith in *Seeing*

Mahler over so many years and consider him my true *Doktorvater*, having been offered his intellectual support ever since I met him.

Seeing Mahler would never have been completed without the help, editorial guidance, and interest of Dr Richard Taruskin. No one has been as morally invested in the success of this project as he has, and this proved to be a precious asset. He caught many an error, is responsible for several insights and connections that I had not seen, and spent so much of his own time fixing my prose. (All remaining infelicities are my own, of course!) I hope that the joint dedication of the book will go a small way to repaying the huge debt that I owe him intellectually, editorially, and personally.

It is one of the sadnesses of academic life that friends once close must now be physically separated by miles, sometimes continents. I feel lucky and grateful that I can thank the following people for their help, support, and encouragement: Elizabeth Bergman, Jennifer Bilfield, James Buhler, Lorenzo Candelaria, Alice Clark, Susie Clark, Daniel DiCenso, Joel Friedman, Ryan R. Kangas, Laura Knittel, Justin London, Alison Nikitopoulos, Natalka Pavlovsky, April Prince, Michael C. Tusa, and Jessica Waldoff. I have taught two Vienna-related seminars at The University of Texas, one in the spring of 2005 and the other in the fall of 2008. All of those students challenged me to constantly rethink my assumptions about the material and all leave their trace in this book.

The wonderful staff at Ashgate Publishing were warm and welcoming from the moment they received my query letter. The entire process has been a pleasant one, made so largely by Heidi Bishop, who never failed to be helpful and caring. My copy editor, Robert Anderson, caught not only errors, but several interpretive conundrums. I am grateful for his unerring eye. Celia Barlow, with whom I worked on layout, the book jacket, and day-to-day logistics, never failed with useful suggestions and attention to detail. I also want to thank my two anonymous readers for improving the text and pointing out several infelicities. To all those behind the scenes who helped to bring *Seeing Mahler* into the light of day, I thank you as well for your hardwork and dedication.

Finally, to Joshua Klein, who can spell better than anyone and writes better than most musicologists let alone physicists: thank you. You were the only one who believed in this from start to finish, even when I did not.

Portions of this book were published by The University of California Press, and I gratefully acknowledge permission to use them here:

"'Ein hypermoderner Dirigent': Mahler and Anti-Semitism in *Fin-de-siècle* Vienna," *19th-Century Music* 18 (1995), pp. 257–76.

"'Polemik im Conzertsaal': Mahler, Beethoven, and the Viennese Critics," *19th-Century Music* 29 (2006), pp. 289–321.

Abbreviations

AM Memories   Alma Mahler, *Gustav Mahler: Memories and Letters*, trans. Basil Creighton, ed. Donald Mitchell and Knud Martner, 4th edn (London: Cardinal, 1990); orig. edn *Gustav Mahler: Erinnerungen und Briefe* (Amsterdam: Allert de Lange, 1940); orig. Eng. edn trans. Basil Creighton as *Gustav Mahler: Memories and Letters* (London: J. Murray, 1946).

AMW Diaries   Alma Mahler-Werfel, *Tagebuch-Suiten, 1898–1902*, ed. Antony Beaumont and Susanne Rode-Breymann (Frankfurt am Main: S. Fischer Verlag, 1997); selections trans. as *Alma Mahler-Werfel Diaries, 1898–1902*, selected and trans. Antony Beaumont (London: Faber and Faber, 1998).

DLG 1973; DLG II; DLG III; DLG IV   Henry-Louis de La Grange, *Gustav Mahler: chronique d'une vie* (3 vols, Paris: Fayard, 1979–1984); Volume 1 trans. as *Mahler, Volume One* (Garden City, New York: Doubleday & Co., Inc., 1973); Volume 2 trans. as *Gustav Mahler, Vienna: The Years of Challenge (1897–1904)* (Oxford and New York: Oxford University Press, 1995); Volume 3 trans. as *Gustav Mahler, Vienna: Triumph and Disillusion* (1904–1907) (Oxford and New York: Oxford University Press, 1999); Volume 4 trans. as *Gustav Mahler: A New Life Cut Short (1907–1911)* (Oxford and New York: Oxford, 2008).

Roller   Alfred Roller, *Die Bildnisse von Gustav Mahler* (Leipzig and Vienna: E.P. Tal & Co., 1922).

Chapter 1
Introduction: "Mahlers Metamorphosen"

In a Viennese cartoon from 1905 the composer Gustav Mahler (1860–1911) is shown dressed up as Wagner, Liszt, Meyerbeer, Schubert, Beethoven, and finally in peasant garb, "orchestrating a folk song" (see Figure 1.1 overleaf). Entitled "Mahlers Metamorphosen" [Mahler's Metamorphoses], it suggests that Mahler lacks creativity and originality because his music is full of melodic reminiscences and borrowings from other composers. The caption jokes that Mahler will now make himself a cipher as well by dressing up and even acting like those he has imitated:

> Nach der Aufführung seiner letzten Symphonie bemerken einige Kritiker daß Mahler sich von Erinnerungen an die von ihm verehrten Meister nicht freimachen konnte, und überdies auch Anleben beim Volksliede gemacht hat. Mahler gedenkt nun bei Wiederholungen seines Werkes auch in den Gesichtszügen und Attitüden jenen Vorbildern zu ähneln die ihn bei der Komposition jeweilig beeindußt haben.

> After the performance of his last symphony, several critics noticed that Mahler could not free himself from the reminiscences of the masters he admired, and, in addition, also had written music in the style of folk songs. Mahler now intends at the repetition of his work also to resemble the features and attitudes of every model who has influenced his with their relevant compositions.

This cartoon is often reprinted in books about Mahler with little or no commentary because modern scholars now identify the use of melodic reminiscence or allusion as one of the hallmarks of Mahler's style. For these scholars, the cartoon represents a straightforward reaction to a Mahler symphony, albeit not a particularly pleasant one.

The cartoon, however, is far from straightforward. By 1900 melodic eclecticism and imitation were thought to be specifically Jewish characteristics. Richard Wagner had written a famous essay in 1850, *Das Judentum in der Musik* [Jewry in Music], in which he claimed that Jewish composers, since they lacked creativity or originality, could only "hurl together the diverse forms and styles of every age and every master."[1] The prevailing cultural stereotype also asserted that Jews were only mimics in other ways as well, such as in their language and behavior, emulating—but never truly understanding—German language and culture. The

---

[1]   Richard Wagner, "Judaism in Music (1850)," *Richard Wagner's Prose Works*, trans. William Ashton Ellis (8 vols, New York, 1966; rpt 1894), vol. 3, at p. 92.

Figure 1.1   "Mahlers Metamorphosen," Theo Zasche, 15 January 1905, *Wiener Caricaturen*, p. 4. Source: Österreichisches Nationalbibliothek, Bildarchiv.[2]

caricature thus makes a subtle reference to Mahler's Jewishness in the guise of a purely musical critique.

It is worth stressing that the listening experience is not—and can never be—a neutral one: like any other perception, it is structured not only by our backgrounds and experiences, but also by our preconceived ideas. Recently, the

---

[2]   The internal captions read: "Bei Wagner-Anklangen; Bei Liszt-Reminiszenzen; In Meyerbeers Erinnerungen; Bei Schubert-Tönen; Bei Zitierung von Beethovens Geist; Bei Instrumentierung des Volksliedes als Wiener Viz." [In Wagner's ringing tones; With Liszt-reminiscences; In Meyerbeer's memory; With Schubert's tones; With citations from Beethoven's spirit; With the instrumentation of the folksong as a Viennese joke.] "Viz" is likely another jab at Mahler: it is the Yiddish-inflected word for "joke." Chapter 3 will discuss language as a marker in more detail.

American conductor Leon Botstein expressed amazement that reviews of the early performances of Copland's Third Symphony were so "subjective":

> In the case of Copland's Third Symphony, what is striking is how reliable the residue of criticism is in revealing commonplace social, political, and cultural prejudices of an unremarkable and commonplace nature well outside the realm of music. At the same time, reading through the generous citations ... one is horrified by the flawed, primitive, and often nonsensical ways in which the music was described, judged, and written about. In the end, one does not even come away convinced that the critical legacy tells us much about what audiences heard or responded to. Once again, we are confronted with how marginal journalistic criticism actually is as historical evidence for musical culture. There are advantages to forgetfulness. When historians exhume the long-buried mass of criticism in the daily press, one is taken aback at what was once written, printed, and taken seriously, if only to satisfy the daunting demands of daily or even weekly, publication. Criticism is essential to history, but the subject may not be music as such but everything that sounds its appearance.
>
> ... In the absence of any recorded evidence, it would be hard to know even what these critics were writing about particularly in the cases of George Szell's or Jascha Horenstein's performances. One's curiosity is piqued but not satisfied ... The criticism itself is rescued from oblivion only by historians ... Only a handful of critics survive as worthy of rereading, and most turn out to be composers or performers, such as Virgil Thomson, Vincent d'Indy, Claude Debussy, and, of course, Schumann and Berlioz ... The narrowness and parochial agendas of critics are all the more reprehensible in a world in which new music of any sort struggles for a voice and recognition.[3]

Botstein's indictment of Copland's early critics is symptomatic of the misunderstanding of reception: he assumes not only that the listening experience is objective and recoverable and that it can be captured in words, but also that it should somehow reflect our own, modern evaluation and understanding of the work. Would we *really* know any more about Copland's Third Symphony if we *did* have, as recordings, the same performances as those that the critics experienced? Could we therefore be more "objective" than they were able to be? To be "horrified" by what early critics wrote is to be confronted by history as "a

---

[3]   Leon Botstein, "Analysis and Criticism," *Musical Quarterly* 85 (2001), pp. 225–31, at pp. 228–9; he is discussing Elizabeth Bergman Crist's article in the same issue, "Critical Politics: The Reception History of Aaron Copland's Third Symphony," pp. 232–63. Crist's point is in fact that the initial reception of Copland's Third Symphony had very little to do with the music per se but rather with the shifting American political landscape after World War II.

foreign country."[4] Perhaps music's immediacy lulls us into the mistaken belief that it will (that it should) mean the same thing to all who hear it—criticism, perhaps most particularly the "nonsensical" kind, forces us to confront that lie.[5]

Reception history can also be distorted into a longing after the "authentic" first experience of a work. Botstein seems troubled by the mundane aspects of the criticism, as if early reviews should offer a key to unlock the meaning of the music itself, as if the experiences of early listeners are "pure" in a way that ours are not or can no longer be. He is "not convinced" that the early reviews of Copland's Third tell us anything about "what the audiences heard or responded to"—but this, I would argue, is true of any review: it always tells us at least as much about the reviewer as it tells us about the music. Writers (whether novelists, concert reviewers, or even musicians) will often reveal their cultural beliefs and values more freely as they attempt to ascribe meaning to musical works than they might in a discussion of more concrete topics.[6] Rather than seeing this as a liability, however, I see it as an opportunity: the historian is thus granted an insight into each critic's underlying belief system. In the case of the Viennese reception of Mahler's works, listeners were bound to hear what they saw in Mahler himself—his Jewishness, his difference. To say this is not to indict those early critics; it is an attempt to see into the foreign country of the past. Nor can a reception historian pick and choose (and dismiss) those critics who are not "worthy of re-reading": to do so is to commit the error of searching for what one wants to find—that is, a validation of one's own opinion of the work in question. Reactions to Mahler's music can illuminate the Viennese fin de siècle in ways that other writings do not—but we cannot begin to understand that culture until we understand how Jews were seen.

Perhaps this is the place to address the issue of Vienna—and Mahler—as a special case. Vienna was, of course, the city that in 1897 elected as its mayor Karl Lueger, a man who openly "relativized anti-Semitism to the attack on liberalism and capitalism."[7] Unlike Georg Schönerer, the head of the Pan-Germans, whose rabid version of antisemitism was too much even for the Viennese, Lueger was a consensus builder who used antisemitic feelings to unite "aristocrats and democrats,

---

[4] As in David Lowenthal, *The Past Is a Foreign Country* (Cambridge and New York, 1985).

[5] For a discussion of the "work concept" and the idea that works of music exist "autonomously" outside of time and space, see Lydia Goehr, *The Imaginary Museum of Musical Works: An Essay in the Philosophy of Music* (Oxford, 1992).

[6] One of Botstein's examples, that of Robert Schumann, offers an opportunity to witness the difficulty of navigating between music and the written word. The flights of fancy that characterize Schumann's writing about the works of other composers never enter his attempts to explain his own compositional project or specific works. See Leon Plantinga, *Schumann as a Critic* (New Haven, 1967).

[7] Carl E. Schorske, *Fin-de-Siècle Vienna: Politics and Culture* (New York, 1981), p. 145.

artisans and ecclesiastics, by confining the uses of racist poison to attacking the liberal foe."[8] While remaining mindful of Vienna's peculiar history in relation to its Jewish population and its unusual place in the history of European antisemitism, I nevertheless oppose the notion that Mahler's experience was an aberration that can be dismissed as irrelevant to the general history of antisemitism. True, Mahler was not just any musician, Vienna not just any town, and the Court Opera not just any theater. Even so, or perhaps even because of these special conditions, the combination of Mahler and Vienna gives us a glimpse of something that might otherwise—in a less public place, with a less prominent figure—remain hidden.

No one, of course, doubts that Mahler's tenure at the Vienna Court Opera (Hofoper) from 1897 to 1907 was made extremely unpleasant by the antisemitic press, and it is relatively easy to find scathing comments—for example, from 1897, when the Viennese daily the *Reichspost* wondered if "the Jews' press" would still support Mahler's appointment to the Hofoper once he began "his Jew-boy antics at the podium."[9] Henry-Louis de La Grange acknowledges in his biography of Mahler that "it must be said that anti-Semitism was a permanent feature of Viennese life."[10] Botstein, in his introduction to the volume *Mahler and His World*, goes further to suggest that "There were certainly anti-Semites who, following Wagner's construct of a Jewish incapacity for creativity, disparaged Mahler as a composer for no other reason than his Jewishness."[11] Edward Kravitt makes a similar point in his book on the late romantic lied: "In spite of Mahler's remarkable skill as a conductor, reviews by Pan-German nationalists remained unremittingly negative. Their criticism was undisguisedly ethnic and often of such crudity as to sound ludicrous today."[12]

Given that most modern scholars acknowledge that antisemitism is an aspect of Mahler reception that cannot be dismissed, why, then, a need for an additional study to focus on this situation? I believe that the shortfall of present scholarship on Mahler and antisemitism has three sources: a misunderstanding of the word "antisemitism"; a lack of consideration regarding how minority cultures find themselves implicated in the dominant discourse; and, finally, how blatant references to Jewishness have been fetishized and dismissed, obscuring the extent to which "ordinary" attitudes about Jewish difference were prevalent and pervasive yet subtle and covert. While all these issues have received subtle treatment outside

---

[8]   Schorske, *Fin-de-Siècle Vienna*, p. 146.

[9]   *Reichspost*, 14 April 1897; cited in Kurt and Herta Blaukopf, *Mahler: His Life, Work, and World*, trans. Paul Baker et al. (London, 1991), p. 125; enlarged edn of *Mahler: A Documentary Study* (London, 1976).

[10]   Henry-Louis de La Grange, *Gustav Mahler, Vienna: The Years of Challenge (1897–1904)* (Oxford and New York, 1995), p. 4.

[11]   Leon Botstein, "Whose Gustav Mahler? Reception, Interpretation, and History," in *Mahler and His World*, ed. Karen Painter (Princeton, 2002), pp. 20–21.

[12]   Edward F. Kravitt, *The Lied: Mirror of Late Romanticism* (New Haven and London, 1996), p. 112.

the field of music, musical scholarship has tended either to ignore them or treat them only superficially and has thus failed to see how deeply it has misunderstood the culture in which Mahler worked and was judged.

To begin with the word itself: antisemitism. For readers in the twenty-first century, the term is forever bound up with the Shoah; it has come to mean hatred, to imply genocide, and to suggest an extreme revulsion that can only be described as a pathology.[13] If we want to write the history of the nineteenth century, however, then we cannot be satisfied with the current usage and implications of the term. Indeed, as George Mosse and others have argued, one cannot understand how antisemitism caused the Holocaust without trying to understand how it was that educated, seemingly moral human beings allowed such a thing to happen.[14] And, as he and others have stressed, it happened because people truly believed that the Jews were somehow different: different in body, in speech, in mannerisms, even in terms of their susceptibility or immunity from certain diseases. Once you believe that a group is essentially different from you (whatever the origins for this belief may be or whatever the attempts to justify it), it becomes easier to withhold empathy, to cease caring what happens to them. In the context in which I am using the term, then, it means just this: the assumption that the Jew was different from the gentile, that those differences were both racial (that is, biological) and visible. To be antisemitic did not necessarily mean one hated the Jews.[15] To be antisemitic in fin-de-siècle Vienna meant to see the Jew as fundamentally different, as an outsider, as someone for whom true assimilation—the erasure of the bodily signs—was forever an impossibility.

The term "antisemitism" itself was invented only in 1879 by Wilhelm Marr as a political slogan, and its ambiguity is well known.[16] However, for some time, many scholars have associated the existence of the new term with a "new" antisemitism, one that is primarily racial (rather than religious) and particularly virulent. The

---

[13]   See, for example, Klaus P. Fischer, *The History of an Obsession: German Judeophobia and the Holocaust* (New York, 1998).

[14]   George Mosse, *Germans and Jews: The Right, The Left, and the Search for a "Third Force" in Pre-Nazi Germany* (New York, 1970), pp. 34–5 and Peter Gay, *Freud, Jews, and Other Germans: Masters and Victims in Modernist Culture* (New York, 1978), pp. 20–21.

[15]   Kravitt, for example, seems to interpret antisemitism through the lens of the post-Nazi experience; see his "Mahler, Victim of the 'New' Anti-Semitism," *Journal of the Royal Musical Association* 127 (2002), pp. 72–94.

[16]   See, for example, Fischer, *The History of an Obsession*, pp. 23–4; Zygmunt Bauman, "Allosemitism: Premodern, Modern, Postmodern," in *Modernity, Culture and "The Jew,"* ed. Bryan Cheyette and Laura Marcus (Stanford, 1998), pp. 143–56; Sander L. Gilman, *The Jew's Body* (London and New York, 1991), pp. 5–6 and the citations provided p. 286, n. 12; on Marr, see Paul Lawrence Rose, "Revolution to Race II: Wilhelm Marr and the Antisemitic Revolution," in *German Question/Jewish Question: Revolutionary Antisemitism from Kant to Wagner* (Princeton, 1990), pp. 279–95 (on the problems of the term, see his p. xviii); and Gilman, *Jewish Self-hatred: Anti-Semitism and the Hidden Language of the Jews* (Baltimore and London, 1986), pp. 211–12.

confluence of the supposedly "new" racial antisemitism with the rise of political antisemitism has caused many historians to treat the end of the nineteenth century as a turning point of sorts, and, given that the endpoint was the Holocaust, the emergence of the "new" antisemitism became a way to understand how it was that a political platform could eventually lead to the attempt to destroy European Jewry.[17]

Recently, however, historians have begun emphasizing the continuity of "Jew-hatred" rather than the invention of something new, calling into question the setting aside of the late nineteenth century for special treatment.[18] Sander Gilman states that he uses the term anti-semitism "as the blanket label for all stages of Jew-hatred as a means of emphasizing the inherent consistency of Western attitudes toward the Jews."[19] By focusing not on a sharp divide but rather on the fact "that continuities do exist between earlier and later varieties of anti-Jewish mentality," it is possible to understand antisemitism as "a real and ongoing category in Western culture which is transmuted from age to age and from location to location."[20] Klaus Fischer and Joshua Trachtenberg both emphasize that the Jews were seen, from the Middle Ages onward, as fundamentally different, and that those categories simply came to be explained as "race" once that was an available concept. I will use the term "antisemitism" to refer to the long history and consequences of treating the Jew in European culture as "other."

The more recent use and acceptance of the term without the hyphen is one way of emphasizing both this continuity of hatred, but also an attempt to get away from the fictive origins of the word. ("Semitic" and "Aryan" were originally language groups, and the "Semitic" languages included the Arab languages. "Anti-Semitism," however, never assumes a hatred of Arabs.) As Shmuel Almog writes:

> So the hyphen, or rather its omission, conveys a message; if you hyphenate your "anti-Semitism," you attach some credence to the very foundation on which the whole thing rests. [That is, the racial foundation.] Strike out the hyphen and you will treat antisemitism for what it really is—a generic name for modern Jew-hatred which now embraces this phenomenon as a whole, past, present and—I am afraid—future as well.[21]

---

[17] Cf. Kravitt, "Mahler, Victim of the 'New' Anti-Semitism," p. 74, for instance, where the distinction between an "old" and "new" antisemitism is used to argue "not only that Mahler confronted a new kind of xenophobia, but that the Viennese and German varieties were different species."

[18] See, for example, Fischer, *The History of an Obsession*, and Joshua Trachtenberg, *The Devil and the Jews: The Medieval Conception of the Jew and Its Relation to Modern Anti-Semitism* (Philadelphia, 1983).

[19] Gilman, *The Jew's Body*, pp. 5–6.

[20] Rose, *German Question/Jewish Question*, p. xviii and Gilman, *The Jew's Body*, p. 5.

[21] Shmuel Almog, "What's in a Hyphen?" *SICSA Report: Newsletter of the Vidal Sassoon International Center for the Study of Antisemitism* 2 (Summer 1989).

Given the pervasiveness and continuity of antisemitism, it should hardly seem surprising that it affected Jewish self-understanding. While the term "antisemitism" is itself problematic, the term "self-hatred" may be even more so.[22] Perhaps, again from our perspective now, it seems to suggest that the Jews were implicated in their own destruction. According to Sander Gilman, "self-hatred results from the outsiders' acceptance of the mirage of themselves generated by their reference group—the group in society which they see as defining them—as a reality."[23] Again, if we want to write history, then we must understand not only the evolving nature of antisemitism, but also how and why a member of that minority might accept views about him or herself that emphasized that group's outsider status. To be self-hating in Vienna meant that one saw oneself through the eyes of the majority and it can be understood, paradoxically, as a drive toward assimilation—to accept one's "difference" in order to move beyond it—even though "One cannot escape these labels because of the privileged group's myth that these categories are immutable."[24]

For example, a number of Mahler's Viennese critics were Jewish. Therefore, it would seem impossible for them either to have been antisemitic or to have directed antisemitic criticism at Mahler. Yet these critics—public figures—desperately wanted to show their understanding of the dominant discourse. Ultimately it matters not whether these critics were "for" or "against" Mahler, but only whether, in describing him or his actions, they resorted to or utilized images that would have been understood by their audiences as "Jewish." Max Graf, for example, draws attention to Mahler's "modernist" tendencies; but, as I have detailed in my study of reactions to Mahler the conductor,[25] a connection was perceived to exist between the Jews and the modern age—Jews were seen as more likely to be "nervous" and to suffer more from the effects of city life. Whatever Graf might say about Mahler or his music, he is simultaneously manipulating well-understood stereotypes in order to signal to his audience his own recognition of Mahler's Jewishness. He can therefore be described as both "antisemitic" and "self-hating" as I have defined them here.[26]

---

[22]   The phrase itself, like antisemitism, postdates its origin: Theodor Lessing, *Der jüdische Selbsthass* (Berlin, 1930) gets credit for its popularization, although the concept dates back into the nineteenth century. See Gilman, *Jewish Self-hatred*, pp. 209–308.

[23]   Gilman, *Jewish Self-hatred*, p. 2

[24]   Gilman, *Jewish Self-hatred*, p. 4.

[25]   K.M. Knittel, "'Ein hypermoderner Dirigent': Mahler and Anti-Semitism in *Fin-de-Siècle* Vienna," *19th-Century Music* 18 (1995), pp. 257–76.

[26]   Cf. Kravitt, "Mahler and the 'New' Anti-Semitism," pp. 83–4; Kravitt not only fails to see how stereotypes can shift and overlap but insists that Graf was "a fervent admirer" of Mahler—a piece of information both questionable (when seen in the light of Graf's other discussions of Mahler), and, ultimately, irrelevant (since many of Mahler's other "fervent admirers" also described him using the basic language of the Jewish caricature). Graf was, incidentally, the father of "Little Hans," the subject of one of Sigmund Freud's

Robert Hirschfeld, another prominent Viennese critic, was also Jewish and often attributed to Mahler actions or qualities that stemmed from the well-understood language of stereotype. Botstein, however, is at pains to argue that Hirschfeld "was more of a threat because he was not an anti-semite, a Christian Socialist, or a German nationalist. His motives and arguments against Mahler could not be dismissed as political and racial."[27] Botstein is correct in that Hirschfeld was not allied with any of these political factions, and indeed wrote for the *Wiener Abendpost*, a supplement to the *Wiener Zeitung*, the "official" paper of the Habsburg capital that bore the privilege of the crown.[28] Botstein does suggest further that, "Hirschfeld's particularly virulent anger at a fellow assimilated Jew working to further fragment the fragile cultural foundation (or at least the illusion of a cultural foundation) of successful assimilation in Vienna was understandable. Mahler (and Klimt) threatened the very basis of Hirschfeld's self-image as a true Viennese."[29] Yet this does not go far enough: assimilation was never truly possible due to the immutable "signs" of race and therefore Hirschfeld's self-image was under siege not by Mahler but by the entire culture. That he directed this anxiety toward Mahler—and that he consistently did so by drawing on the language of antisemitism—makes him a fascinating case study. The background of the critic is therefore immaterial to my study. Far more important to me is the language used when discussing Mahler and the potential for essentializing Mahler—that is, reducing him to a category.

Finally, we have failed to recognize the less overt references to Mahler's Jewishness and thus downplayed their importance for Mahler reception. Recent scholarship has illuminated the extent to which ideas about Jewish difference were expressed in ways that are often no longer recognized as such. Gilman's work investigates how the Jewish caricature relied on a complex network of stereotypes, any one or a combination of which could signal "Jewish" to the intended audience. Indeed, it is precisely because the signs are doubled, that they could be read "straight" or do—and did—seem ambiguous, that they are so discursively powerful. For example, Wagner's *Das Judentum in der Musik* is often dismissed as harmless because it does not include a specific list of "Jewish" traits

---

most famous cases: see Lebrecht, *Mahler Remembered* (New York and London, 1987), pp. 101–2; the case is discussed in "Analysis of a Phobia in a Five-year-old Boy," in vol. 10 of *The Standard Edition of the Complete Psychological Works of Sigmund Freud* (24 vols, London: Hogarth Press and the Institute of Psycho-Analysis, 1953–74).

[27] Leon Botstein, "Music and Its Public: Habits of Listening and the Crisis of Musical Modernism in Vienna, 1870–1914," PhD diss., Harvard University, 1985, pp. 1145–6.

[28] Kurt Paupié, *Handbuch der Österreichischen Pressegeschichte 1848–1959*, 2 vols (Vienna and Stuttgart, 1960), vol. 1, pp. 119–22.

[29] Botstein, "Music and Its Public," p. 1133; the linking of Mahler and Gustav Klimt, a visual artist and one of the founders of the Secession in Vienna, was a relatively common trope of the period. As will be discussed in Chapters 4 and 5, Hirschfeld was not alone in making this connection.

or techniques in music—but to have done so would have made the essay less useful by its very specificity. Its vagueness proves far more damaging in that it can be used as a universal stick with which to beat the chosen target. That antisemitic stereotypes were often turned against those we now think of as particularly antisemitic themselves illustrates the slipperiness of the language as well as the power of these images to serve the negative pole in any comparison. To be overtly antisemitic in Vienna was to ensure that your discourse could easily be dismissed as lunatic ravings; far more effective and influential to use the language in a covert manner that did not unmistakably ally yourself with the far, pan-German, right.

My book will attempt what Marc Weiner, in *Richard Wagner and the Anti-Semitic Imagination*, calls "cultural archeology": to reconstruct what Mahler's audiences expected, saw, and heard, given the biases and beliefs of turn-of-the-century Vienna.[30] My goal is not to identify hostile discussions or overt attacks, but rather to reveal the extent to which authors resorted to beliefs in Jewish difference. My book shares with Weiner's an attempt to overcome the resistance of many modern scholars and critics to the idea that such an antisemitic "horizon of expectation" did exist in the culture of Vienna (and, of course, elsewhere in Europe) and that, even if such a culture no longer exists or has ceased to be obvious to us, it nevertheless structured the expectations of those who saw and heard Mahler. Neither am I insisting, as Weiner does not insist, that every listener necessarily responded to these assumptions of Jewish difference or chose to act upon them. It is important to understand where these categories originated and that their intended meaning in their original context was far from neutral: this language was deployed for its ability to signify on two levels at once. It telegraphed specific antisemitic content even as it appeared simply to describe.

* * *

The theoretical background for this study takes two forms. The first is the work done by Sander Gilman and others on how the Jewish body came to be depicted, caricatured, and imagined to be "other," and what the iconographic or corporeal signs of that difference were thought to be. Like these scholars, I am not concerned with distinguishing between those aspects which were "real" and those which were "imaginary"; nor am I interested in simply labeling descriptions of Mahler or reviews of his music as "antisemitic" or not. I am focused instead on understanding what the socially constructed image of the Jew constituted, how it was manipulated for different ends, and how these signs were all thought to be both visible and immutable. Some signs were physical (stature, noses, feet, eyes, smell); some were less tangible (language, essence, gesture, gait)—but all were thought to be the inescapable signs of race that conversion or conviction could not erase.

---

[30]   Marc A. Weiner, *Richard Wagner and the Anti-Semitic Imagination* (Lincoln and London, 1995), p. 28.

The second important ideological backdrop is Richard Wagner's essay *Das Judentum in der Musik* (1850, revised 1869). Although some have claimed that the essay did not provide a model for critics seeking to react to the music of Jewish composers, I show how Wagner's language provided powerful metaphors to address the presumed inferiority of Jewish music. In his essay, Wagner carefully described what he believed to be wrong with Jewish music: 1. Jewish composers were not creative, but could only imitate other composers; 2. in attempting to hide their lack of creativity, Jewish composers would often strive for an "elaborate surface;" and 3. Jewish composers, with no source for creativity, could not manipulate large-scale musical forms in a convincing manner. In addition, I place Wagner's writings in the context of other antisemitic writings to emphasize that Wagner's statements—while authoritative and influential—were neither unique nor original.

In order to reconstruct the Vienna that saw Mahler, I have chosen as my source material concert reviews, for the most part those published by Viennese writers in Viennese newspapers; cartoons and caricatures published in humor magazines; and anecdotes and reminiscences of Mahler. The second deals primarily with images, anecdotes, and reminiscences. Chapters 4 and 5 utilize almost exclusively newspaper reviews of musical events: the Viennese premieres of the first six of Mahler's symphonies, those being the works that were performed in Vienna while he was still the director of the Hofoper; and, for comparative purposes, the reviews of Strauss's tone poem premieres in Vienna. I have not included discussions by musicians (such as Zemlinsky or Schoenberg) or musical scholars (for example Guido Adler or Heinrich Schenker), nor have I looked at Mahler's own music or delved into the history of Vienna or its Jewish population. Mahler, because of his prominent public position, provides a unique lens through which we can see how Jews were perceived in Vienna. I am interested not in extremes but in the everyday, and I believe that the sources that I have chosen allow us to glimpse that "world of yesterday"—charming, yes, but menacing at the same time—in a way that no others can.

The newspaper reviews reflect both the position of music within this society, and the position of Mahler within its musical culture. Reviews appear in two places: either as a feuilleton at the bottom third of the first page of the newspaper, which would usually then extend to the bottoms of both pages two and three; or, several pages into the paper in the "Theater and Art" section, usually close to the sports news (but before the economic market reports).[31] Although not universally the case, Viennese premieres, in most of the papers, would warrant a feuilleton; repeat concerts, out-of-town concerts, rehearsals would usually receive a shorter review inside the paper. In general, as Mahler's fame grew, more and more of his concerts would receive front-page treatment, and more of his out-of-town

---

[31]   On the importance of the feuilleton, see Stefan Zweig, *The World of Yesterday* (New York, 1943; rpt Lincoln, 1964), pp. 99–110; Karl Kraus famously hated and denounced the form; see his pamphlet *Heine und die Folgen* (Munich, 1910).

concerts—especially the premieres—would be covered. This escalation continued even after Mahler left Vienna for New York.

Each of the major papers had at least one music critic, although some larger or more arts-oriented papers may have had two or more. The major figures were: Julius Korngold (*Neue Freie Presse*); Robert Hirschfeld (*Wiener Abendpost*, supplement to the *Weiner Zeitung*); Max Kalbeck (*Neues Wiener Tagblatt*); Hans Liebstöckl (*Reichswehr*); Max Graf (*Neues Wiener Journal* and other papers and journals); and Theodor Helm (*Deutsche Zeitung* and *Musikalisches Wochenblatt*). Several other names such as Max Vancsa and Hans Geisler also recur relatively frequently, although they wrote for smaller or specialized music papers (such as the *Neue musikalische Presse*, which was published in Vienna). Reviews also appeared in other papers such as the *Fremden-Blatt* (Albert Kauders), *Reichspost* (generally unsigned), and *Die Zeit* (Richard Wallaschek). Viennese writers occasionally contributed pieces to newspapers or journals in other cities, the most common being the *Musikalisches Wochenblatt* (Leipzig) and *Die Musik* (Berlin). In general, few writers wrote only for one paper or journal, and several could be contributing to the same publication.[32]

I do not claim to have looked at every newspaper or every review of every concert. I have purposely avoided those papers that were the most virulently antisemitic or overtly nationalistic such as the *Deutsches Volksblatt*, *Ostdeutsche Rundschau*, or the *Alldeutsches Tagblatt*. The *Deutsche Zeitung*, while it did advertise itself as the only antisemitic daily newspaper in Vienna, was the most restrained of these and also had a relatively wide circulation. It also had a history as a more liberal paper, leaning toward the nationalistic and antisemitic only with the installation of Dr Theodor Wähners as editor in 1882.[33] In all cases, I have made every effort to collect reviews from the major papers cited above and to gain input from all the major critics in order to maintain a consistency across all concerts.

---

[32]   On the history and political leanings of the many Viennese newspapers, see Kurt Paupié, *Handbuch der Österreichischen Pressegeschichte 1848–1959*, vol. 1: *Wien*; see also Sandra McColl, *Music Criticism in Vienna, 1896–1897: Critically Moving Forms* (Oxford, 1996), pp. 11–22 (on the critics, pp. 22–32); some information on both the papers and critics is also provided in Karen Lindsley Painter, "The Aesthetics of the Listener: New Conceptions of Musical Meaning, Timbre, and Form in the Early Reception of Mahler's Symphonies 5–7," PhD diss., Columbia University, 1996, pp. 344–64. See also Elizabeth Riz et al., *Biographische Beiträge zum Musikleben Wiens im 19. und frühen 20. Jahrhundert* (Vienna, 1992); Julius Korngold, *Die Korngolds in Wien* (Zürich and St Gallen, 1991); Andrea Harrandt, "Gustav Schonaich: Ein Wiener Falstaff, Musikkritiker und Bohemien," *Musicologica austriaca* 13 (1995), pp. 77–125 and "Gustav Schonaich: Ein Wiener Musikkritiker aus dem Bruckner-Kreis," *Mitteilungen der Österreichischen Gesellschaft für Musikwissenschaft* 20 (July 1989), pp. 28–31; Franz Endler, "Julius Korngold und die Neue Freie Presse," PhD diss., Universität Wien, 1981; Peter Grunsky, "Epigone oder gescheiterter Reformer? Richard Heuberger in historischer Sicht," in *Brahms-Kongress Wien 1983* (Tutzing, 1988), pp. 187–98.

[33]   Paupié, *Pressgeschichte*, vol. 1, p. 158.

This project does not involve extended analyses or close readings of Mahler's works. In this study, I wish to emphasize my premise that early reviewers were reacting not to his music but rather to the figure of Mahler. Especially when a critic is being vague, I identify the musical moment about which he is speaking, but I strongly maintain that Mahler's music is not "just this way." Indeed, it is as an attempt to distance ourselves from that mentality, to see the critics' language for what it is, and to show just how far the listening experience can be taken off track by preconceived ideas that this book contains no musical examples, no musical discussions.

Seeing Mahler comprises five subsequent chapters. Chapter 2 is constructed around two witnesses who knew Mahler well: Alfred Roller, a founding member of the Secession; and Alma Schindler, Mahler's wife. The first part discusses a lengthy essay by Roller written for inclusion in his book, *Die Bildnisse von Gustav Mahler*. In it, Roller seems consciously to refute some Jewish stereotypes in relation to his description of Mahler's body while almost inadvertently reinforcing others. Woven into my discussion of Roller's essay is an examination of Jewish stereotypes in light of Mahler and his reception, including other reactions to Mahler's physiognomy. Roller's essay challenges our modern understanding of the term "antisemitism": Roller was not only a friend (he was invited to spend summers with Mahler and family at their second home in the Alps), but also a collaborator (he worked with Mahler on several productions at the Hofoper between 1904 and 1907). Even though he values Mahler as a friend and artist, he is nonetheless controlled by his society's understandings of Jewish difference, emphasizing again that "antisemitism" and "hatred" were not interchangeable terms. His view is contrasted to that of Alma's, with particular emphasis on the relationship between her diaries and her 1940 book, *Gustav Mahler: Memories and Letters*. Alma gives us a glimpse of the seldom-seen uncensored views of upper-middle-class Viennese prejudices and allows us to speculate on how it was that Alma managed to overcome her own biases and marry Mahler. The image she presents of Mahler has been influential, but it is now possible to see, from her *Diaries*, the extent to which that image relies on Jewish stereotypes. Perhaps our own portrait of Mahler's personality needs to be revised and Alma's discarded—or at least treated with the cautious skepticism that it deserves.

Chapter 3 provides a detailed examination of Richard Wagner's ideas and places those ideas into the larger context of assumptions about the supposed lack of Jewish creativity in general. Chapter 4 then provides an examination of Viennese reviews of Mahler's symphonies nos. 1-6 in light of Wagner's statements in particular and Jewish stereotypes in general. Early critics of Mahler's symphonies criticize them as eclectic, formless; his melodies are banal and trivial; he lacks ideas and uses orchestration to hide this or borrows melodies from other composers. Examining early reviews in light of Jewish stereotypes thus highlights the extent to which descriptions of his music can be—and continue to be—driven by expectations or preconceived ideas.

Chapter 5 is a discussion of the reception history of Richard Strauss's tone poems in Vienna. As a composer who was often compared to Mahler, in particular with regard to his huge orchestras and skill at orchestration, Strauss raises questions about just how easily the reviews of Mahler can be seen to reveal "antisemitic" intent. In 1904, however, a series of Mahler and Strauss concerts in Vienna during a short period of time gave critics the opportunity to compare these two composers directly. Critics typically excuse Strauss's decisions: Strauss can make choices, even if the critics do not always agree with them; Mahler, on the other hand, can do only what his nature allows him—he could not change his style even if he desired to do so. Chapter 5 also illustrates how antisemitic stereotypes were often employed in ways that seem contradictory or paradoxical to us today. A short conclusion examines Theodor W. Adorno's influence and the continuing prevalence of the Jewish stereotype, even today.

* * *

For a decade Mahler was perhaps the most important musician in Vienna—he directed both the Philharmonic and the Hofoper, made sweeping changes to the latter, and even his enemies acknowledged that he improved the quality of the operatic productions. But despite his obvious talent and his clear musical results— and even despite the fact that he had converted—Mahler's Jewishness inevitably caused anxiety in many influential Viennese circles. That anxiety may have found an outlet in the language of antisemitism, a language that saw Jews as different in body, mind, and essence. Given the fin-de-siècle context, we need to question what the Viennese saw. Did they see Mahler the man, the musician, the composer? Or did they see Mahler the Jew?

It is one of the unacknowledged tragedies of German Jews after emancipation that their own self-definition is dismissed as immaterial. Whatever Mahler—or Felix Mendelssohn, or Heinrich Heine, or Karl Marx—thought about his own relationship to Judaism, their selves were bound to be defined by others. Their contemporaries would have dismissed their conversions as insincere; today scholars dismiss them as irrelevant. Attempts to determine the extent to which these men professed the Jewish faith, or were at least ambivalent about their Christianity,[34] are by definition treating Judaism like the antisemites did—as a race, not a religion. To a large extent, who and what Mahler was is irretrievable. Therefore, I would like to make clear that my study is not concerned with what Mahler thought about himself, what his beliefs were, or even how he "really" was. I am interested only in how he was viewed through the eyes of others.

---

[34]   For example, Eric Werner, *Mendelssohn: A New Image of the Composer and His Age*, trans. Dika Newlin (New York, 1963); but see Jeffrey S. Sposato, "Creative Writing: The [Self-] Identification of Mendelssohn as Jew," *The Musical Quarterly* 82 (1998), pp. 190–209.

Chapter 2
Die Bildnisse von Gustav Mahler

The Jew's Body

"Unattractive, puny, ugly, a fidgeting bundle of nerves"—these are the expressions commonly used to describe Mahler's outward appearance. They are inaccurate and only *occasionally* derive from the man himself.[1]

In 1922 Alfred Roller, the Secession artist who collaborated with Gustav Mahler on several new productions at the Hofoper in Vienna between 1904 and 1907, published a book of photographs of Mahler entitled *Die Bildnisse von Gustav Mahler* [Pictures of Gustav Mahler]. As a preface to the collection, Roller provided an essay that begins with the details of Mahler's clothing and ends with an examination of his religious beliefs, making the journey from outer to inner man. The description has been called "the most acute and accurate in existence"[2] —Roller, after all, saw Mahler as simply another artistic subject. However, the essay is valuable with regard to the study of Mahler and antisemitism in ways heretofore unrevealed. For example, in the quote above, it seems that Roller is specifically arguing against the stereotype in Mahler's case—"unattractive, puny, ugly, a fidgeting bundle of nerves" can all easily be shown to be recognizably "Jewish" traits. Yet by suggesting that they "only *occasionally* derive from the man himself," he is unconsciously betraying his own entrapment in Vienna's antisemitic culture. Roller's essay provides an encapsulation of how pervasive images of Jewish difference were in Mahler's Vienna, and how the assumptions

---

[1] Alfred Roller, *Die Bildnisse von Gustav Mahler* (Leipzig and Vienna, 1922), p. 9 (hereafter Roller): "'Unansehnlich, schwächlich, häßlich, zappelndes Nervenbündel'—das sind gangbare Schlagworte über Mahler's äußere Erscheinung. Sie sind unzutreffend und nur teilweise durch ihn selbst veranlaßt." As translated in Norman Lebrecht, *Mahler Remembered* (New York and London, 1987), pp. 149–65, italics added; all translations from Lebrecht unless otherwise indicated. Pages will be cited first in the German, followed by the citation to Lebrecht's translations: thus 9/149. On Roller himself, see Manfred Wagner, *Alfred Roller in seiner Zeit* (Salzburg, 1996). Jens Malte Fischer also discusses Roller's essay in his book *Gustav Mahler: Der fremde Vertraute, Biographie* (Vienna, 2003), pp. 11–23, although he treats it as a one source among many in order to discuss how Mahler might have appeared physically.

[2] Lebrecht, *Mahler Remembered*, p. 149.

of Jewish difference shaped the discourse about Jews—even when, as is the case with Roller, the observer was not only sympathetic but a friend.

Many scholars have pointed out that the Vienna in which Mahler lived from 1897 to 1907 was far from being a typical European city.[3] As Stephen Beller has noted, "Vienna was the only European capital at the time to have an elected antisemitic municipal government."[4] The Viennese elected Karl Lueger as mayor in 1895—the Christian Socialist candidate who ran on a specifically antisemitic platform—but the Emperor, Franz Joseph, had refused to ratify the choice until 1897.[5] In addition to the city's overtly antisemitic government, the geographical situation in Vienna made it a particularly explosive space for political life. Being the Western city furthest east, it became a gateway for all immigrants fleeing persecution, becoming a stopover point for some, a permanent home for many others. The rise in Jewish (but also other ethnic) immigration to Vienna after the 1867 emancipation, particularly after the 1881 assassination of Czar Alexander II and the ensuing Russian pogroms, may have contributed to the success of Lueger's antisemitic platform.[6] "Between 1880 and 1910 Vienna's population

---

[3]   On Vienna and the Jews, see Carl Schorske, *Fin-de-Siècle Vienna: Politics and Culture* (New York, 1980); Robert S. Wistrich, *The Jews of Vienna in the Age of Franz Joseph* (Oxford et al., 1989); Stephen Beller, *Vienna and the Jews, 1867–1938: A Cultural History* (Cambridge and New York, 1989); Leon Botstein, *Judentum und Modernität: Essays zur Rolle der Juden in der deutschen und österreichischen Kultur*, 1848 bis 1938 (Vienna, 1991); Peter Gay, *Schnitzler's Century: The Making of Middle-class Culture, 1815–1914* (New York, 2002); and *Was wir umbringen: 'Die Fakel' von Karl Kraus*, ed. Heinz Lunzer et al. (Vienna, 1999). On fin-de-siècle Vienna more generally, see Schorske, *Fin-de-Siècle Vienna*; John W. Boyer, *Culture and Political Crisis in Vienna: Christian Socialism in Power, 1897–1911* (Chicago and London, 1995); Peter Vergo, *Art in Vienna, 1898–1918: Klimt, Kokoschka, Schiele, and Their Contemporaries*, 2nd edn (Oxford, 1981); Allan Janik and Stephen Toulmin, *Wittgenstein's Vienna* (New York, 1973); Brigitte Hamann, *Hitler's Vienna: A Dictator's Apprenticeship* (New York and Oxford, 1999); and, on the musical scene, see Margaret Notley, "Musical Culture in Vienna at the Turn of the Twentieth Century," in *Schoenberg, Berg, and Webern: A Companion to the Second Viennese School*, ed. Bryan R. Simms (Westport, CT and London, 1999), pp. 37–71; and Camille Crittenden, *Johann Strauss and Vienna: Operetta and the Politics of Popular Culture* (Cambridge and New York, 2000).

[4]   Beller, *Vienna and the Jews*, p. 188.

[5]   Schorske, *Fin-de-Siècle Vienna*, pp. 144–5. For an excellent and concise discussion of Viennese mayoral politics, see Ryan R. Kangas, "Remembering Mahler: Music and Memory in Mahler's Early Symphonies," PhD diss., The University of Texas at Austin, 2009, pp. 21–7.

[6]   Hamann, *Hitler's Vienna*, particularly Ch. 10 "Jews in Vienna" but also *passim*; and on the Eastern/Western opposition and its relation to antisemitism, see Steven E. Ashheim, *Brothers and Strangers: The East European Jew in German and German Jewish Consciousness, 1800–1923* (Madison, 1982).

almost doubled,"[7] creating housing and food shortages and overstressing the vastly underdeveloped Viennese infrastructure. As Klaus Fischer comments, "Vienna was probably the most racially paranoid capital of Europe; it was here that fears of Slavic encirclement and rumors of Jewish conspiracies combined to produce a very volatile atmosphere that could easily be exploited."[8]

Scholars have acknowledged that Mahler was attacked by the antisemitic press as soon as his appointment as director of the Hofoper was made public: the *Deutsche Zeitung*, for example, asked if it were wise "to appoint a Jew to the German Opera of a city in which a strong movement against the fearsome Jewification of art is just cutting a path?"[9] (The *Deutsche Zeitung*, it should be noted, advertised itself as Vienna's only antisemitic daily paper.) The focus on such overt attacks, however, has obscured the much more insidious tacit antisemitism. In nineteenth-century Europe, the term "Jew" was not a religious category but a racial one: being Jewish had nothing to do with belief and everything to do with their immutable difference from other "peoples." In *The Jew's Body*, Sander Gilman concludes that, "no aspect of the representation of the Jewish body … whether fabled or real, is free from the taint of the claim of the special nature of the Jewish body as a sign of the inherent difference of the Jew."[10] Therefore any reference to one or more of these accepted differences would have been understood as implicitly "Jewish." As Peter Gay has similarly pointed out, the Jew "appeared to concentrate … all the qualities that … Germans found most unmanageable and most unsettling," and antisemitism became "an irrational protest against the modern world."[11] For the German reader and writer "Jewishness" was accepted as "the central category

---

[7]   Hamann, *Hitler's Vienna*, p. 277.

[8]   Klaus P. Fischer, *The History of an Obsession: German Judeophobia and the Holocaust* (New York, 1998), p. 113.

[9]   *Deutsche Zeitung*, 10 Apr. 1897, p. 7; cited in Sandra McColl, *Music Criticism in Vienna, 1896–1897: Critically Moving Forms* (Oxford, 1996), p. 101. Henry-Louis de La Grange, *Gustav Mahler: Chronique d'une vie* (3 vols, Paris, 1979–84) includes a number of concert reviews from Mahler's years in Vienna, many of which are overtly antisemitic. The title has been translated into English as four volumes, of which the last three are currently in print: vol. 2, *Gustav Mahler, Vienna: The Years of Challenge (1897–1904)* (Oxford and New York, 1995), vol. 3, *Gustav Mahler, Vienna: Triumph and Disillusion (1904–1907)* (Oxford and New York, 1999), and vol. 4, *Gustav Mahler: A New Life Cut Short (1907–1911)* (Oxford, 2008). The translation of vol. 1, which appeared in 1973 as *Mahler, Volume One* (Garden City, NY, 1973), will be reissued, updated, and revised now that the fourth volume has appeared. The English edition will thus include material not present in the French. Citations from de La Grange will be from the English translations, except where noted, and indicated as DLG 1973, DLG II, DLG III, and DLG IV.

[10]   Sander L. Gilman, *The Jew's Body* (New York and London, 1991), p. 38.

[11]   Peter Gay, *Freud, Jews, and Other Germans: Masters and Victims in Modernist Culture* (Oxford and New York, 1978), pp. 20–21.

of 'racial' difference,"[12] and, as Gay suggests, "the point of the caricature was not ... to sum up actual characteristics, but to identify a convenient target for inconvenient emotions."[13]

While the stereotyped Jewish image or caricature is one that always functioned as the marker of ultimate difference, that marker never had a single meaning; often its use seems paradoxical to us today. For example, Margaret Notley has pointed out that Brahms—or chamber music in general—could be culturally coded as "Jewish" in order to criticize perceived "rational" or "unfeeling" qualities.[14] Yet the cartoon "Darwinistische Entwicklungslehre" [Lesson in Darwinian Evolution] shows a Jewish caricature (complete with skullcap, dark curly hair, prominent nose, and shofar) evolving into Richard Wagner, often identified as in the opposite political camp of Brahms (see Figure 2.1). Here, although the artist has depicted Wagner as a Jew—ironic in the face of Wagner's vehement and public antisemitism—the whole enterprise is consistent with the function of the image: the cartoonist is implying that Wagner has strayed down the wrong path. The Austrian philosopher Otto Weininger called Wagner "the bitterest Antisemite," who was "obliged to overcome the Jewishness within him before he found his special vocation." Weininger's contention that hatred of Judaism "leads the Aryan to a knowledge of himself and warns him against himself" is unlikely to be the message of "Darwinistische Entwicklungslehre"—here the artist seems to imply a different statement of Weininger's, that Wagner "cannot be held free from an accretion of Jewishness even in his art."[15] Thus, the caricature's power lay precisely in its flexibility and its well-understood function as a negative symbol. As George Mosse has argued, the ubiquity of the image helps to explain the subsequent "surrender to National Socialism's antisemitism by even the more respectable elements of the population."[16] He emphasized that the stereotypes of "Aryan" versus "Jew" "did not seem at all absurd to many respectable members of the community who embraced them. Such racial attitudes, ridiculous to most Western intellectuals, had in fact been prepared by popular novelists for more than a century before National Socialism came to power."[17]

It should be stressed that Roller was not just one of Mahler's collaborators at the Hofoper, but a friend who was invited to spend summers with Mahler and his

---

[12]   Gilman, *The Jew's Body*, p. 96; Gilman is citing Theodor Fritsch, *Handbuch der Judenfrage* (Leipzig, 1935), p. 408.

[13]   Gay, *Freud, Jews, and Other Germans*, p. 20.

[14]   Margaret Notley, "Brahms as Liberal: Genre, Style, and Politics in Late Nineteenth Century Vienna," *19th-Century Music* 17 (1993), pp. 107–23.

[15]   Otto Weininger, *Geschlecht und Charakter: Ein prinzipielle Untersuchung* (Vienna, 1903); quotations are from the anonymous English translation, *Sex and Character* (London, 1906), pp. 305–6.

[16]   George Mosse, *Germans and Jews: The Right, The Left, and the Search for a "Third Force" in Pre-Nazi Germany* (New York, 1970), p. 34.

[17]   Ibid., pp. 34–5.

Darwiniſtiſche Entwicklungslehre.

Abb. 432. Wie aus Roof Wägeles, Schofarbläſer in Leipzig, allmählich — Richard Wagner wurde. Von Th. Zajacskowſki aus dem „Floh".

Figure 2.1 "Darwinistische Entwicklungslehre" ["Lesson in Darwinian Evolution"]. Th. Zajacskowski, *Floh*, n.d. Source: Karl Storck, *Musik und Musiker in Karikatur und Satire; eine Kulturgeschichte der Musik* (Oldenburg im Grossherzogtum: G. Stalling, 1911?), plate 432.[18]

family on the Wörthersee. Therefore, Roller's conscious rejection of some of the Jewish stereotypes and his unconscious acceptance of others were not intended as criticism of Mahler. Indeed, his essay is valuable for my purpose here precisely because it reflects the extent to which these assumptions about Jewish difference were considered "reality." In the following, I will show how Roller's essay both denies and reinforces certain stereotypes about "the Jew's body" in regard to Mahler's physical appearance by comparing his language to explications of the culturally accepted stereotype or caricature. Roller's description—consciously or unconsciously—examines Mahler's body in light of those commonly held assumptions.

Mahler's Body

The most obvious aspects of the stereotype are those physical characteristics that were thought to be "Semitic." Oskar Panizza (1853–1921), a German writer perhaps most famous for the blasphemy trial surrounding his play *Das Liebeskonzil*, wrote a short story in 1893 titled "Der opererirte Jud'." The main character is Itzig Faitel Stern, a Jewish student, who desires to become a German.[19] Panizza's story,

---

[18] The caption reads: "Wie aus Roof Wägeles, Schofarbläser in Leipzig, allmählich—Richard Wagner wurde." ["How Roof Wägeles, shofar blower in Leipzig, by degrees became Richard Wagner."] *Floh* was a popular Viennese humour magazine. A shofar is a ram's horn that has been treated to very high temperatures and is used in certain synagogue services, most notably at Rosh HaShanah, the Jewish New Year.

[19] Oskar Panizza, "Der Operirte Jud'," trans. as "The Operated Jew" by Jack Zipes in his *The Operated Jew: Two Tales of Anti-Semitism* (New York and London, 1991),

because it lacks any subtlety whatsoever, provides us with a virtual compendium of antisemitic stereotypes. Stern's very appearance is of central importance—his slightly yellow skin, his eyes, his curly black hair, and his lips and nose:

> Itzig Faitel was a small, squat man. His right shoulder was slightly higher than his left, and he had a sharp protruding chicken breast [*einer spitz zulaufender Hühnerbrust*], upon which he always wore a wide heavy silk tie ornamented by a dull ruby and attached to a breast plate ...[20]
>
> Itzig Faitel's countenance was most interesting ... An antelope's eye with a subdued, cherry-like glow [*ein Gazellen-Auge von kirschen-ähnlich gedämpfter Leuchtkraft*] swam in wide apertures of the smooth velvet, slightly yellow skin of his temples and cheeks. Itzig's nose assumed a form which was similar to that of the high priest who was the most prominent and striking figure of Kaulbach's painting "The Destruction of Jerusalem"[21] ... His lips were fleshy and overly creased; his teeth sparkled like pure crystal ... If I may also add that my friend's lower torso had bow-legs whose angular swing was not excessive, then I believe that I have sketched Itzig's figure to a certain degree. Later I'll talk about the curly, thick black locks of hair on his head.

Panizza's description of Stern—and the story itself—is a particularly extreme example, yet it nonetheless reflects a general belief at the end of the nineteenth century that the Jew was not just different, but visibly so—and the aspects of his difference were marked on his body for all to see.

Despite the fact that Panizza's story is clearly overdetermined, the physical stereotypes that constituted the Jewish caricature would have been immediately recognizable, even if the word "Jew" remained unmentioned. For example, a Viennese cartoon from 1897 criticized Mahler's directorship of the Hofoper (see Figure 2.2). Here, the Germanic gods Freya and Wotan have dark curly hair, prominent noses, large lips (Wotan has *payess*, or side locks, and a hat). The caption reads: "In our opera Freya and Wotan will soon look like this!" The cartoonist depends on his audience recognizing the obvious signs of race. Indeed, the cartoon makes no sense unless the tacit racial message is understood. While Panizza

---

pp. 47–74; original story published in Panizza, *Visionen. Skizzen und Erzählungen* (Leipzig, 1893). The story was reprinted in 1914 and again in 1919; see Zipes, p. 127. Panizza's play *Das Liebeskonzil* (1894) led to a blasphemy charge brought by the Munich authorities and he was tried in 1895 and imprisoned for a year; see Zipes, pp. 91–2. See also Peter D.G. Brown, *Oskar Panizza: His Life and Works* (Las Vegas, Bern, and Frankfurt, 1983).

[20]   See Exodus 28 on the clothing for Aaron as High Priest.

[21]   Wilhelm von Kaulbach (1804–1874), *Der Zerstörung von Jerusalem*; the figure of the High Priest is in the direct center of the painting. Source: Fritz von Ostini, *Wilhelm von Kaulbach* (Bielefeld und Leipzig, 1906), plate between pages 20 and 21.

Figure 2.2   "In unserer Oper werden die Freya und der Wotan bald so aussehen!"
Kikeriki, 12 October 1897. Source: Hans Christoph Worbs, *Das Dampfkonzert* (Wilhelmshaven: Heinrichshofen, 1982), p. 259.

might be dismissed as a madman or a pamphleteer,[22] the presence of recognizable stereotypes in "high" literature is potentially more dangerous. The more subtle the image, the easier it becomes to explain away or to ignore altogether. In Thomas Mann's 1905 story "Wälsungenblut" [The Blood of the Walsungs], for instance, his twins exhibit characteristic stereotypes, yet they are never explicitly identified as Jews: "They were very like each other, with the same slightly drooping nose, the same full lips lying softly together, the same prominent cheek-bones and black, bright eyes." The danger lies in that this can be read—and dismissed—as neutral physical description. Such a description seems innocently to reflect reality, thus subtly reinforcing the stereotypes without seeming to do so.[23]

---

[22]   Oscar Panizza (1853–1921) was institutionalized in 1905 for mental disorders possibly stemming from a syphilitic infection. He later died there of a heart attack; see Zipes, *The Operated Jew*, pp. 87–109.

[23]   Thomas Mann, *Death in Venice and Seven Other Stories*, trans. H.T. Lowe-Porter (New York, 1989), p. 290. Other aspects of Mann's story serve to reinforce the twins, Siegmund and Sieglinde, as Jewish; Mann's story will be discussed in more detail in Chapter 3. See also Sander L. Gilman, *Love + Marriage = Death: And Other Essays on Representing Difference* (Stanford, 1998), pp. 140–43.

That these differences were believed to be real, that is, scientifically verifiable, can be seen in the work of the anthropologist Francis Galton, who attempted to capture "the Jewish physiognomy" with a series of multiple exposure photographs published in 1885. These famous photographs, cited by many scientists of the time (including Sigmund Freud), were thought to capture the "essence" not merely of Jewish external features but also of the (different) nature of the Jew. Commentaries on the photographs pay close attention to the eyes, their "cold, scanning gaze" identified by Galton.[24] That the Jew was alleged to have different eyes than the gentile is reported as early as the seventeenth century—as in Robert Burton's *The Anatomy of Melancholy*, which mentions the "goggle eyes" of the Jew.[25] In the case of Stern, his eyes are not human but rather those of an animal—the "antelope's eye with a subdued, cherry-like glow"—an image that captures the position of the Jew within German society (*Gazellen* are prey, not predators) but that nonetheless implies a hidden, sinister nature. That gaze—the "evil eye"—was said to reflect the pathology of their souls.[26] Hans Günther, in his 1922 *Rassenkunde des jüdischen Volkes*, discussed the "sensual," "threatening," and "crafty" nature of the Jewish gaze.[27]

Joseph Jacobs, a Jewish social scientist, also found something recognizably "Jewish" in the gaze captured in Galton's photographs: "Cover up every part of the composite A but the eyes, and yet I fancy anyone familiar with Jews would say: 'Those are Jewish eyes.'" In an article on "Anthropological Types" in the *Jewish Encyclopedia*, Jacobs describes "Jewish" eyes as follows:

> [These] eyes themselves are generally brilliant, both eyelids are heavy and bulging, and it seems to be the main characteristic of the Jewish eye that the upper lid covers a larger proportion of the pupil than among other persons. This may serve to give a sort of nervous, furtive look to the eyes, which, when the pupils are small and set close together with semistrabismus, gives keenness to some Jewish eyes. The lymph-sac beneath the eye is generally fuller and more prominent than among non-Jews.[28]

---

[24]   See the commentary in Sander L. Gilman, *The Case of Sigmund Freud: Medicine and Identity at the Fin de Siècle* (Baltimore and London, 1993), pp. 42–9. The photographs originally appeared in *Photographic News* 29 (17 & 24 Apr. 1885), unnumbered insets.

[25]   Robert Burton, *The Anatomy of Melancholy, What It Is. With All the Kindes, Causes, Symptomes, Prognostickes, and Severall Cures of It* (Oxford, 1621), p. 80.

[26]   See Gilman, *The Case of Sigmund Freud*, pp. 42–64; and, "The Image of the Hysteric," in Gilman et al., *Hysteria beyond Freud* (Berkeley, 1993), esp. pp. 406–17; the belief in potential pathology is Francis Galton's. That the Jew possessed the evil eye can be found in S. Seligmann, *Der Böse Blick und Verwandtes: Ein Beitrag zur Geschichte des Aberglaubens aller Zeiten und Völker* (2 vols, Berlin, 1910–11), vol. 1, p. 86.

[27]   Hans F.K. Günther, *Rassenkunde des jüdischen Volkes*, 2nd edn (Munich, 1930; 1st edn, 1922), pp. 210–11, 217.

[28]   Joseph Jacobs, *Studies in Jewish Statistics* (London, 1891), p. xxxiii; cited in Gilman, *The Case of Sigmund Freud*, p. 45; Maurice Fishberg and Joseph Jacobs, "Types,

Note that Jacobs's description folds into itself far more than just a physical description: the eyes reflect the "nervous, furtive" nature of the Jew. Roller's description of Mahler's "gaze," on the other hand, seems subtly to contradict Jacobs assertions:

> It was not entirely Mahler's fault that this was the only face that many people saw and that they never really got to know any but the "nasty Mahler." He was short sighted, and, as the pictures show, wore glasses from boyhood. Sometimes spectacles, sometimes a pince-nez. By the end of his life they were usually rimless spectacles with oval lenses and gold frames. They made the area surrounding the eyes look bigger than the eyes themselves ... All round his eye sockets, the features jutted well forward. His tear sacks were small and flat. There had been an energetic lift to his upper eyelids ever since he had attained maturity, giving him a very wide-awake appearance. If they drooped a little, that was a sign that he was beginning to grow tired. They were a pair of eyes that registered intelligence, honesty and an ability to hold their own.[29]

As if recognizing the resemblance of the young Mahler to those boys in Galton's photographs, Roller emphasizes that "since he had attained maturity," his eyes seemed "very wide-awake." The careful description of not just the eyes but the surrounding features emphasizes their "normality." By attributing the effect of Mahler's gaze to his glasses, Roller protects Mahler from the assumptions about Jewish eyes, suggesting that had people known Mahler better, they would have realized their mistake.[30] Here, Roller appears both to acknowledge the reigning Jewish stereotypes and to try to distance Mahler from them.

Anthropological," in *The Jewish Encyclopedia: A Descriptive Record of the History, Religion, Literature, and Customs of the Jewish People from the Earliest Times to the Present Day* (New York and London, 1906), vol. 12, p. 294.

[29] Roller, 23/161: "Es war nicht ausschließlich Mahler Schuld, daß manche Leute bloß dieses Gesicht zu sehen bekamen und einen anderen als den 'häßlichen Mahler' überhaupt nicht kannten. Mahler war kurzsichtig und trug, wie die Bilder zeigen, von Jugend an Gläser. Bald Brillen, bald Klemmen. Zuletzt gewöhnlich ovale Brillen ohne Rundfassung, mit goldenem Bügel. So wirkte die Umgebung des Auges mehr als dieses selbst ... Der Augenhöhlendrand trat überall stark hervor. Die Tränensäcke waren klein und flach. Das obere Augenlid war seit den Mannesjahren mit dem Ausdruck heller Wachheit energisch gehoben. Sank es ein wenig, so bedeutete das beginnende Ermüdung—Bilder 52, 54, 55. Es war das ein Paar kluger, aufrichtiger Augen, die standhalten konnten." Note that Roller's essay is a commentary on the photos, to which he refers throughout his text; Lebrecht's translation has removed these references.

[30] As I have discussed previously, many artists used Mahler's glasses to create the menacing impression of a stare in their drawings or caricatures. While Roller wants us to believe that if the eyes did droop, it was a sign of tiredness and not an indication of Mahler's "normal" visage (and therefore not his "race"), one could read the passage as

As Panizza's description of Itzig Faitel Stern implies, the Jewish body was seen as ugly. The comparisons to animals (the "chicken breast," the "antelope's eye"), the juxtaposition of Stern's crooked body with his beautiful clothes, and the use of seemingly positive adjectives to describe features that are clearly meant to be negative (the "smooth velvet, slightly yellow skin", the "fleshy and overly creased" lips compared to the teeth that "sparkled like pure crystal") all serve to emphasize the unaesthetic effect of Stern upon the witness. According to Gilman, "in the world of nineteenth-century science, the great chain of being that was seen to stretch from the most human to the least human was also a chain of beauty." The racial character of beauty, codified in the eighteenth century by Petrus Camper and Johann Kaspar Lavater, placed Jews and Africans together at the bottom because "the Jew's physiognomy was understood to be closer to that of the African than to that of the European."[31] In his description of Vienna from the 1780s, Johann Pezzl links the Jew and the black man:

> There are about five hundred Jews in Vienna … Excluding the Indian fakirs, there is no category of supposed human beings which comes closer to the Orang-Utan than does a Polish Jew … Covered from foot to head in filth, dirt and rags, covered in a type of black sack … their necks exposed, the color of a black man, their faces covered up to the eyes with a beard, which would have given the High Priest in the Temple chills …[32]

The comparison to the animal serves to place the Jew and the black African together at the nadir of the evolutionary scale, seeing them as not only unattractive but as non-human.[33] Gilman emphasizes that the assumption that Jews and blacks were either closely related or intermixed "becomes a commonplace of nineteenth-century ethnology":

---

emphasizing the opposite: that when tired, Mahler let his guard down and revealed his true physiognomy.

[31] Gilman, *Making the Body Beautiful: A Cultural History of Aesthetic Surgery* (Princeton, 1999), pp. 85 and 89; Petrus Camper (1722–89) and Johann Kaspar Lavater (1741–1801).

[32] Cited in Gilman, *The Jew's Body*, p. 172.

[33] Note, however, that no matter how repulsive, the Polish Jew, Pezzl believes, is still higher than the "Indian fakir"; see Steven E. Aschheim, *Brothers and Strangers*, particularly pp. 3–31 on the creation of the "Ostjude"; for the Viennese context, see Hamann, *Hitler's Vienna*, pp. 325–59. Pezzl's distancing of the Jews from those of the Temple period suggests what Gilman identifies as the Christian insistence on "the Christian demand that the Jews of the Torah prefigure (and thus are replaced by) the Christian experience, [thus removing] the discourse of the Jews about their own history from their own control." *The Jew's Body*, p. 18.

Both non-Jewish and Jewish anthropologists of the fin de siècle write of the "predominant mouth of some Jews being the result of the presence of black blood" and the "brown skin, thick lips and prognathism" of the Jew. It is not only the skin color that enables the scientist to label the Jew as "black," but also the associated anatomical signs, such as the shape of the nose.[34]

Roller, on the other hand, is at pains to reveal the ways in which Mahler's physiognomy is un-Jewish and, indeed, beautiful. Besides describing Mahler's eyes in a way that distances them from the accepted stereotype, he also writes about Mahler's ears, lips, nose, and teeth in such a way as to make them the antitheses to Stern's:

Mahler had a quite unusually short skull from front to back: you could say it had absolutely no rear segment. The impetuousness of his nature expressed itself in the bulging curve of his temples and the older he grew, the more this dominated his features. The structure of the skull, together with the thrusting lower jaw and the way the wavy locks of his naturally curled hair—which was dark all over— stood up over his forehead gave his head its striking similarity to an antique mask of tragedy.

From his thirtieth year, Mahler wore no beard. Only in the summer months, to save himself the trouble of shaving, he sometimes had a short-trimmed moustache. One summer when I met him he had a magnificent beard, thick, dark grey overall but with two fiery streaks of lighter grey extending down from the corners of his mouth. But bowing good-humouredly to the general protests, he soon emerged beardless again. That way his strong, healthy teeth showed up better. They were white and regular. No dentist got any employment from them until the last few years of his life, and not much then either ... The fine hooked nose was not as prominent in life as on the death-mask, where the general wasting of the face tends to exaggerate it ...

His ears were small and close to the head, with particularly intricate and delicately modeled folding and completely free-standing lobes. His lips were classically shaped, and their immediate area had that multiplicity of detail which is produced by the habit of very carefully articulated speech. They were thin, and, when he was wearing his customary sober expression, usually closed. It was only when he was listening intently that they stood slightly open. But if Mahler was disgruntled, angry or out of sorts, he would pull his mouth out of shape, taking half his lower lip between his teeth, wrinkling his brow and tightening the folds of his nose. Pulled about like this, his face took on such a distorted grimace that he really did become the "nasty Mahler" ...

---

[34] Gilman, *Making the Body Beautiful*, p. 89. Weininger, *Sex and Character* (p. 303) writes that "The Jewish race ... appears to possess a certain anthropological relationship with both negroes and Mongolians. The readily curling hair points to the negro; admixture of Mongolian blood is suggested by ... a yellowish complexion."

This spare visage was a true mirror of every internal emotion of its owner, which is why different people have described it so differently depending on their relationship with Mahler. The mask-like quality is referred to almost universally.[35]

Such attention to the characteristics of Mahler's face is not necessarily striking in and of itself, given that Roller is an artist and therefore used to paying attention to both detail and beauty. Woven into this discussion, however, are some interesting contradictions to the accepted stereotypes—for example, that Jewish ears are recognizable. Hans Günther claimed that Jewish ears are "large, red," that they "stick out" and have "fleshy lobes."[36] Roller's description seems to counter each of these charges in turn. The extent to which the shape of the ears was believed to

---

[35]   Roller, 21–3/160–61: "Mahler war ganz ungewöhnlich kurzschädelig. Er hatte sozusagen überhaupt keinen Hinterkopf. Die Impetuosität seines Wesens drückte sich in dem mächtigen Kuppelgewölbe der Stirne aus, die mit zunehmendem Alter des zusammen mit dem energischen Unterkiefer und dem über die Stirn emporstrebenden, bis an das Ende dunklen, in schlangenartigen Strähnen natürlich gelockten Haar, gibt dem Kopf jene bezeichnende Ähnlichkeit mit einer antiken tragischen Maske. – Vom 30. Lebensjahr an erscheint Mahler völlig bartlos. Bloß in den Sommermonaten trug er manchmal, um sich die Mühe des Rasierens zu ersparen, einen gestutzten Schnurrbart—Bild 44. Einmal traf ich ihn im Sommer auch mit einem mächtigen, eisenfarbigen, starren Vollbart, den von den Mundwinkeln herab zwei hellgraue Flammen durchzogen. Dem allgemeinen Protest lachend gefügig, erschein er aber bald wieder bartlos. So kam das starke, gesunde Gebiß zur Geltung. Es war weiß und regelmäßig. Der Zahnarzt bekam erst in den letzten Lebensjahren daran zu tun, und da nicht viel … Die prachtvolle Hakennase wirkte im Leben nicht so mächtig wie an der Totenmaske, wo sie infolge der allgemeinen starken Abmagerung des Gesichtes vergrößert erscheint. Aber sie war doch viel schärfer als etwa auf dem Bilde 78, das eine durch Retouche verweichlichte Vergrößerung ist. Ihre Kontur erscheint am richtigsten in den Bildern 63, 64 und in den letzten Aufnahmen 79 und 80. Ihre Modellierung stellt sich am besten im Bild 65 dar. Die Ohren waren klein, anliegend, hatten vollkommen freistehende Läppchen und besonders reich und zierlich modellierte Muscheln. Sehr edel waren die Lippen geschnitten. Ihre Umgebung zeigte den Formenreichtum, den die Gewohnheit sehr klar artikulierten Sprechens hervorbringt. Sie waren schmal und für gewöhnlich mit dem Ausdruck der Festigkeit geschlossen, bloß beim achtsamen Lauschen – Bild 50 – leicht geöffnet. War Mahler verstimmt, geärgert, innerlich angewidert, so zog er den Mund ganz schief, nahm die halbe Unterlippe zwischen die Zähne und zog Stirn- und Nasenfalten kraus. So verzerrt erschien das Gesicht ganz entstellt, einer Fratze gleich, und er war wirklich 'der häßliche Mahler.' So zeigen ihn die beiden Momentaufnahmen, Bild 35, auf dem Wege aus der Oper nach der Vormittagsarbeit, und Bild 36, in der Augustinerstraße aus der Intendanz zurückkehrend …

Diese magere Antlitz war ein treuer Spiegel jeder inneren Regung seines Trägers, weshalb es von vielen Menschen, je nach der Verschiedenheit ihrer Beziehungen zu Mahler, sehr verschieden geschildert wird. Das Maskenhafte wird fast allgemein erwähnt."

Here and elsewhere Lebrecht's paragraphing differs from the original, but it has been retained.

[36]   Cited in Gilman, *Making the Body Beautiful*, p. 126.

be a sign of Jewish difference is illustrated by the fact that Hitler had apparently been convinced that Josef Stalin was a Jew and wanted to analyze photographs of him in order to determine if his earlobes were "ingrown and Jewish, or separate and Aryan."[37] In addition, Roller describes Mahler's lips as thin and "classically shaped," unlike those of the twins in Mann's story. Indeed the sheer amount of detail serves to personalize this portrait and to emphasize its uniqueness, thus distancing any physical traits from the possibility of stereotype. Roller concedes that Mahler had a "fine hooked nose"—perhaps the quintessential sign of a "Jewish" face—but suggests that it did not dominate his features.[38] He is careful to distance Mahler's "real" face with that represented by the death mask, where he believes that the nose is more prominent. The anxiety here seems to be the two-dimensional photographs versus the three-dimensional death mask: obviously, the photos could be said, more than the mask, to misrepresent the size of Mahler's nose. That Roller suggests the reverse, pointing to the "wasting" of the features as a possible cause, indicates that he is aware of or at least uncomfortable with the nose as an important "sign" of difference.

Mahler's head also receives attention from Roller, possibly because the size of the head was seen as another marker of Jewish difference. Richard Wagner, in 1851, described the character Mime—who can be shown to exhibit other Jewish stereotypes—as having a head that was "abnormally large."[39] Elsewhere Roller asserts that "[Mahler's] thick hair, allowed to grow fairly long at Frau Alma's wish, made his head appear too large." Like the illusion created by his glasses, Mahler's "real" self is masked and he appears more "Jewish" than he actually is. And, in the case of the size of his head, it seems to be the result of Mahler merely trying to please his wife, something for which he can hardly be blamed even if he realizes that it contributes to his unaesthetic appearance.

Overall, the impression of Mahler's face is likened to an "antique mask of tragedy," an image which immediately calls forth ideas of Greek physical perfection and beauty. It is worth pointing out, however, that the image of the

---

[37] Ibid., p. 130. Gilman is citing Alan Bullock, *Hitler amd Stalin: Parallel Lives* (New York, 1992), p. 537.

[38] On "Jewish" noses, see Gilman, *Making the Body Beautiful*, pp. 85–118 and 119–37 and *The Jew's Body*, pp. 169–93.

[39] Mark Weiner, *Richard Wagner and the Antisemitic Imagination* (Lincoln and London, 1995), p. 6. Many drawings and caricatures of Mahler depict him with an unnaturally large head. For example, Oscar Garveus's drawing shows Mahler's head as more than a third of his entire height—clearly not the standard artistic proportion. Enrico Caruso's caricature of Mahler from 1908 exaggerates this even more: here the head is in fact bigger than the entire body. Likewise, in the caricature by Faragó, Mahler's body is only a fraction of the size of his head. See Gilbert Kaplan, ed., *The Mahler Album* (New York, 1995), plate 241 (Garvius), plate 235 (Caruso), and plate 240 (Faragó).

mask was double-edged: it was a common trope that Jews, lacking any real self, were the best actors because they could easily take on the aspects of another.[40]

While the stereotype does in fact most often concern the male Jew, the Jewish body is feminized when compared to the gentile body. Indeed, many commentators insist upon "feminine" aspects, from a characteristic "break" in their voice to their softness or "unsoldierly" nature.[41] During the Middle Ages, it was even believed that male as well as female Jews experienced menstruation.[42] The source of the perceived difference was the circumcised penis, which was thought both to define the Jew and to mark him as different; it became the locus of anxiety.[43] The variety of cultural meanings ascribed to circumcision were many: it was seen as a mark of tribal identity, as both a protection against and a cause of disease (specifically syphilis), and as the source of powerlessness.[44] Circumcision was often linked to castration, a link which Freud discusses in the case of "Little Hans," among others: "If—says the child—I can be circumcised and made into a Jew, can I not also be castrated and made into a woman?"[45] Otto Weininger believed that "Judaism is saturated with femininity," and "that the most manly Jew is more feminine than the least manly Aryan."[46] Carl Jung claimed that male Jews are feminized: "They have this peculiarity in common with women; being physically weaker they have to aim at the chinks in the armor of their adversary."[47]

---

[40] I discuss the idea of masking the self (or "passing") in "'Polemik im Concertsaal': Mahler, Beethoven, and the Viennese Critics," *19th-Century Music* 29 (2006), pp. 289–321, and in Chapter 3. It is unclear if Roller is suggesting that Mahler was consciously trying to "mask" his Jewish difference or that observers, because they did not know him well, mistook his face for a "mask." Even if, as is most likely, Roller meant the link to be a positive one and to invoke the Greek ideal, the image itself is ambivalent.

[41] Walter Rathenau, "Höre Israel!" in *Schriften*, 2nd edn (Berlin, 1981), pp. 89–93; he uses the term "weichliche Rundlichkeit der Formen" on p. 92. The essay was originally published in *Die Zukunft* on 6 Mar. 1897. On Rathenau, see Amos Elon, *The Pity of It All: A Portrait of the German-Jewish Epoch, 1743–1933* (New York, 2002), pp. 232–6. Günther cites Rathenau on p. 251 of *Rassenkunde des jüdisches Volkes*, adding the adjective "unsoldatisch." The linking of (male) Jews to women is a common theme throughout the period. Gilman discusses this theme extensively in *Freud, Race, and Gender* (Princeton, 1993), chs 1 and 2. See also Nancy A. Harrowitz and Barbara Hyams, eds, *Jews and Gender: Responses to Otto Weininger* (Philadelphia, 1995).

[42] Joshua Trachtenberg, *The Devil and the Jews: The Medieval Conception of the Jew and Its Relation to Modern Anti-Semitism*, 2nd paperback edn (Philadelphia and Jerusalem, 1983), p. 50.

[43] Sander L. Gilman, *Freud, Race, and Gender*, pp. 49–92.

[44] Ibid., pp. 56–69.

[45] Cited in Gilman, *Freud, Race, and Gender*, p. 77; Freud cites this fear as the "deepest root" of antisemitism.

[46] Weininger, *Sex and Character*, p. 306.

[47] Carl G. Jung, *Collected Works*, ed. Herbert Read et al., trans. R.F.C. Hull (20 vols, London, 1957–79), vol. 10, p. 165; Jung is of course reacting specifically to Freud and

Roller several times in his essay contradicts any assumption that Mahler was "weak" or unmasculine. Roller describes a typical summer day, which allows him to stresses his friend's strength and ability to endure hard work:

> So long as he believed his heart was sound (that is, up to 1907), he was not only an avid walker but an outstanding swimmer, a powerful oarsman and an agile cyclist. At Maiernigg by the Wörthersee, his summer residence for seven years, he would rise at 5:30, take his first swim alone, then hasten through secret paths to his small composing-house deep in the woods, where his breakfast awaited. Then followed around seven hours of uninterrupted work …
>
> His swim usually began with a high dive. Then he swam under water and did not reappear until he was far out in the lake, bobbing about comfortably like a seal. Rowing a boat with Mahler was no pleasure. He had a very powerful stroke, and pulled too fast; his strength enabled him to keep going for a long time. [48]

In perhaps the most astonishing passage in the essay, Roller takes care to describe Mahler's naked body:

> While Mahler was sunbathing, which he was very keen on, I had the opportunity to study his naked body closely. It was very tidily formed and very masculine in its proportions. His shoulders were broader than one would imagine from seeing him in clothes, and perfectly symmetrical. His hips were very narrow and his legs, which were by no means too short, had beautifully formed and regularly spaced axes, firm, clearly developed muscles and just a light covering of hair. There was no sign of any prominent veins. His feet were small with a high instep and short regularly shaped toes, without a blemish.

---

psychoanalysis. Jung came to believe that the latter was a tainted project because of its origin in a "feminized psyche."

[48]   Roller, 20/159: "Seine Rede war männlich." 14/154: "Dieser Körper war von großem Ebenmaß und ausgesprochen männlichen Proportionen."

16/156: "Solange er an sein gesundes Herz glaubte, also bis zum Jahre 1907, war er nicht nur ein leidenschaftlicher Fußgeher, sondern auch ein vorzüglicher Schwimmer, ausdauernder Ruderer und geschickter Radfahrer. In Mayernigg am Wörthersee, das ihm durch sieben Jahre als Sommersitz diente, erhob er sich um halb sechs Uhr morgens, hatte einsam sein erstes Bad und eilte dann rasch auf versteckten Pfaden zu seiner tief im Wald verborgenen Komponierhütte, wo das erste Frühstück für hin vorbereitet war. Dann folgten etwa sieben Stunden ununterbrochener Arbeit."

17/157: "Sein Bad begann gewöhnlich mit einem mächtigen Kopfsprung. Dann schwamm er lange unter dem Wasser und weit draußen im See kam er erst wieder zum Vorschein, sich behaglich im Wasser wälzend wie eine Robbe. Mit Mahler gemeinsam zu rudern war kein Vergnügen. Er hatte einen sehr kräftigen Streich und einen viel zu schnellen Schlag. Aber seine Kraft befähigte ihn, diese Anstrengung lange anzuhalten."

His chest stood out strongly with very little hair and well-defined musculature. His belly, like the rest of his body, bore no trace of excess fat, the central line of muscle was plainly visible and the outline of the other muscles as clear as on an anatomical model. In the course of my profession, I have seen a great many naked bodies of all types and can testify that at the age of forty Mahler had the perfect male torso strong, slim beautifully made, although the total body length was probably not quite seven and a half times the vertical head diameter. The first time I saw him without clothes, I could not refrain from expressing my surprise at such a fine display of muscle. Mahler laughed in amusement because he realized that I too had been misled by the general talk about his poor physical shape. The most beautifully developed part of him, quite an outstanding sight because it was so well delineated, was the musculature of his back. I could never set eyes on this superbly modeled, sun-tanned back without being reminded of a racehorse in peak condition.

His hands were real workman's hands, short and broad with unmanicured fingers ending as if they had been chopped off. The nails—it must be said—were mostly bitten short, often right down to the skin, and only gradually did Frau Alma have any success in her campaign against this bad habit. His arms were thin, at least in proportion to their great strength—because contrary to general opinion, Mahler was muscularly powerful. Many people saw him from time to time vault up on to the stage out of the orchestra pit via the ramp. He was also capable without great strain of carrying his sick sister all the way from the street up to their flat on the third floor. Standing for long periods in the restricted space of the conductor's podium, often with no railing and high above the heads of the audience in the stalls, was probably also quite a feat of strength.[49]

---

[49]   Roller, 154–5/14–16: "Ich konnte im Sonnenbad, das Mahler eifrig pflegte, seinen nackten Körper aufmerksam studieren. Dieser Körper war von großem Ebenmaß und ausgesprochen männlichen Proportionen. Die Schultern waren breiter, als der bekleidete Körper vermuten ließ, und vollkommen symmetrisch gebaut. Das Becken war sehr schmal. Die Beine, keineswegs besonders kurz, hatten kurz, hatten absolut schön und regelmäßig, gestellte Achsen, harte, klar entwickelte Muskel und schwache Behaarung. Übertriebene Adernausprägung fehlte gänzlich. Die Füße waren klein mit hochgebautem Rist und kurzen, regelmäßigen, vollkommen fehlerfreien Zehen. Die Brust hatte kräftige Wölbung, geringe Behaarung und sehr klar gezeichnete Muskelansätze. Der Bauch war, bei starker Betonung des geraden Bauchmuskels, ohne jeden sichtbaren Fettansatz, wie übrigens der ganze Körper, und zeigte die Inskriptionen so deutlich wie bei einem Mustermodell. Ich habe infolge meines Berufes eine große Zahl nackter Menschenkörper aller Art beobachtet und erkläre, daß der vierzigjährige Mahler einen tadellos schönen, kräftig-schlanken Manneskörper besaß, der allerdings kaum ganz siebeneinhalb Kopflängen gemessen haben mochte. Ich konnte, als ich ihn zum erstenmal nackt sah, eine Bemerkung der Überraschung über diese Muskelpracht nicht zurückhalten. Mahler lachte gutmütig, da er merkte, daß auch ich durch das allgemeine Geschwätz über seine dürftige Körperlichkeit beeinflußt worden war. Am schönsten entwickelt, geradezu sehenswert wegen der Klarheit ihrer Formen, war die Rückmuskulatur. Ich konnte diesen prachtvoll modellierten, braungebrannten

Roller implicates himself in the assumption that Mahler was "weak" or "unsoldierly" by admitting his astonishment when seeing Mahler without his clothes. Note also that, by insisting on Mahler's love of sunbathing, Roller implies that Mahler's skin was not naturally dark. He is also careful to describe the shape of Mahler's feet. Günther said the Jewish gait "can have something soft or sneaking about it"—a "groping, dragging, slouching gait." He also argued that some observers recognized Jews merely by observing them walk.[50] Just as criminals and epileptics were said to have a gait that marked them as degenerate, so were the Jews said to have a "Jewish" gait, and it was widely believed during the nineteenth century that Jews were predisposed to flat feet. Although the condition of flat or crooked feet may be related to the devil's "cloven hoof," the specious condition served to bar Jews from the armed forces—and thus from being considered true citizens. [51] To return to Panizza's description of Stern: "Itzig always raised both thighs almost to his midriff so that he bore some resemblance to a stork," and it often "appeared as though he were veering down the sidewalk ... in a diagonal direction."[52] Panizza also describes Stern as having "bow legs." Thus unaesthetic "Jewish" movements, products of an inferior body, provide yet another sign of recognizability.

Roller's authority is that of an artist, someone who, as he tells us, has seen countless naked subjects in the course of his artistic training and career. Roller knows the "correct"—and therefore most beautiful—proportions of the human

---

Rücken nie ansehen, ohne an ein fites Rennpferd erinnert zu werden. Seine Hand war eine rechte Arbeiterhand, kurz und breit, und die Finger ohne Verjüngung wie abgehackt endigend. Die Fingernägel—es muß leider gesagt werden—waren meist kurz abgebissen, oft bis aufs Blut, und erst allmählich bleiben Frau Almas Bemühungen gegen diese Unart siegreich. Schlank waren die Arme, wenigstens im Verhältnis zu ihrer großen Kraft. Denn Mahler war im Gegensatz zu der verbreiteten Vorstellung sehr muskelstark. Viele sahen ihn gelegentlich aus dem Orchester über die Rampe auf die Bühne hinaufvoltigieren. Er vermochte aber auch ohne besondere Mühe seine leidende Schwester von der Straße in die im dritten Stockwerk gelegene Wohnung zu tragen. Übrigens war das lange Stehen auf der schmalen, oft geläznderlosen Plattform des Konzertdirigenten, hoch über den Köpfen der Parterrebesucher (Bild 43), sicher auch eine körperliche Kraftleistung."

   [50]   Günther, *Rassenkunde des jüdisches Volkes*, p. 252: "Der 'jüdische' Gang kann etwas Leises oder Schleichendes haben; Schleich spricht von einem 'tappenden, ziehenden, schlürfenden Gang.' ... Es gibt Beobachter, die einen vor ihnen hergehenden Menschen am Gange mit großer Sicherheit als Juden erkennen können"; see also Nancy Harrowitz, *Antisemitism, Misogyny and the Logic of Cultural Difference: Cesare Lombroso and Matilde Serao* (Lincoln and London, 1994).

   [51]   Gilman, *The Jew's Body*, pp. 38–59 and 48–9; see also his *The Case of Sigmund Freud*, pp. 113–68 and Weiner, *Richard Wagner and the Anti-Semitic Imagination*, pp. 261–72. Günther states that "Der Gang manches Juden ist durch eine Plattfutzanlage bedingt" and cites statistics about the rates of flat feet among Jewish soldiers; *Rassenkunde*, p. 252.

   [52]   Zipes, *The Operated Jew*, pp. 48–9.

body, and he can therefore objectively attest to Mahler's beauty.[53] Even so, Roller's invocation of Mahler's nakedness is startling and strange. And, once he uncovers Mahler's body, the failure to address the obvious issue of circumcision inadvertently emphasizes its association with castration: Roller's avoidance only draws attention to its absence. Roller's attempt to construct a "masculine" Mahler thus relies on the ultimate feminizing act. What is astonishing is not by any means Roller's failure to describe Mahler's penis—we would hardly expect that in any case—but in the act of revealing Mahler's nakedness, Roller himself calls attention to something he cannot discuss. Mahler could of course be in a bathing costume, therefore leaving the entire question moot. Even if that were true, however, by using the adjective *nackt* [naked] Roller seems to want the issue left ambiguous. He could have easily told us that Mahler was partially clothed. In any event, the reliance upon aesthetic argument seems to add more strength to Roller's assertion of Mahler's visible masculinity. Certainly given his authority as an artist, but perhaps also because the inclusion of this eyewitness account is so bizarre, we are seduced into giving credence to Roller's description.

Nevertheless, Roller's further description of Mahler's personal habits serves to reinforce the masculine image:

> Mahler at that time gave the impression of being utterly healthy. He slept splendidly, relished his cigar and in the evening enjoyed a glass of beer. Spirits he abstained from completely. Wine he drank on special occasions, preferring Mosel, Chianti or Asti. One or two glasses sufficed to make him light-hearted and he would then invent puns which, in Frau Alma's expression, fabulously entertained their inventor.
>
> But for all his sensual pleasures, including those of the table, he was a man of great moderation. You never saw him do anything in excess. He abhorred drunkenness, as much as obscenity or indecency. The strict cleanliness that he kept about his person was observed, without prudishness, in his speech and doubtless also in his thoughts.
>
> In middle life, Mahler underwent a serious intestinal operation that left him with extensive internal scarring. This obliged him to be particularly careful about his food and to follow a strict diet. But he ate well and derived much pleasure from food. Lots of fruit, especially apples and oranges, plenty of butter, plain vegetables and pasta, very little meat and only from farm animals. He avoided game and anything that came from the wild. Since anything outside his careful diet made him too unwell to work, he was exaggeratedly cautious, even finicky, at table, particularly if he was just completing a composition and had only a few

---

[53]   See Gilman, *Making the Body Beautiful*, p. 87: "For [Lorenz] Oken, bodies are not to be judged against other real bodies but against the ideal forms of bodies in art."

more days of vacation left. In general he was very good at enduring aches and pains. Sometimes he would enter the podium with a terrible migraine.[54]

One of Roller's more noteworthy observations is Mahler's incapacity for liquor: Immanuel Kant had written that "Women, clergymen, and Jews ordinarily do not become drunk, at least they carefully avoid all appearance of it, because they are weak in civic life and must restrain themselves (for which sobriety is required.)"[55] In Panizza's story, all of Stern's attempts to become German are undone at his wedding where he becomes drunk and reverts to his "true" self. In Mahler's case, alcohol brings out another, softer, side of him—it is unclear if Roller is implying that this is Mahler's true nature. Certainly, Mahler's reaction to alcohol is not severe or dangerous: his bad puns can hardly be called unraveling; in fact, it seems to make him more harmless, more childlike. According to Weininger, however, "Jews and women are devoid of humor but addicted to mockery," a view that, given the prominence that Weininger's work received after his suicide in 1903, would have been well known in Mahler's Vienna.[56]

---

[54] Roller, 17–18/157–8: "Mahler machte zu jener Zeit den Eindruck eines kerngesunden Menschen. Er schlief vortrefflich, liebte seine Zigarre und genoß gern des Abends ein Glas Bier. Schnäpse mied er gänzlich. Wein trank er nur bei besonderen Anlässen. Besonders gern Mosel, Chianti, oder Asti. Ein oder zwei Glas machten ihn schon aufgeräumt und er brachte dann Wortwitze vor, über die er, um Frau Almas Worte zu gebrauchten, sich selbst fabelhaft unterhielt. Aber bei aller Sinnenfreudigkeit, die er auch den Genüssen der Tafel entgegenbrachte, war er von größter Mäßigkeit. Nie merkte man an ihm ein Zuviel. Trunkenheit war ihm ein Abscheu ebenso wie jede Unfläterei oder Anstößigkeit. Die strenge Reinlichkeit, die er an seinem Körper pflegte, bewahrte er, ohne jede Prüderie, auch im Gespräch und sicher auch in seinen Gedanken.

Er hatte in seinen mittleren Mannesjahren eine schwere Darmoperation zu überstehen gehabt, die ausgedehnte innere Narben zurückgelassen hatte. Dies zwang ihn, seiner Ernährung besondere Aufmerksamkeit zu widmen und eine strenge Diät zu beachten. Aber er aß gern und mit Genuß. Viel Obst, besonders Äpfel und Orangen, viel Butter, leichte Gemüse und Mehlspeisen, wenig Fleisch und immer nur das von Haustieren. Wild und das Fleisch freilebender Tiere mied er vollkommen. Da ihn jeder Diätfehler arbeitsunfähig machte, war er—besonders wenn er an der Beendigung eines Werkes tätig war und nur noch wenige Ferientage vor sich sah—bei Tisch übertrieben vorsichtig, ja ängstlich. Im allgemeinen war er gegen körperliches Ungemach sehr widerstandsfähig. Er erschien mitunter trotz quälender Migräne am Dirigentenpult ..."

[55] Cited in Gilman, *The Jew's Body*, p. 204.

[56] Weininger, *Sex and Character*, p. 319; Weininger committed suicide at the age of 23 in the Schwarzspanierhaus, where Beethoven had died. Mahler's preferences in wine might suggest that Mahler was not a wine connoisseur; whether Roller means it here to imply that Mahler was a peasant or simply above such fussiness is unclear. I would like to thank Mr Bernard Klein for his insights regarding this subject. The avoidance of wild game could be seen as being in accordance with kashrut, the Jewish dietary laws, or, alternatively, as a "feminine" diet. Max Graf, in 1900, compared Mahler to Hans Richter, stating that Richter had "more roast beef and less nerves in his body"—he, of course, was evaluating

Yet Roller again inadvertently undermines his masculine image when he discusses Mahler's speaking voice:

> In fact, Mahler's voice functioned in two separate registers, one directly above the other. A very sonorous baritone when he was speaking in a relaxed manner and a ringing tenor that came into play when his excitement began to grow. His voice could be raised to a very high volume without losing its deeper tones. This was demonstrated, for example, during his celebrated theatrical storms. "Please don't think I am really angry," he told me after I was taken aback the first time, "but being fierce is the only weapon I have for keeping the sort of order you need." Subsequently I learned to recognize by the sound of his voice whether he was putting it on or whether he was really becoming heated. In the latter case his voice would suddenly soar into the higher register with a kind of break: it would happen whether his excitement was of joy or anger, or whether it sprang from intense involvement in a subject of conversation. After 1907 his higher voice was to be heard less and less. His increasing melancholy caused the lower register to predominate more and more, and that is why it could seem that his voice had actually altered.[57]

As Gilman writes, "the feminizing 'break of the voice,' the inability to speak in a masculine manner, is one of the standard stigmata of degeneration born by the homosexual in late-nineteenth-century medicine and popular culture."[58] The image of the homosexual and that of the Jew overlap in the realm of medical science, where both groups are seen as "neurasthenic or hysteric, they are easily

---

them as conductors; see my "'Ein hypermoderner Dirigent': Mahler and Anti-Semitism in *Fin-de-siècle* Vienna," *19th-Century Music* 18 (1995), pp. 257–76, p. 270.

[57] Roller, 20/159: "In Mahlers Stimme lagen nämlich zwei Register unvermittelt nebeneinander. Ein sehr sonores baritonales, in dem sich seine ruhige Rede bewegte, und ein klingendes, tenorales, das bei gesteigerter innerer Lebhaftigkeit benützt wurde. Die Stimme konnte zu großer Kraft gesteigert werden, die berühmten Theater-Donnerwetter. 'Glauben Sie nur nicht, daß ich mich wirklich geärgert habe,' sage er mir nach dem ersten solchen Wetter, das ich miterlebt und das mich etwas verschüchtert hatte, 'aber ich habe leider kein anderes Mittel als Strenge, um die nötige Ordnung aufrecht zu halten.' Und in der Folge lernte ich am Klang der Stimme erkennen, ob es sich um 'Theater' handelte oder ob er wirklich erregt war. Dann nämlich sprang die Stimme sofort mit einer Art Bruck in die höhere Lage über, einerlei, ob die Erregung freudiger oder ärgerlicher Art war oder gesteigertem Interesse am Gesprächsstoff entsprang. Nach dem Jahre 1907 war die höhere Stimme immer seltener zu hören. Die zunehmende Gelassenheit seines Wesens ließ immer ausschließlicher die tiefere Lage erklingen und so konnte die Täuschung entstehen, als habe die Stimme sich geändert. –"

[58] Gilman, *Freud, Race, and Gender*, p. 164; he discusses the "break" in the voice, the claims that a high number of Jews were homosexuals, and the surprisingly common belief that male Jews menstruated (pp. 77–98 and 12–48). He also cites Adolf Jellinek who claimed "that bass voices are much rarer than baritone voices among the Jews," p. 43.

excited, suffer from headaches, suffer from all sorts of sensations in their limbs, are often unwilling to work."[59] Mahler's inability to control his voice, to keep it in one register, marks him as "other." His impassioned voice is feminine, and even after 1907 it only seemed as if his voice "had actually altered." When Roller suggests that he could tell if Mahler was truly angry or merely being "theatrical," he is claiming to be able to see through to Mahler's real self. Like the image of the mask, this is double-edged, suggesting that, while Mahler may have had a true self, he nevertheless chose to hide it. Roller's insight comes from his own essential self, his ability to see through Mahler's "mask."

Erinnerungen an "Mahler"

Whereas Roller's portrait of Mahler was not particularly influential—his book was published in a limited edition and not generally available in English until 1987—the same cannot be said of the multiple editions and translations of Alma Mahler's *Gustav Mahler: Memories and Letters*. Given her position of importance in Mahler's life during his last decade, and given its seeming openness, always delivering the good with the bad—never hiding, for example, Mahler's demand that she give up composing or even trying to hide her own affairs later in their marriage—Alma's Mahler is seductively close and believable in a way that Roller's Mahler can never be.

The extent to which Alma's is "a one-sided record," however, should be kept in mind, despite our reliance on her as a primary source of information for Mahler's biography.[60] Norman Lebrecht states that "She deliberately misleads too often for

---

[59]   Ibid., p. 165; on the quality of the Jewish voice as related to being homosexual, see also Gilman, "Strauss and the Pervert," in *Reading Opera*, ed. Arthur Groos and Roger Parker (Princeton, 1988), pp. 306–27.

[60]   The quote is Donald Mitchell, "Introduction to the 1969 American Edition," *Gustav Mahler: Memories and Letters*, ed. Donald Mitchell and Knut Martner, trans. Basil Creighton, 4th English edn, with additional notes and commentaries (London, 1990; original edn, *Gustav Mahler: Erinnerungen und Briefe* [Amsterdam, 1940]; orig. Eng. trans. by Basil Creighton as *Gustav Mahler: Memories and Letters* [London, 1946]), p. xxxix [hereafter quotes will be from 1990 edition and be cited as AM Memories]; Mitchell, however, goes on to defend Alma against de La Grange 's article in *The Saturday Review* (29 Mar. 1969), where de La Grange presented what he called his "New Image" of Mahler. He had compared the *Memories* to the then unpublished *Diaries* and had noted that Alma's book represented "the most serious distortions of the truth." Mitchell takes de La Grange to task, claiming that "it must surely be an eccentric person, who, after reading Alma Mahler's biography in its entirety, can seriously hold the view that, in substance and intent, it presents a hostile portrait of her husband" (p. xl). He also defends Alma on the grounds that her portrait of the composer was based "on an acquaintance a good deal more intimate than Baron de La Grange's." Mitchell's criticism is typical both in its desire to believe the substance of Alma's story and also in its inability to hear in her text its

her book, compulsively readable though it remains, to be used as the principal basis for considering Mahler's character."[61] My concern, however, is not trustworthiness so much as her ambivalence toward Mahler's Jewishness, which I believe has not been sufficiently explored. Indeed, I would argue, it is only when the *Memories* are read in tandem with Alma's now published *Diaries* that the vague sense of unease that pervades her book—the ambiguous nature of her feelings toward Mahler—reveal themselves as discomfort with his "racial" heritage. In their correspondence that forms the introduction to the English edition of the *Diaries*, Anthony Beaumont and Susanne Rode-Breymann write that "doubtless the most critical area of her *Weltanschauung* is the problem of Judaism ... The diaries include remarks which ... cannot go to press without comment."[62] The *Diaries* present in unexpurgated form what the *Memories* have whitewashed and censored for a very different world: first published in Amsterdam in 1940 and translated into English in 1946, even Alma had to know that it was no longer acceptable to give voice to the casual antisemitism that had preceded, indeed enabled, the Shoah. Yet the remnants of everyday, fin-de-siècle Viennese antisemitism structure the portrait of Mahler presented in the *Memories*, and to ignore them is to accept a view of Mahler that remained uneasy, to say the least, with his "race."

The odd undercurrent of ambivalence toward Mahler is discernable in even the opening of the *Memories* and runs throughout the entire book—something that scholars, even those who treat its claims warily, nevertheless tend to ignore. She announces at the beginning that:

> I did not want to meet Mahler. In fact I had purposely and with considerable difficulty avoided meeting him that summer, because of the stories people told about him. I knew him well by sight; he was a small, fidgety man with a fine head. I was acquainted also with the scandals about him and every young woman who aspired to sing in the opera. I had been to the concert when he conducted his First Symphony [18 November 1900], a work I had thoroughly disliked and even

---

deep ambivalence toward her subject. With the publication of the *Diaries* (complete in the German edition), de La Grange's claims can now be vindicated. Lebrecht (in *Mahler Remembered*, p. xiii) remarks that "the scholarly consensus that Alma 'is nearly always reliable where she speaks of aesthetic judgements or emotional reactions; [but] it becomes risky to trust her in question of fact or chronology' is no longer tenable." He is quoting Kurt Blaukopf, *Gustav Mahler*, trans. Inge Goodwin (London, 1974), p. 259. It is unclear why he believes her aesthetic judgments are without bias. Peter Franklin (*The Life of Mahler* [Cambridge, New York, and Melbourne, 1997]) only rarely questions the basic veracity of Alma's account (see, for example, pp. 14 and 15 compared to the following).

[61]   Lebrecht, *Mahler Remembered*, p. xiii.

[62]   *Alma Mahler-Werfel Diaries, 1898–1902*, selected and trans. Antony Beaumont from the German edn (London: Faber and Faber, 1998), p. xvi; this comment is contained in the Eng. edn only.

angrily rejected. At the same time, he was of importance to me as a conductor and I was conscious of his mysterious and powerful fascination.[63]

Aspects of her description of him—"a small, fidgety man with a fine head," the implication of sexual excess, the inability to compose yet a talent for conducting, all combined with his "powerful fascination"—resonate with the Jewish caricature, while at the same time remaining neutral enough to be pass as simple description. Nevertheless, Alma's recollection of her first meeting with Mahler as if by chance is disingenuous: her diaries reveal that she had been hoping for a meeting for several years. As early as 4 December 1898, she writes, "As for Mahler—I'm virtually in love with him." She esteems him as a conductor, calling him "a genius through and through."[64] Her ambivalence towards him is also stated more strongly, and she writes on 11 July 1899 that, "Anyway I feel absolutely no urge to meet him. I love and honor him as an artist, but as a man he doesn't interest me at all. I wouldn't want to lose my illusions, either."[65] She is also less charitable regarding the premiere of Mahler's first symphony, calling it "an unbelievable jumble of styles—and an ear-splitting, nerve-shattering din." When she describes her first meeting with him, she calls him "dreadfully restless" and writes that "he stormed about the room like a savage."[66]

Alma's *Diaries* are full of explicit comments about Jewish difference. For example, in the entry for 2 December 1900, she recounts going to the Hotel Rabl on the Fleischmarkt to hear Max Burckhard "give a dramatic reading of his 'Bürgermeisterwahl'":

> At the reception desk we were met by Jewish committee members, who eagerly led us to a long, smoke filled room packed with working-class Jews.—He read well. The play is fine and effective. It was so funny: the fellow who opened the proceedings, a lad of no more than twenty years, blathered of the workers' incredible thirst for knowledge, of the spectre of reactionism, of the influence of the clergy etc., all in the strongest possible Jewish accent, in the most obvious Yiddish slang. Finally he apostrophized Burckhard as a fine man who had

[63]   AM Memories, p. 3.

[64]   Alma Mahler-Werfel, *Tagebuch-Suiten, 1898–1902*, ed. Antony Beaumont and Susanne Rode-Breymann (Frankfurt am Main, 1997), p. 155; selections translated as *Alma Mahler-Werfel Diaries, 1898–1902*, by Antony Beaumont from the German edn (London, 1998), p. 76; hereafter AMW Diaries; page numbers will be cited German/English; thus AMW Diaries, p. 155/76: "In den Mahler bin ich effectif—verlieb." and pp. 191–2/96: "Mahler is durch und durch genial." In both versions, square brackets, [], are used to indicate later additions by Alma, although it is unclear at what point those glosses were made. In 1962–63, she apparently contemplated publication of the diaries and many of the emendations and deletions date from that period; see the English translation, p. 469.

[65]   AMW Diaries, p. 318/163.

[66]   AMW Diaries, p. 724/443.

come to open their eyes [*sie zu belehren*].—B. made his entrance to thunderous applause. Why on earth did he give that reading? Surely not because he cares about this degenerate race. Was it just vanity? What do I know? Enough—I just wouldn't consider it worthwhile to squander my vocal chords, my good temper like that, for no return. He was so exhausted that he had to go home …[67]

In addition to her obvious remarks about "this degenerate race" and the "Jewish accent," the Jewish audience at the reading is parasitic, soaking up knowledge but giving nothing back, leaving Burckhard exhausted. Alma suggests that there is something wrong with Burckhard (his vanity?) that he does not understand that he is squandering himself and his art. This sentiment is more clearly stated regarding an earlier lecture that took place on 18 November when she had written: "I must admit though, that the bad company he keeps is causing his pure, Aryan blood to semitify. He's even beginning to look Jewish. I just can't help it. My sympathy for him has waned considerably."[68] The signs of difference that reveal the Jews have begun to alter Burckhardt's own physiognomy; Aryan blood is no protection from their "bad company." Alma is typical in her granting that, while the Aryan (Burckhard) can be brought down, the Jews cannot rise—even here where the emphasis is clearly on education: "the workers' incredible thirst for knowledge," the fact that Burckhard had come to "to instruct them." Alma's question to herself—she asks "Bildung?" after wondering why Burckhard would give the reading—is missing from the English translation, and while she could be

---

[67]   AMW Diaries, p. 594/351; the German contains a few words that are missing in the English: "Beim Eingang empfingen uns einige jüdische Com<m>itäter, die uns bereitwillig in einen langen, rauchigen Saal führten, vollgepropft von jüdischen Arbeitern.—Er las gut. Das Stück ist fein und wirkungsvoll. Ja—zu komisch war der, der die Sitzung eröffnete, ein Bengel mit 20 Jahren, der von dem unglaublichen Wissen<s>durst der Arbeiter, von dem Gespenst der Reaktion, von Clericalismus etc. im denkbar jüdischesten Jargon, in denkbar jüdischester Sprachen schwatzte. Zum Schluss apostrophierte er Burckhard als einen braven Mann, der gekommen ist, sie zu belehren. Darauf bestieg B. unter Bravorufen das Podium.

Eigentlich—warum hat er gelesen? Bildung? Um die dieser degenerierten Rasse kann es ihm doch nicht zu thun sein. Ist es vielleicht nur Eitelkeit? Was weiß ich? Genug—mich würde es nicht die Mühe lohnen—meinen Hals, meine Stimmung 2 Stunden für nichts und wieder nichts zu vergeuden. Er war so hin, dass er nach Hause gehen musste …" (Translation slightly emended; the translator has inverted the phrases "im denkbar jüdischesten Jargon" and "in denkbar jüdischester Sprachen schwatzte.")

Max Burckhard (1854–1912) was, from 1890, the director of the Burgtheater in Vienna, a playwright, and one of Alma's admirers—he both courted and proposed to her.

[68]   AMW Diaries, p. 586/345: "Ich muss aber gestehen, dass sein reines arisches Blut von seinem schlechten Umgang wesentlich versemitiert ist. Auch sein Blick hat etwas jüdisches. Ich kann mir nicht helfen. Und [aber] meine Gefühl für ihn sind wesentlich verringert."

querying Burckhard's own desire for education, she could also be questioning the workers' desire—or ability for—knowledge.

The Mahler of the *Diaries* should not be isolated from Alma's portrait of Alexander Zemlinsky, and it is only when viewed from this angle that one gets a sense of not only how difficult it was for Alma to overcome her own prejudices but also of how and why she did manage to do precisely this in the case of Mahler. Alma first mentions Zemlinsky in her diary on 26 February 1900: interestingly enough, one of the topics of conversation was Gustav Mahler and their mutual admiration for him. She describes Zemlinsky as "dreadfully ugly, almost chinless—yet I found him quite enthralling." When she confides to him that *Tristan* is her favorite work of Wagner's, this so delights him that "he became entirely transformed. He grew truly handsome. Now we understood each other."[69] Even after Alma begins studying composition with Zemlinsky her attraction to him remains conflicted. On 7 January 1901, after he rebukes her for flirting with him during a lesson, she confides, "And he's right. *What* do I want of him? Yes, I like him—beyond words ... But when he arrived—his incredible ugliness, his smell. And yet—when he's there, I get strangely excited."[70] That the Jew had a distinctive and unpleasant smell was another antisemitic canard, dating back to the Middle Ages. The *foetor judäicus*, or "odor of the Jews," is, as Gilman points out, "linked with the sexualized image of the goat. For Jews, like the Devil, are horned like goats and have a goat's tail and goat's beard."[71] The link is clear in Alma's diary where she juxtaposes Zemlinsky's smell with her own strange excitement. She cannot seem to decide if she finds him attractive or ugly, and one imagines that she is trying to see him without his "Jewish" face. Only a few months later, trying to imagine herself married to him, she writes:

---

[69] AMW Diaries, pp. 463–4/253–4: "Er ist furchtbar hässlich, hat fast kein Kinn—und doch gefiel er mir ausnehmend." "Drauf war er so erfreut, dass er nicht widerzuerkennen war. Er wurde ordentlich hübsch. Jetzt verstanden wir uns." She also claims again here that she "longed to meet" Mahler. While Alma claims that Zemlinsky became beautiful at the moment that she believes that they are of one mind, on 17 Dec. 1901, more than a month after her first official meeting with Mahler, she writes: "Strange though: yesterday I was calm and remained so, looked at [Zemlinsky], and suddenly felt, with a shudder, just how ugly he is, how strongly he smells etc. [Midsummer-night's dream!] All things I'd never noticed before. That is strange. [?!]" While obviously her statement is untrue—she repeatedly makes note of his "ugliness"—the timing here is interesting: does she begin to see him as more "Jewish" at the same moment that Mahler becomes less so in her eyes?

[70] AMW Diaries, p. 614/366; "Und er hat recht. *Was* will ich denn von ihm? Ja er gefällt mir—unsagbar gut...Aber wie er kam—seine unglaubliche Hässlichkeit, sein [scheusslicher] Geruch. Und dabei—bin ich merkwürdig aufgeregt in seiner Nähe." The later gloss on "Geruch"—hideous, revolting—is not reflected in the English translation.

[71] Gilman, *Jewish Self-hatred*, p. 174; Weiner, *Richard Wagner*, pp. 194–259 and Adorno and Horkheimer, *Dialectic of Enlightenment* (New York, 1991), p. 189, also discuss smell. See also Trachtenberg, *The Devil and the Jews*, pp. 47–50.

"how ridiculous it would look … he so ugly, so small—me so beautiful, so tall."[72] On 27 April, she asks, "is he one of those little half-Jews who never succeed in freeing themselves from their roots?" The picture postcard that prompted this is of a coffee house in the Leopoldstadt, the Jewish district.[73] That summer, while rumors flew among family and friends that she was going to marry him, she herself seems incapable of taking that irreversible step:

> [Saturday 28 July 1901]
> p.m. My feelings for him are stronger than ever. I have never loved him more—*never*. I would love him even more—freer, less inhibitedly—if that ominous word "marriage" were not beckoning from afar. For the idea of marrying him, of bearing his children—little, degenerate Jew-kids [*kleine degenerierte Judenkinder*] … On the other hand, I would be perpetuating his name. I love the word "Zemlinsky."[74]

Despite her strong feelings, it is the idea of marriage to him and his children that she rejects: that is, the societally approved necessary step to consummate a union and its possible consequences. Indeed, the tension between her very real attraction to him and her own feelings that the marriage would be unacceptable suggests that Alma, while she chafed under those societal constraints, nevertheless felt some obligation to them. Her comments about perpetuating his name and loving the word "Zemlinsky" suggest an attempt to decontextualize both Zemlinsky himself and her love for him: if only marriage—and children—were simply about perpetuating a name. Her struggle is a microcosm of the tensions inherent in fin-de-siècle Vienna: antisemitism is not about hatred but about the inability to see the Jew as anything but "other," separate from both oneself and society at large. One wonders if Zemlinsky understood her better than anyone: when she reminds him

[72] AMW Diaries, p. 660/399: "Und ich dachte mir so—wenn ich mit Z. dor am Altar stehen würde—wie lächerlich das doch sein würde … Er so hässlich—so klein, ich so schön—so groß."

[73] AMW Diaries, pp. 665/402–3: "Er hat mich gestern diese Ansichtskarte geschickt— und die hat meiner Liebe sehr geschadet. Ein Cafeehaus im II. Bezirk—Leopoldstadt … Ob er zu den kleinen Halbjuden gehört, die ihr ganzes Leben nicht von ihrer Judenschaft loskommen?" The postcard was from the Café Haus Maendel (II., Praterstrasse 33); see AMW Eng. edn, p. 402, fn. 9. The Leopoldstadt (now the 2nd District) was the original Jewish ghetto, erected in 1623, after the expulsion of the Jews from the Innenstadt. The Jews were completely expelled from Vienna in 1670 under Leopold I, but brought back only a few years later. "As late as 1900, approximately one third of all Viennese Jews lived [in the Leopoldstadt]." Hamann, *Hitler's Vienna*, pp. 325–6.

[74] AMW Diaries, p. 694/421.

that she had written that she wanted to be the mother of his children, "he kissed me on the forehead, & said he would never have expected it of me."[75]

Although Alma later famously stated that Mahler was a "Christgläublicher Jude"—a Jew who believed in Christ—her diary entries about Mahler are similarly conflicted. She is seduced by his status and importance, but cannot overcome her own prejudices. Less than a month after formally meeting him for the first time, in the entry for 3 December 1901, she writes the following:

—I'm on first name terms with Mahler now [*Ich bin mit Mahler per Du*— literally, "I am using the familiar second person with Mahler"]. He told me how much he loved me, and I could give him no reply. Do I really love him?—I have no idea. Sometimes I actually think not. So much irritates me:

his smell,

the way he sings,

the way he speaks [can't roll his rrrr's].

… He's a stranger to me. Our tastes differ …

And I don't know what to think, how to think—whether I love him or not— whether I love the director of the Opera, the wonderful conductor—or the man … Whether, when I subtract the one, anything is left of the other. And his art leaves me cold, so *dreadfully* cold [*Und seine Kunst, die mir so unendlich ferne liegt—so furchtbar ferne*]. In plain words [*auf deutsch*]: I don't believe in him as a composer. And I'm expected to bind my life to this man … I felt nearer to him from a distance than from near by.

I shudder.

… You can get used to a lot of things—given time … but patience is not Mahler's strong point.—

What should I do?[76]

---

[75] AMW Diaries, p. 724/443: "Er küsste mich auf die Stirn u. sagte, dass er das nie in mir vermuthet hätte." Although the date of this entry is unclear because of a missing page in the manuscript, it appears to have been just after Alma had met Mahler for the first time.

[76] AMW Diaries, pp. 731–2/449: "—Ich bin mit Mahler per Du. Er sagte mir, wie er mich liebe, und ich konnte ihm kein Antwort geben. Ja, liebe ich ihn und denn? – Ich habe keine Ahnung. Manchmal glaube ich direct—nein.

So *vieles* irritiert mich:

sein Geruch,

sein Vorsingen,

einiges in seinem Sprechen! [ohne rrrr]

… Er ist mir Fremder. Unser Geschmacksrichtungen gehen auseinander.

…

Und ich weiß nicht, was in mir ist, wie's in mir ist—ob ich ihn liebe, ob ich nicht liebe—ob der Director, der herrliche Dirigent derjenige ist—oder der Mensch … Ob, wenn ich von dem Einen abstrahiere, für das Andrer etwas Bliebt. Und seine Kunst, die mir so unendlich ferne liegt—so *furchtbar* ferne. Auf deutsch: Als Componist glaube ich nicht an

Alma seems to be struggling with her own ideas of difference: smell, voice, lack of creativity—all are traits ascribed by her culture to the Jews.[77] She is clearly drawn to him but repulsed at the same time, wary of his art and of what it would mean to commit herself to him. To put Alma's diary entry in perspective, Roller had described Mahler's speaking voice very differently:

> Incidentally, Mahler spoke a fine, pure form of German that was completely free of any foreign intonation, and he uttered clear, redounded sentences that did not sound at all bombastic. His delivery was very masculine. His "r"s were quite strongly emphasized and rather guttural. [78]

It is unclear whether Alma and Roller are making the same claim regarding Mahler's *r*s. However, Roller is obviously emphasizing that Mahler did not speak with a Yiddish or any other accent (*fern ... von jeglichem Fremdklang* = lit. "free from a single foreign sound")[79] and did not have a "Jewish" (that is a high) voice (this despite his insistence on Mahler's two "registers"). Given these contradictions, the beginning of Alma's diary entry thus looks more like a laundry list of Jewish traits than a description, a way of voicing her own anxieties rather than necessarily describing Mahler himself.

For Alma, marrying Mahler held the same taboos as marrying Zemlinsky: their union could only produce "kleine degenerierte Judenkinder." Her metaphor of distance emphasizes their racial difference. In the entry from 3 December, that idea of distance is clearer in the German: a better translation might be, his art "lies so infinitely far from me—so frightfully far." Despite being *per Du* with him, all she feels are unbridgeable gaps, not just between herself and him, but also between the Director and the man, between herself and his music. Her concern about his "otherness" comes up elsewhere in her diaries. For example, only a few days later she comments, "Never in my life have I met anyone as alien as he. How alien [and yet so close!] I cannot say. Maybe that's one of the things that attracts me to

---

ihn. Und soll mein Leben an den Menschen binden ... Er ist mir von ferne eigentlich näher gestanden, wie von nah.

Mir grauts. –

... Viel macht die Gewohnheit, viel die—Zeit ... aber <u>Geduld</u> ist nicht Sache meines Mahler.

Was soll ich thun?"

[77]   "Lack of creativity" as a potential sign of Jewish inferiority will be discussed in Chapter 3.

[78]   Roller, pp. 20/159–160: "Übrigens sprach Mahler ungemein fesselnd und anschaulich in klaren, wohlgefügten Sätzen, fern von jedem Schwulst und in einem schönen, reinen, von jeglichem Fremdklang vollkommen freien Deutsch. Seine Rede war männlich. Das 'R' wurde etwas stark betont und ein ganz klein wenig gaumig gesprochen."

[79]   The role of language, Yiddish, and accented speech as "signs" will be discussed in Chapter 3.

him."[80] As with her attraction to Zemlinsky, it seems at least partially motivated precisely by the things that repel her. Yet she adds, "but he should let me be as I am." His foreignness is both exotic and a threat: she goes on to say that "already I'm aware of changes in myself, due to him. He's taking much away from me and giving me much in return. If this goes on, he'll make a new person of me. A better person? I don't know. I don't know at all."[81] Like Burckhard, she is becoming different. She leaves the meaning of that difference ambiguous.

Obviously, Alma did decide to marry Mahler, so how did she manage to overcome the ambivalence that she could not put aside in the case of Zemlinsky? In the *Memories*, Alma writes about the past while presuming the reader's knowledge of her own future; there is no need to explain why she decided to marry him since of course she did. The *Diaries*, however, allow us to see the process that lay behind her decision. On 9 December, she reports that Felix Muhr told her:

> that Gustav was suffering from an incurable disease and that he was weakening perceptibly.—Dear God, I shall nurse him like a child. I will not be the cause of his downfall. I shall restrain my longing and my passion—I want to cure him—let him recuperate through my strength and youthfulness.
> My beloved Master ...[82]

The next day, she reports that she "didn't get a wink of sleep all night" because of her worries about "Gustav's ill health." In her mind, it seems that his "weakness" made him childlike, and, one might dare say, less threatening. She envisions herself as the person who can save him—but from what? The "cure" that she offers—her "strength and youthfulness"—while opposed to his age and weakness, can also be seen as the forces of assimilation. Mahler can be "cured" of his Jewishness by marriage, by allowing him to enter *her* society. Far from being the cause of his downfall, then,

---

[80] AMW Diaries, p. 733/451: "Ich habe in meinem Leben noch keinen Menschen getroffen, der mir fremder war wie er. Aber so fremd [und so nah!], ich kanns gar nicht sagen. Vielleicht ist gerade das ein Moment, das mich hinzieht zu ihm." Here as elsewhere, her additions are interesting: reading over her diaries again many years later, perhaps she felt that her words seemed cold; or, from that distance in time and space, they would no longer be understood as she originally meant them—or even that she no longer meant them in that way.

[81] Ibid.: "Nur mich soll er lassen, wie ich bin. Und ich fühle bereits deutlich die Umwandlungen, die in mir durch ihn vorgehen. Vieles nimmt er mir, vieles gibt er. Geht das so fort, so macht er einen andern, neuen Menschen aus mir. Einen Besseren? Ich weiß es nicht. Ich weiß überhaupt *gar* nichts."

[82] AMW Diaries, p. 738/456: "Muhr sagte mir heute, ein Arzt habe ihm gesagt, Gustav sei unheilbar krank, u. siene Kräfteabnahme sei merklich.—Ach Gott, ich will ihn hüten wie mein Kind. An mir soll er nicht zu Grund gehen. Ich will mein Sehnen u. meine Leidenschaft zügeln—heilen will ich ihn ... gesunden soll er an meiner Kraft und Jugend." Muhr, an architect, was another suitor of Alma's, and de La Grange suggests that his comments were motivated out of jealousy; DLG II: 441.

she envisions herself as *his* savior. After this, her expressions of his mastery over her ("my beloved Master," "my Savior!") may suggest the very opposite.

Yet her reinventing of him as a child in need of her assistance is only the peripeteia: the epiphany is his letter to her demanding that she give up her music. Prior to this, she still confessed to her diary her desire for Zemlimsky, reported her flirtations with Burckhard, Louis Adler, and Muhr—in general, showed no sign of having made up her mind. Despite more sympathetic feelings toward Mahler, she had yet to make a choice. It is odd, given Alma's self-portrait in the *Memories*—where the loss of her art is the wound that never heals—that the deciding factor for her was the command to renounce her compositional aspirations, which apparently arrived as a letter on 20 December.[83] The next day, 21 December, she rereads the letter, asking her diary, "What if I were to *renounce* [my music] *out of love* for him?" Then she seems to make up her mind: "Yes—he's right. I must live *entirely* for him, to make him happy. And now I have a strange feeling that my love for him is deep & genuine."[84] Only three days after receiving his letter, she reports their "official" engagement.

In *Memories and Letters*, Alma often places herself in an intermediary, acculturating role. She maintains, for example, that Mahler instructed her to let him know if he used his hands too much while speaking. It is clear from the context in which Alma provides this information that she associates excessive gesticulation with "Jewishness."[85] In her book, she writes that Mahler "was not a man who ever deceived himself" about his Jewish heritage and how he understood that others "would not forget he was a Jew" even if he had been baptized. She goes on to say that neither "did he wish it [his Jewishness] forgotten, even though he frequently asked me to warn him when he gesticulated too much, because he hated to see others do so and thought it ill bred."[86] Mahler cannot control his own behavior, nor can he recognize when he might be offending others. He requires Alma to help him assimilate into polite (Viennese, gentile) society. Likewise, Roller had noted that it was Alma who had campaigned to get Gustav to stop biting his nails. Alma's (self-proclaimed) role is to tame Mahler, to make him—visibly, at least—less Jewish.

Henri-Louis de La Grange places Alma's moment of decision regarding her engagement to Mahler much earlier, as a consequence of Mahler's private dedication to her of his 8 December performance of *The Magic Flute*; he also

---

[83]   Alma claimed to have destroyed this letter, but the original is in the Moldenhauer archive; see DLG II: 448–52. His Chapter 12 deals with Mahler's meeting and engagement to Alma (pp. 417–70).

[84]   AMW Diaries, p. 745/462: "In der früh seinen Brief durchgelesen—und so warm kams auf einmal über ich. Wie wars, wenn ich *ihm zu Liebe verzichten würde*?" "Ja—er hat recht. Ich muss ihm *ganz* leben, damit er glücklich wird. Und ich fühle jetzt gar seltsam, dass ich ihn tief u. echt liebe."

[85]   On gesticulation as a sign of neurasthenia—to which Jews were said in the nineteenth century to be more at risk—see my "'Ein hypermoderner Dirigent,'" esp. pp. 263–7.

[86]   AM Memories, p. 101.

suggests that it was Anna Moll's attempts to convince her daughter to break with Mahler that "in fact helped her to decide to give in, since Alma had consulted her mother only in order to test her loyalty."[87] Nevertheless, it seems likely that it was both the possibility of reconceiving (and making harmless) Mahler's Jewishness along with the opportunity to prove her love to him (and the world?) that allowed Alma to accept the engagement. She had earlier commented in her diary that she was annoyed that Zemlinsky did not "dare" call her by her first name—and she detested "people who don't dare."[88] Whether Alma is grateful for the opportunity to prove her love or whether she sees Mahler's demand as a sign of his strength is unclear. In any event, it must be remembered that Alma's favorite opera was *Tristan*: perhaps the prospect of placing herself in the self-sacrificing role of Isolde was irresistible.

Paul Lawrence Rose offers another perspective on *Tristan*—that its anti-Jewish message comes in the form of self-sacrifice: "redemption [in *Tristan*] is the annihilation of the self and the egoistic will: and of course, the supreme embodiments of egoism are the Jews, with their God made in the image of their own will." Rose relates *Tristan* to the earlier and unset libretto *Jesus of Nazareth* where "authentic love (according to the *Jesus* texts) must be given rather than received, and this is indeed the nature of sexual love, which is actually related to death." In Rose's reading, then, Alma's act was one of asserting power over Mahler by being the one to choose "redemption."[89]

As Lebrecht states, she portrays Mahler in the *Memories* "as prematurely old, in poor health, and a confirmed virgin"—all patently untrue.[90] Her own self-deception—perhaps willful blindness or else the overwhelming desire to construct her own "childlike" Mahler—is interesting. In the passage from the *Memories* regarding her first meeting with Mahler, she does mention that she knew of the scandals about him and young women at the opera, although she later denies that he was anything but a virgin. Again, her diaries are revealing: in the entry of 13 December she mentions Mahler's many affairs but has then added, "Later I discovered it was all lies!"[91] Given her deep unease regarding what we now recognize as the assumed nature of the Jew, perhaps our mistrust of her portrait should be more general. For example, in her book she describes what she calls the "full-dress review" by Mahler's friends, where Mildenburg asks her opinion of Mahler's music and she replies: "'I know very little of it, but what I do know I don't like.'" Her diary, however, states simply: "This evening:

---

[87] DLG II: 438–9; 453. Also note that Alma between 8 and 21 Dec. reports to her diaries her continuous flirtations with various men.

[88] AMW Diaries, p. 660/399, in the entry for 19 Apr. 1901: "Ich hasse alle Menschen, die sich nicht //getrauen//…" "Getrauen" has been crossed out by Alma.

[89] Paul Lawrence Rose, *Wagner: Race and Revolution* (New Haven and London, 1992), pp. 170–71 and 55.

[90] Lebrecht, *Mahler Remembered*, p. xiii.

[91] AMW Diaries, p. 741/458: "[War alles unwahr, wie ich festellen konnte!]"

at Gustav's. His friends … all conspicuously Jewish. I could find no bond … amused myself by stunning them with unprecedented impertinence, said I didn't care for Gustav's music etc." Given that this scene takes place after their first successful sexual encounter, is it not reasonable to see her qualms displaced onto his Jewish friends and his music? Having renounced everything for him, she is now in power. She has yet to discover her pregnancy (she writes in the *Memories* that "all my self-assurance was undermined by the psychological effects of becoming pregnant before being married"), has yet to understand fully the consequences of being married to a man like Mahler. The story of their marriage, in a sense, becomes Alma's struggle to regain that fleeting sense of power over Mahler—his Jewishness, her fear—that she had felt for those few days in January, and it is against this backdrop, then, that her portrait of Mahler in *Memories and Letters* needs to be read.

Race Matters

Being Jewish meant being visible; conversion appeared to offer a solution, yet it could not erase bodily signs. In Panizza's story, Stern tries to become a German but fails. Not only does he bleach and straighten his hair, but he also has his bones broken and reset, wears a corset to minimize his "Jewish" movements, takes speech therapy to remove all traces of his Yiddish accent, and even attempts to purchase a German soul. In the end, the experiment is a failure, and Stern lies "crumpled and quivering, a convoluted Asiatic image … a counterfeit of human flesh."[92] The Jewish response to this story illustrates the extent to which even Jews had internalized the biological immutability of race. In Salomo Friedlaender's rebuttal, "The Operated Goy," written in 1922, the protagonist, the antisemitic Count Rehsok, desires to become a Jew in order to win the love of the beautiful Rebecca.[93] The Count undergoes the reverse of Stern's operations: his bones are made crooked, his nose is given an artificial hump, his feet are made flat, he learns Yiddish with all its accompanying gestures. His conversion (including circumcision) is not complete in Rebecca's eyes until he *looked* like a Jew. For Friedlaender and Panizza alike—more generally, for both philosemites and antisemites—racial difference was real, and, being biologically based, ineradicable.

Mahler himself, of course, had converted to Catholicism and had been baptized on 23 February 1897—but he had no illusions about what his "official" conversion meant in Vienna. In a discussion regarding the appointment of young conductors at the Hofoper, Mahler said (in regard to Leo Blech): "It won't work, unfortunately, even if he has been baptized as you say. For the anti-Semites, I still count as a

---

[92] Zipes, *The Operated Jew*, p. 74.
[93] Mynona (Salomo Friedlaender), "Der operirte Goj: ein Seitenstück zu Panizzas operirtem Jud'," trans. from the Yiddish and published in Zipes, *The Operated Jew*, pp. 75–86. "Rehsok" is of course "kosher" backwards (Reschok/Koscher in the original).

Jew despite my baptism, and more than one Jew is more than the Vienna Court Opera can bear." Similarly, in regard to the possible appointment of Bruno Walter: "I can't engage him because he is a Jew. Admittedly by race only, as he has long since been baptized a Protestant. But unfortunately, it is the race that matters."[94]

Alma positions herself as the cultural agent of assimilation that will bring Mahler's Jewishness under control, yet her portrait of him infantalizes that part of him that she cannot abide. She must insist on his virginity, just as she must insist on his childishness, pettiness, naïveté, and weakness, because to believe anything else would be to acknowledge the threat, sexual or otherwise, of the Jew. On the other hand, Roller is the "objective artist," giving us a picture that must be authentic because the author, unlike Alma, seems to have no agenda other than the aesthetic. Illustrated with photographs that are referred to in the German but not the English, it seduces with detail. Yet while Roller may not have been an antisemite, indeed, may not have even have thought about Mahler *as a Jew*, his essay nevertheless betrays his unconscious absorption of those cultural markers of difference, even as he tries to explain them away. Their "Mahler"—like so many of the portraits from this time, this place—cannot but be a product of the culture that produced it, the Vienna where being Jewish had little to do with religion and everything to do with differences constructed by race.

Whatever one thinks of Alma, or her self-serving prose, or the nature of her relationship with Mahler, she nonetheless gives us a glimpse of the otherwise internal monologue of ambivalence that characterized Viennese love and hate for Mahler. Without her diaries, we would never see what lay beneath Stefan Zweig's "world of security." For him to have written that he never "experienced the slightest suppression or indignity as a Jew" while growing up in Vienna, the most antisemitic of cities, is to acknowledge that antisemitism was being expressed in ways more casual and less overt than Zweig was aware.[95] Both Alma and Roller emphasize the belief in Jewish difference, albeit in divergent ways and for conflicting purposes. Indeed, they show us not only how to speak openly about Jewishness, and but also how to express oneself behind closed doors.

---

[94] Ludwig Karpath, *Begegnung mit dem Genius: denkwürdige Erlebnisse mit Johannes Brahms—Gustav Mahler—Hans Richter, und vielen anderen bedeutenden Menschen* (Vienna and Leipzig, 1934), trans. in Lebrecht, *Mahler Remembered*, pp. 107, 105–6.

[95] Stefan Zweig, *The World of Yesterday*, no trans. given (New York and London, 1964; orig. New York, 1943), p. 5; it is also the title of Ch. 1. On p. 1, he calls it "The Golden Age of Security." Zweig, it must be said, was a rather naïve and self-centered man. The quote about never experiencing antisemitism is on p. 25.

Chapter 3
Das Judentum in der Musik

A "Useless Model"

While Mahler's Jewish background may seem unimportant now—or indeed, something to be purposely excluded from discussion—such a lack of knowledge of or interest in the cultural situation makes it impossible to understand the reception of Mahler's music during his lifetime.[1] For those critics writing while Mahler still lived in Vienna, Jewishness was *the* fact that determined how Mahler would behave, look, speak, walk, and conduct, and how he would write music. As noted in Chapter 2, the work of Sander Gilman and others leaves little doubt that an extensive set of expectations existed that foretold or described Jewish behavior. It seems unlikely that in music of all things—perhaps, after language the most important bearer of German identity—Jewish composers were not perceived as a serious threat. I have discussed elsewhere how these stereotypes influenced how

---

[1]   I am hardly the first to study either Mahler and antisemitism or Mahler and Jewishness; see, for example, Raymond Knapp and Francesca Draughton, "Gustav Mahler and the Crisis of Jewish Identity," *Echo* 3 (2001), available at www.echo.ucla.edu; Draughton, "Mahler and the Music of Fin-de-siècle Identity", PhD diss., University of California at Los Angeles (2002); Susan Filler, "Mahler as a Jew in the Literature," in *Dika Caecilia: Essays for Dika Newlin*, ed. Theodore Albrecht (Kansas City, 1988); Vladimír Karbuskicky, "Gustav Mahlers musikalisches Judentum," *Hamburger Jahrbuch für Musikwissenschaft* 16 (1999), pp. 179–207, trans. and ed. Jeremy Barnum as "Gustav Mahler's Musical Jewishness," in his *Perspectives on Gustav Mahler* (Aldershot, 2005), pp. 195–216; Karen Painter, "Contested Counterpoint: 'Jewish' Appropriation and Polyphonic Liberation," *Archiv für Musikwissenschaft* 58 (2001), pp. 201–30. I do not know why Karbuskicky chooses the word "Judentum" in his title—he makes no mention of Wagner, if that was his intent—and while the German might be more neutral now, that word had menacing overtones in the nineteenth century: "jewry" is a better translation than "Jewishness." Even more alarming, he quotes Rudolf Louis's most infamous line about Mahler's music as if it were a neutral judgment: Mahler's music "*jüdelt*. In other words, it speaks the language of German music but with an accent, with the intonation and above all with the gestures of the Easterner, the all-too-Eastern Jew." To this Karbuskicky claims that "Even [sic!] Mahler's anti-Semitic enemies have detected [the Hasidic] trait in his music." Rudolf Louis, *Die deutsche Musik der Gegenwart* (Munich and Leipzig, 1909), p. 182: "Das heißt: sie spricht musikalisches Deutsch, aber mit einem Akzent, met dem Tonfall und vor allem mit der Geste des östlichen, des allzu östlichen Juden." I would translate the last phrase as "of the eastern, the all too eastern Jew." Rev. edn 1912. I will not dwell on the limitations of the other studies.

Mahler was seen as a conductor.[2] Was there also a vocabulary to describe the way the music of a Jewish composer would *sound*? The most obvious candidate for such a role is Richard Wagner's essay of 1850, *Das Judentum in der Musik*, but it has been largely ignored by musicologists, in part because such a description was not Wagner's goal, and in part because he presented only vague examples.

It is my contention, however, that critics did in fact treat Wagner's essay as a handbook or guide for describing the music of Jewish composers, and that examination of Wagner's language in the essay can illuminate many of the earliest reviews of Mahler's music, and perhaps the reviews of other Jewish composers as well. I do not argue that Wagner was the originator of such language or its only source; nor do I imagine that other models did not exist. Yet Wagner occupied a position in the musical world that ensured his work would be read and relied upon by other writers. Wagner's essay not only collects many images of Jewish inferiority in one place, but it also relates those images specifically to music. How is it, then, that its significance for later criticism has been overlooked?

Part of the answer to that question lies in the nature of the essay itself, and part lies in the nature of Wagner scholarship. Scholars outside music have long recognized Wagner's important position in the history of antisemitism, but while Wagner's antisemitism cannot be erased, even by Wagner's staunchest defenders, there has been reluctance within musical scholarship to see it as an integral part of his artistic output. In particular, scholars have wanted to protect Wagner's works from the charge that they contain images or characters that are meant to be read as antisemitic, let alone that the works carry messages of "Aryan" superiority. The standard strategy to defend the goal of separation has been to isolate Wagner's life from his works, and to assert that while his views were repugnant, they nonetheless leave no trace in his art. Recent publications by Barry Millington, Paul Lawrence Rose, and Marc Weiner have attempted to reconnect Wagner with his own writings, showing, against the prevailing apologist trend, that Wagner's music dramas make extensive use of accepted Jewish stereotypes.[3] Perhaps because the life-and-works battle has raged so fiercely,[4] the question of Wagner's influence on musical criticism remains largely unexplored. And while the argument continues as to whether it is

---

[2]   See my "'Ein hypermoderner Dirigent': Mahler and Anti-Semitism in *Fin-de-siècle* Vienna," *19th-Century Music* 18 (1995), pp. 257–76 and "'Polemik im Conzertsaal': Mahler, Beethoven, and the Viennese Critics," *19th-Century Music* 29 (2006), pp. 289–321; the first discusses images and descriptions of Mahler on the podium; the second discusses Mahler's years as the director of the Vienna Philharmonic (1898–1901), in particular, his revision of the orchestration of works, most famously, Beethoven's Ninth Symphony.

[3]   Barry Millington, "Nuremburg Trial: Is there Anti-Semitism in *Die Meistersinger?*" *Cambridge Opera Journal* 3 (1991), pp. 247–60; Paul Lawrence Rose, *Wagner: Race and Revolution* (New Haven and London, 1992); and Marc A. Weiner, *Richard Wagner and the Anti-Semitic Imagination* (Lincoln and London, 1995).

[4]   The reaction to Weiner has been particularly vicious; see, for example, Thomas Grey, "Bodies of Evidence," *Cambridge Opera Journal* 8 (1995), 185–97; review by Pamela M.

Wagner's music itself that carries antisemitic messages or only his plots and/or characters that do, the discussions of Wagner's written views have centered largely on how those writings fit into the history of antisemitism in general.[5]

Did Wagner's views influence other *musical* writers? Here the problem lies not with the secondary scholarship but rather with the essay itself. Pamela Potter has gone so far as to say that Wagner cannot be used as a model to examine criticism:

> After 1933, antisemitism became a multipurpose political weapon for attacking any opposing point of view ... But while racial antisemitism started to take root in many academic disciplines, pursuing such a line in musicology was problematic. The best known tract on Jews and Music, Wagner's 1850 essay *Das Judentum in der Musik*, served as a useless model and any examples of musicological work that attempted to bind music to any race were haphazard and inconclusive ... By 1930, attempts to apply racial theories to musicology were virtually nonexistent.[6]

Despite the fact that Potter speaks here of Nazi musicology, her position that Wagner was a "useless model" is the prevailing one. The reason for this belief is Wagner's apparent failure in *Das Judentum in der Musik* to provide concrete musical examples to support his claims. Wagner mentions no specific musical characteristics or traits and refers only to Mendelssohn by name and Meyerbeer by implication.

It is a mistake, however, to assume that without a taxonomy of Jewish music— Wagner's stated goal being a critique of what he calls the "be-jewing" ("Verjudung") of German art—his essay fails to identify what is wrong with Jewish music *as music*. Out of context, Wagner's claims do seem vague and unspecific. However, placed within the essay's broader assumptions regarding Jewish difference, and given the general currency of those assumptions in nineteenth-century Europe, Wagner's opposition of impoverished surface and privileged depth furnishes a powerful metaphor to describe all types of Jewish inferiority. Marc Weiner has discussed the importance of this image for Wagner,[7] and within the essay it allows Wagner to criticize everything from the status of Jews as outsiders to their

---

Potter, published by H-German@msu.edu (January 1996), and Lisa Norris, "Jewish Dwarfs and Teutonic Gods," published by H-Judaic@h-net.msu.edu (September 1997).

[5] See, for example, Jacob Katz, *The Darker Side of Genius: Richard Wagner's Anti-Semitism* (Hanover and London, 1986); Paul Lawrence Rose, *German Question/Jewish Question: Revolutionary Antisemitism from Kant to Wagner* (Princeton, 1990); Sander L. Gilman, *Jewish Self-hatred: Anti-Semitism and the Hidden Language of the Jews* (Baltimore and London, 1986), esp. pp. 209–211; and Jens Malte Fischer, *Richard Wagners "Das Judentum in der Musik": Eine kritische Dokumentation als Beitrag zur Geschichte des Antisemitismus* (Frankfurt am Mein and Leipzig, 2000).

[6] Pamela M. Potter, "Anti-Semitism in German Musicology, 1900–1945: Theory and Practice," paper read at the 60th Annual Meeting of the American Musicological Society, 28 October 1994, Minneapolis; unpaginated typescript.

[7] Weiner, *Richard Wagner*, pp. 39–44.

incapacity to be truly creative, and ultimately to claim that their music was not and could never be expressive.

The same language and oppositions can be found in critics writing about Mahler; in each case, specific musical "problems" are linked to the lack of Jewish creativity, to the status of the Jew as the outsider in a culture that he does not understand, and to the insufficiency of feeling or absence of a musical "kernel" that would indicate a poet rather than a mere thinker. In Mahler's case, these deficiencies include his melodic eclecticism, his failure to manage large-scale forms, and his attempts to hide his lack of originality under the cloak of orchestration. In what follows, by carefully examining his language, I will attempt both to explain Wagner's ideological position vis-à-vis Jews as composers and to show how his essays might be been seen as prescriptive for later criticism.

Das Judentum in der Musik was originally published pseudonymously in 1850, then reissued under Wagner's own name in 1869.[8] Much has been made of the years 1848–50 as a watershed in the development of Wagner's antisemitic thinking, but, as Weiner points out, one can find references to racial distinctions as early as 1841 and throughout Wagner's writings until his death.[9] Wagner employs the metaphors noted above interchangeably with specific references to Jewish inferiority. For this reason, some of Wagner's essays, seeming less explicitly antisemitic than *Judentum*, are not recognized as such. Although *Judentum* reveals Wagner's basic ideological position regarding the Jews, it should be noted that none of the ideas expressed in *Das Judentum in der Musik* are original with Wagner, nor are those assertions confined in his writings to this essay alone. The essay raises many complex issues, including that of its relationship to Wagner's own personal situation and his larger output. My focus will be on why Wagner believed the Jews to be incapable of composition and creativity, what in particular he adduced as the signs of that inferiority, and the extent to which Wagner was merely a compiler—not a creator—of the images presented in the essay.

---

[8]   Richard Wagner, "Judentum in der Musik," *Richard Wagner's Prose Works*, trans. William Ashton Ellis, 8 vols (New York and London, 1966; rpt 1894); the essay is in vol. 3, pp. 75–122 (the 1850 original ends on p. 100) and Ellis translates it as "Judaism in Music." While this is technically correct, a better translation would be "Jewry in Music." Ellis and Jens Malte Fischer, *Richard Wagners "Das Judentum in der Musik,"* both compare the 1869 version to the 1850. The differences amount to wording, added sentences in the case of the 1869 version, and the addition of a long, rambling postlude for the later version. A note regarding the Ellis translation: while many find it distasteful and difficult, I believe it does a better job of conveying the difficulty of the original German than a cleaner translation would.

[9]   Weiner, *Richard Wagner*, pp. 53–65.

Wagner's *Das Judentum in der Music*

Perhaps the central image in Wagner's ideology of race is the idea of community. For Wagner, a community is a group of people who share certain similarities of language, appearance, and habit. Weiner stresses, however, that the differences are far more important: "the unified community comprised of similar members defines itself by rejecting what is different."[10] Wagner defines Greek drama as the perfect artwork because it was said to be a reflection of the community itself. When the Greeks beheld the tragedy, they in a sense beheld themselves, saw themselves reflected back: the Greek community watched the drama "in order ... to understand itself ... to dissolve its being, its community ... into innermost unity and thus in the noblest deepest peace to be that once again which a few hours before it had also been in restless excitement and isolated individuality."[11] The drama was thus both descriptive, in that it showed the Greeks to themselves, and prescriptive, in that it was the guarantor or vehicle of social transformation. "Art ... is nothing other than the fulfillment of a longing to recognize oneself in a represented, admired, or beloved object, to find oneself again in the phenomena of the outer world through their representation."[12] Wagner's own theories regarding musical drama are an attempt to recapture both the prescriptive and descriptive aspects of Greek drama.

Defining the German community, however, proved a more complicated task than describing the ancient Greek. In his essay *Was ist deutsch?* [What is German?], published in 1878, Wagner agreed that the true origin of those people who began to call themselves "Deutsche" is not known, and his definition therefore relied upon the continuity of language and habits: "'Deutsche' is the title given to those Germanic races which, upon their natal soil, retained their speech and customs."[13] The Germans are nothing more than a collection of peoples who remained on one side of the Rhine and "continued to speak their ure-mother-tongue [sic]."[14] Defining the German community is thus tantamount to rejecting those who did not share the "speech and customs" of the Germans.

Thus, the Jew's inability to compose, Wagner believed, originated in their status as eternal outsiders, those who are rejected as different. Wagner reiterates in *Das Judentum in der Musik* the dogma that Jews were everywhere foreigners: "The Jew has stood outside the pale of any ... community, stood solitarily with his Jehova in a splintered soilless stock." Because language requires "an historical community," the Jew may speak the language of his chosen country, but will do so "always as an alien." Thus, their outsider status bars them from true understanding, and also from expression; the Jew is kept from "expressing himself idiomatically,

---

[10] Weiner, *Richard Wagner*, p. 50.

[11] Wagner, *Kunst und die Revolution*, cited in Weiner, p. 38.

[12] Wagner, *Oper und Drama*, cited in Weiner, p. 37.

[13] Wagner, *What is German?*, in *Prose Works*, vol. 4, pp. 149–69; quote is p. 159.

[14] Wagner, *What is German?*, p. 152.

independently, and conformably to his nature."[15] Art, like language, also originates in and requires a community: Wagner states that "the true poet, no matter in what branch of art, still gains his stimulus from nothing but the faithful, loving contemplation of instinctive Life, of that life which only greets his sight amid the folk."[16] The poet gives voice to the unconscious thoughts of the community, and the community then recognizes itself as reflected in that artistic endeavor. The Jew, however, lacking that community, is thus without art: "Alien and apathetic stands the educated Jew in [the] midst of a society he does not understand, with whose tastes and aspirations he does not sympathise, whose history and evolution have always been indifferent to him." In such a situation, the Jew becomes a thinker, or "backward looking poet," constantly seeking to fit himself into "his learnt and paid for culture."[17]

Throughout his essay, Wagner equates the Jews' inability to compose with their inability to command any European language as a native: both—composition and language—Wagner believes, the Jew knows only as "learnt, and not mother tongues."[18] The Jews' attempts at communication he describes as "outlandish and unpleasant," and as a result, "when we hear this Jewish talk, our attention dwells involuntarily on its repulsive *how*, rather than on any meaning of its intrinsic *what*." According to Wagner, the message is lost because its mode of expression is so conspicuously odd. Even when the Jew attempts to speak true German, Wagner betrays himself as a Jew by his accented speech. Wagner emphatically states that it is this circumstance—the awkwardness of presentation and its consequent demand of attention—that must be born in mind when discussing the "music-works of modern Jews."[19]

Wagner uses the distinction between *how* and *what* to further suggest that the Jew is incapable of any *what* at all. "European art and civilization ... have remained to the Jew a foreign tongue," because the Jew, standing outside the community and denied its essence, has no access to the source of art.[20] The Jew can only listen "to the barest surface of our art, but not to its life bestowing inner organism," and "therefore the most external accidents on the domain of musical life and art must pass for its very essence."[21] In this second use of "*how* vs. *what*," the Jew is left to focus on the "how," since, as Wagner puts it, "the *how* was the only 'moment' left ... to care for."[22] Whereas in the discussion of language, Wagner implied that the message was lost because of the foreignness of the Jew's speech, here he emphasizes that there is—and can be—no message whatsoever. The Jews' music

---

[15]   Wagner, *Judentum*, p. 84.

[16]   Ibid., p. 89.

[17]   Ibid., p. 88.

[18]   Ibid., p. 84.

[19]   Ibid., p. 85; italics orig.

[20]   Ibid., p. 84.

[21]   Ibid., p. 92.

[22]   Ibid., pp. 88–9; italics orig.

is, as a result, all "coldness and indifference ... triviality and absurdity;" and the listener is offended by "the entire want of purely-human expression."[23]

In his discussion of Wagner's opera *Die Meistersinger von Nürnberg*, Weiner provides a powerful example by reading Beckmesser's use of language. The character of Beckmesser can be seen to embody Jewish stereotypes, and, in the opera, Beckmesser's attempt to steal Walther's prize-song results in a garbled mess precisely because Beckmesser cannot fully understand what he is singing/saying. Weiner considers *Meistersinger* as a whole to be the "scenic representation of ideas expressed in essays such as 'Das Judentum in der Musik' [and] 'Was ist Deutsch.'" Thus Walther's lines from the final act:

Morgentlich leuchtend in rosigem Schein,
voll Blüt' und Duft
geschwellt die Luft
voll aller Wonnen
nie ersonnen,
ein Garten lud mich ein
Gast ihm zu sein.

[Beaming with morning's rosy splendor, and filled with blooms and scents, with all the joys as yet unknown, a garden beckoned me to be its guest within.]

become in Beckmesser's version:

Morgen ich leuchte in rosigem Schein
voll Blut und Duft
geht schnell die Luft;–
wohl bald geronnen,
wie zerronnen,–
im Garten lud ich ein–
garstig und fein.

[Tomorrow I shine in rosy shimmer, full of blood and aroma the air goes quickly;--surely soon curdled, as if evaporated,--in the garden I invited--ugly and fine.][24]

Weiner calls Beckmesser's version "a linguistic tour de force dramatizing both the Jew's inability to understand and to appropriate German art and therefore to adequately and truthfully 'reflect' the German's essence in an aesthetic creation." Yet when Walther sings, the *Volk* spontaneously join in the last lines of his song—a

---

23 Ibid., pp. 93 and 85.
24 Weiner, *Richard Wagner*, pp. 66–71; on the character of Beckmesser, see also Millington, "Nuremburg Trial," cited above.

song that they could not know—illustrating not just the rejection of foreign elements but the innate recognition of the self and "thus the borders of the community."[25]

Having no music of their own except for the music of the ancient synagogue—"an expression whose content has long-since ceased to be the breath of feeling" and has grown "senseless and distorted"—the Jewish composer has no choice but to imitate others:

> Just as words and constructions are hurled together in this jargon with wondrous inexpressiveness, so does the Jew musician hurl together the diverse forms and styles of every age and every master. Packed side by side, we find the formal idiosyncrasies of all the schools, in motleyest chaos.[26]

For example, when Mendelssohn chose to write oratorios, "he was obliged quite openly to snatch at every formal detail that had served as characteristic token of the individuality of this or that forerunner whom he chose out for his model,"[27] since he had no creative capacity himself. Wagner also claims that the "forerunner" that Mendelssohn had chosen for a model—J.S. Bach—was far easier to imitate than Beethoven. Therefore, Mendelssohn lacks even the capacity required to effectively imitate other styles. Likewise, "through his indifference to the spirit of any tongue," Meyerbeer is denied creativity: "Not one departure is his own, but each he has eavesdropped from his forerunner, exploiting it with monstrous ostentation."[28] The lack of Jewish creativity, as attested by Mendelssohn and Meyerbeer, stems from their lack of community; since they have no *Volk* to draw on for inspiration, they have no choice but to imitate others. To mimic implies lack of feeling or expression, and Wagner compares Jewish composers to parrots, who "reel off human words and phrases, but also with just as little real feeling and expression as these foolish birds."[29]

The problem with Jewish music, as with language, is that it lacks depth. But it is not enough for Wagner to assert that this metaphor adequately describes Jewish music—the inferiority of Jewish music must immediately be recognized. Wagner believed that either intentionally or instinctively, the Jew would try to hide his music's lack of feeling and emptiness:

---

[25]   Weiner, *Richard Wagner*, pp. 70–71, and 71.

[26]   Wagner, *Judentum*, pp. 90 and 92; the claim that synagogue music has "kept its fixity of form and substance" and therefore never has been "quickened through renewal of its substance" (90) may be an echo of Luther's claims that the Jews insist on maintaining "their error": that is, of rejecting Jesus. See Gilman, *Jewish Self-hatred*, p. 66.

[27]   Wagner, *Judentum*, p. 94.

[28]   Wagner, *Opera and Drama*, in *Prose Works*, vol. 2, pp. 88–9. Meyerbeer is discussed by name in *Opera and Drama*, but not *Judentum*. The two works are roughly contemporary: *Opera and Drama* (1850–52); *Judentum* (orig. 1850).

[29]   Wagner, *Judentum*, p. 89.

As in these productions, the sole concern is talking at all hazards, and not [with] the object which would make that talk worth doing, so this clatter can only be made at all inciting to the ear by offering at each instant a new summons to attention, through a change in outer expressional means.[30]

Wagner gives the example of Mendelssohn, who endeavors "to speak out a vague, almost nugatory content as interestingly and spiritedly as possible."[31] Likewise, Meyerbeer, though unnamed in the essay, tricks his audiences "by taking that jargon which we have already characterised, and palming it upon his ennuyed audience as the modern-piquant utterance."[32] As cited above, Wagner charged not only that Meyerbeer stole his ideas from others, but, in addition, that he exploited them "with monstrous ostentation."[33]

The secret of Meyerbeer's music, claims Wagner, was *Effekt*, or "a working without a cause," and the result is "so appalling an emptiness, shallowness and artistic nothingness, that ... we are tempted to ... set ... his musical creativity at zero."[34] The charge of "Effekt" is what Wagner most associates with Meyerbeer. Taking the librettos of Eugene Scribe—who has been forced "to cobble up those bombastical, rococo texts"—Meyerbeer confronts them "In cold-blooded care ... calmly meditating as to which piece of the monstrosity he could fit out with some particular tatter from his musical store-room, so strikingly and cryingly that it should appear quite out-of-the-ordinary."[35] In contrast to Weber who desired "a Drama that could pass ... into his noble, soulful melody," Meyerbeer, on the other hand, "wanted a monstrous piebald, historico-romantic, diabolic-religious, fanatico-libidinous, sacro-frivolous, mysterio-criminal, autolyco-sentimental dramatic hotch-potch."[36] In other words, he wanted only to create an "Effekt" and to stir his audience from their "disease of boredom."[37] For Wagner it is not just the lack of coherence—note the contradictions in his description of Meyerbeer's hotch-potch—or its longing after "Effekt": what really bothers Wagner is his belief that Meyerbeer was out to fool his audience, to deceive them into thinking that they were actually getting something when in fact they were getting nothing. Boredom, states Wagner, "is not redeemable by sips of Art"; it can only be "duped into another form of boredom."[38]

Wagner never unambiguously identifies orchestration as "Effekt," but in *Opera and Drama,* he does criticize Berlioz for making possible its exploitation. Thanks

---

[30]   Ibid., p. 92.
[31]   Ibid., p. 95.
[32]   Ibid., p. 97.
[33]   Wagner, *Opera and Drama*, pp. 88–9.
[34]   Ibid., pp. 95 and 100.
[35]   Ibid., pp. 93 and 95.
[36]   Ibid., p. 94.
[37]   Wagner, *Judentum*, pp. 96–7.
[38]   Ibid., p. 97.

to Berlioz's "positively astounding knowledge," composers could now create "the most wonderful effect, from the emptiest and most un-artistic content of their music-making, by an unheard [of] marshaling of mere mechanical means."[39] Thus the problem was not simply orchestration or even "Effekt," it was the use of such an orchestra to dress up "the emptiest and most un-artistic content." Orchestration could potentially be seen in the context of Wagner's essay as representing the impoverished surface, and the Jew's orchestration would ultimately reveal itself in its dishonesty or subterfuge, attempting to hide, ornament, or make enticing its utter lack of true expressive power.

Recalling his image of a *how* rather than a *what*, Wagner claims that Mendelssohn, in an attempt to create musical forms in the manner of Beethoven, "reduces these achievements to vague, fantastic shadow-forms, midst whose indefinite shimmer our freakish fantasy is indeed aroused, but our inner, purely-human yearning for distinct artistic sight is hardly touched with even the merest hope of a fulfillment."[40] Mendelssohn's—and thus Jewish—music fails because it does not accomplish what Wagner thinks art should, namely the reflection of the self. Because Jewish art is merely imitating a culture to which it does not belong, the result can only be meaningless, superficial, and empty. Some, like Meyerbeer, can choose to compensate for this lack of meaning or substance by dressing up the surface; others, like Mendelssohn, are effective only when they acknowledge inability or failure and their music thus expresses a "soft and mournful resignation." In Mendelssohn's case, that resignation is his only possibility of true feeling and therefore of true music—"a gentle individuality."[41]

Passing and Paranoia

Wagner was certainly not the first writer to posit the inferiority of the Jews in terms of their lack of creativity. One of the common antisemitic tropes during the Middle Ages was the Jew as the "parasite" living "off the productive labor of their Christian neighbors." As Klaus Fischer writes:

> Repeated in various versions over the centuries, the myth held that Jews, unlike Christians, did not engage in productive or soilbound occupations but preferred to live off the fat of the land in urban centers where they engaged in purely speculative or abstract money manipulation. The abbot of Cluny, Peter the Venerable, already charged the Jews in the twelfth century with being an urban

---

[39] Wagner, *Opera and Drama*, p. 76.

[40] Wagner, *Judentum*, p. 96.

[41] Ibid., p. 96; Ellis notes that "gentle" (Zartsinningen) was used in the 1869 version; "noble" (edlen) in the original.

people living off the labor of hard-working Christian peasants and cheating them in unfair money transactions.[42]

Of course, because of the prohibition against owning land and participating in the guilds, very few occupations were open to the Jews—although, as Joshua Trachtenberg has pointed out, the belief that Jews held the monopoly on money lending is a myth.[43] Martin Luther, whose ideas and German translation of the Bible would have a profound and lasting effect on German thought, wrote in his essay "Against the Jews and Their Lies" that "They let us work with the sweat of our brow ... while they stuff themselves, guzzle and live in luxury from our hard-earned goods. With their accursed usury they hold us and our property captive ... They are our masters and we their servants."[44] While it was Wagner who coined the term "Verjudung," its true father was Luther. In addition to revealing the initial insecurity regarding national identity, he also represents the transformation of the "Jewish Question" from one of redemption (through conversion or salvation) into one of a parasitic Jewish culture feeding off its German host.[45] Wagner's ideas regarding the Jewish lack of creativity and the necessity for them to steal the ideas of others stems from the "realization" that the Jews could not in fact be "redeemed" and must therefore be eliminated in some other manner. Wagner's *Judentum* ends with the image of Ahasverus, or Wandering Jew, the Christian symbol for the unredeemable Jew who is forced to wander the earth eternally as punishment for rejecting Jesus. Wagner had written "But bethink ye, that one only thing can redeem you from the burden of your curse: the redemption of Ahasuerus [sic]—*Going under!* [*Untergang*]"[46] How literally Wagner—or any other writer who called for Jewish destruction (as did Martin Luther when he wrote in the above-cited essay that "We are at fault for not slaying [the Jews]")—meant this has been a matter of debate. What is important is that Wagner's image of the Jewish parasite, taking but not giving, was not the first.

Another influential writer, Karl Marx, as early as 1844, also wrote about the lack of Jewish creativity as parasitic, but with a slightly different twist:

> Judaism could not create a new world; it could only draw the new creations and conditions of the world into the province of its own activity, since practical need,

---

[42] Klaus P. Fischer, *The History of an Obsession: German Judeophobia and the Holocaust* (New York, 1998), p. 35; see his discussion of the anti-Jewish tropes of the medieval period, pp. 29–37.

[43] Joshua Trachtenberg, see his Ch. 13, "The Attack upon Usury," in *The Devil and the Jews: The Medieval Conception of the Jew and Its Relation to Modern Anti-Semitism*, 2nd paperback edn (Philadelphia and Jerusalem, 1983), pp. 188–94.

[44] Cited in Paul Lawrence Rose, *German Question/Jewish Question*, pp. 6–7.

[45] Ibid., pp. 40–43; Rose traces the Ahasverus image to *Verjudung*.

[46] Wagner, *Judentum*, p. 100; the original 1850 ending.

whose understanding is only at the level of self-interest, is passive and incapable
of extending itself in directions of its own choosing … [47]

Here, not only is the Jew characterized as incapable of creating "a new world," but
he also seems uninterested even in new creations unless they serve "practical need"
or his own "self-interest." While Wagner was willing to grant that both Meyerbeer
and Mendelssohn want, on some level, to create new art—they simply are incapable
of doing it because they *can* not—Marx, on the other hand, implies that Judaism
has no use for art unless it can be seen to have some pragmatic value.

The philosopher Ludwig Wittgenstein echoes this view almost a hundred years
later when he writes: "It might be said (right or wrongly) that the Jewish mind does
not have the power to produce even the tiniest blade of grass; its way is rather to
make a drawing of the flower or blade of grass that has grown in the soil of another's
mind and to put it into a comprehensive picture."[48] He sadly prefaced this with the
statement that "I think there is some truth in my idea that I only think reproductively.
I don't believe I have ever *invented* a line of thinking."[49] Wittgenstein, raised as a
Christian, claimed to have had one Jewish grandparent yet always felt that "they
knew about me."[50] Adolf Hitler had written in *Mein Kampf* that "the Jewish people,
despite all apparent intellectual qualities, is without any true culture, and especially
without any culture of its own. For what sham culture the Jew today possesses is the
property of other peoples, and for the most part is ruined in his hands."[51]

Yet a lack of creativity, even for Wagner, was not the root of the problem. The
fear of *Verjudung* is the fear of "passing," that these works of Jewish art may be
mistaken for real, German artworks. It incensed Wagner that fake artworks might
be mistaken for real ones, that:

> The Jew, who is innately incapable of enouncing himself to us artistically [*uns
> künstlerisch kundzugeben*] through either his outward appearance or his speech,
> and least of all through his singing, has nevertheless been able in the widest-spread
> of modern art-varieties, to wit in Music, to reach the rulership of public taste.[52]

Verjudung is ultimately the fear of the Jew's ability to mask himself, to make
himself invisible to the German and to go unnoticed in German culture. While

---

[47]   Karl Marx, "On the Jewish Question (1843)," in *Early Writings*, trans. Rodney
Livingstone and Gregor Benton (New York, 1975), p. 240.

[48]   Cited in Sander Gilman, *Smart Jews: The Construction of the Image of Jewish
Superior Intelligence* (Lincoln and London, 1996), p. 140. Wittgenstein cites from *Culture
and Value*, ed. G.H. von Wright (Oxford, 1980).

[49]   Ibid., p. 139; italics orig.

[50]   Gilman, *Smart Jews*, p. 138; he actually had three and would thus be considered
"Jewish" under the Nazi purity laws.

[51]   Adolf Hitler, *Mein Kampf*, trans. Ralph Manheim (Boston, 1943), pp. 302–3.

[52]   Wagner, *Judentum*, p. 87.

Wagner's essay—and every antisemitic pamphlet and publication—enumerates the ways in which the Jew will ultimately betray his difference, it is clear that Wagner was not quite as certain about this as he wanted to suggest. Although Wagner may have originally been thinking of one specific Jewish composer when writing these words—Meyerbeer, on whom Wagner blamed his failure in Paris—anxiety about Jews not only making their way into German culture but even "ruling" it was not simply Wagner's paranoia. Thus, Wittgenstein continues the thought quoted above:

> We aren't pointing to a fault when we say this and everything is all right as long as what is being done is quite clear. It is only when the nature of a Jewish work is confused with that of a non-Jewish work that there is any danger, especially when the author of the Jewish work falls into the confusion himself, as he so easily may.[53]

The ability of the Jew to adapt—and thus "pass"—appears in Otto Weininger's work *Sex and Character* (1903), in his chapter "Judaism."[54] Weininger was of course primarily concerned with gender differences, but he also argued, famously, that women and Jews share many characteristics:

> The congruity between Jews and women further reveals itself in the extreme adaptability of the Jews, in their great talent for journalism, the "mobility" of their minds, their lack of deeply-rooted and original ideas, in fact the mode in which, like women, because they are nothing in themselves, they can become everything ...
>
> At this point the comparison between the Jew and the woman breaks down; the being-nothing and the becoming-all-things differs in the two. The woman is material which passively assumes any form impressed upon it. In the Jew there is a definite aggressiveness ... he adapts himself to every circumstance and every race, becoming, like a parasite, a new creature in every host, although remaining essentially the same. He assimilates himself to everything, and assimilates everything ... [55]

Nevertheless, according to Weininger, "these activities are always relative and never seated in the creative freedom of the will."[56] Wittgenstein, James Joyce, Sigmund Freud, Franz Kafka, Karl Kraus—almost every major thinker of the fin-de-siècle had read and was influenced by Weininger's writings. His spectacular

---

[53]   Gilman, *Smart Jews*, p. 140.

[54]   Otto Weininger, *Geschlecht und Charakter: Ein prinzipielle Untersuchung* (Vienna, 1903); quotations are from the English translation, *Sex and Character*, trans. unknown (London, 1906). On Weininger's thought, see also Chandak Sengoopta, *Otto Weininger: Sex, Science, and Self in Imperial Vienna* (Chicago, 2000).

[55]   Weininger, *Sex and Character*, p. 320.

[56]   Ibid., p. 320.

suicide soon after the publication of his dissertation only contributed to his posthumous fame.

Oskar Panizza's story "Der opererierte Jud'" (1893), discussed in Chapter 2, neatly combines these two assumptions: that the Jews were incapable of true art and could only mimic or steal the ideas of others—and yet, in that attempt would nevertheless inevitably reveal their difference. The final task in the main character Stern's ordeal to become a real German is that he must acquire a German soul. As he is of course incapable of true feeling or understanding, he can accomplish this only by learning to mimic the surfaces:

> [In order to gain possession of the German soul] he began reciting pathetic and sentimental passages by poets, especially in social gatherings of the ladies' salons, and he astutely observed the position of the mouth, breath, twinkle of the eyes, gestures, and certain sighs that emanated so passionately and strenuously from German breasts satiated with feelings ... These words would be accompanied by some brusque movements, both hands pressed on the left side of the breast. It was really a very clever way to pour out emotions. Of course, his eyes would rest lifelessly in their sockets like rotten cherries. Yet he was able to deceive many people. He learned to inhale and exhale superbly.[57]

Even in the attempt to become a real German, Stern can only mimic, can achieve only the *how* but not the *what*. He is "very clever" and "able to deceive many people," but his eyes, as Hans F.K. Günther claimed, revealed the essence of his soul: that is, it was all a charade.[58] For those who knew to look closely enough, Stern's German soul was only an act.

This belief is likewise reflected in Thomas Mann's short story "Wälsungenblut" [The Blood of the Walsungs] (1905), also discussed in Chapter 2 in relation to the physical stereotypes. The character Siegmund is described as incapable of artistic accomplishment precisely because of "the conditions of his existence":

> But in the forenoon [Siegmund] had worked. He had spent the hour from ten to eleven in the atelier of his professor, an artist of European repute, who was developing Siegmund's talent for drawing and painting, and receiving from Herr Aarenhold two thousand marks a month for his services. But what Siegmund painted was absurd. He knew it himself; he was far from having any glowing expectations on the score of his talent in this line. He was too shrewd not to know

---

[57]   Oskar Panizza, "Der Operirte Jud'," trans. as "The Operated Jew" by Jack Zipes in his *The Operated Jew: Two Tales of Anti-Semitism* (New York and London, 1991), pp. 61–2.

[58]   Hans F.K. Günther, *Rassenkunde des jüdischen Volkes*, 2nd edn (Munich, 1930; 1st edn 1922), p. 217: "Diese Kennzeichnungen des 'jüdischen Blicks' gehören aber zum Teil schon nicht mehr zu einer Schilderung leiblicher Merkmale, sondern zu einer des seelischen Ausdrucks."

that the conditions of his existence were not the most favourable in the world for the development of a creative gift ... Siegmund had been born into superfluity, he was perfectly adjusted to it. And yet it was the fact that this superfluity never ceased to thrill and occupy him, to give him constant pleasure. Whether consciously or not, it was with him as it was with his father, who practised the art of never getting used to anything.[59]

As if echoing Wagner, Mann stresses that Siegmund's failure is not lack of hard work or even lack of desire: Siegmund will never become an artist because of his cultural predilection for "superfluity" (surface) stands in the way of true artistic expression (depth). Noteworthy also is Mann's information that Siegmund's father is paying "two thousand marks a month" for the services of Siegmund's teacher. Wagner had identified the monetary aspect of the Jew's wish to acquire culture as one would acquire any other object: "to the genteeler Jew his learnt and payed-for culture could only seem a luxury, since at bottom he knew not what to be about with it."[60] Unlike Stern, however, Siegmund seems to realize his inadequacy. Worse still, he is satisfied with it, his "superfluity," which gives "him constant pleasure." For Mann, the Jew is not only incapable, but indifferent to his own deficiency. "Talking at all hazards," as Wagner had said, is the sole concern, and, despite his "giftedness," the Jew is incapable of true feeling. Weininger repeats almost verbatim Wagner's idea that the Jewish artwork can reveal neither true passion nor true calm: "[The Jew] reaches neither the heights nor the depths. His restraint becomes meagerness, his copiousness becomes bombast. Should he venture into the boundless realms of inspired thought, he seldom reaches beyond pathos."[61]

It must be understood that the fear is fundamentally paradoxical—it is the idea that the Jews were both essentially different and yet somehow "passing" as Germans. Therefore, if Wagner's idea of *Verjudung* represents a fear that the Jews were "passing" (and, therefore, supposedly able to infiltrate German culture and gain control of it), Wagner then counters this fear by asserting that the Jew can never truly "pass": even when the "cultured" Jew has "taken the most indicible pains to strip off all the obvious tokens of his lower co-religionists"—even going as far as baptism—[those signs] nevertheless show "an impertinent obstinacy in cleaving to him."[62] In other words, no matter how hard the Jew tries to "pass," he will nevertheless reveal himself as a Jew.

For example, when the Jew attempts to speak true German, it was thought, his Jewishness is obvious from his accented speech.[63] For Wagner, *Mauscheln*, the supposed speaking of German with a Yiddish accent, is not just ugly—he famously

---

[59]   Thomas Mann, "Blood of the Walsungs," in *Death in Venice and Seven Other Stories*, trans. H.T. Lowe-Porter (New York, 1989), p. 299.

[60]   Wagner, *Judentum*, p. 88.

[61]   Weininger, *Sex and Character*, p. 322.

[62]   Wagner, *Judentum*, pp. 87 and 89.

[63]   Gilman, *Jewish Self-hatred*, pp. 139–48.

describes it as "a creaking, squeaking, buzzing, snuffle,"[64]—but ineffective: in the resulting "intolerably jumbled blabber," any message is lost because the language is corrupted. Not only are words used incorrectly and phrases twisted, but there is a "want of purely human expression."[65]

Yiddish, largely believed to be a corrupt form of German, was regarded as a threat precisely because of its similarity to German. Language for Wagner—and other German nationalists—arose out of an historical community, and "only he who has unconsciously grown up within the bond of this community, takes also any share in its creations." The Jew, barred from this community, knowing these languages "merely as learnt and not as mother tongues," would reveal his inferiority by being incapable of "expressing himself idiomatically, independently, and conformably to his nature." While "the Jew [may speak] the language of the nation in whose midst he dwells ... he speaks it always as an alien."[66] Those who insisted that the Jews were destined to remain as Schopenhauer put it, "nowhere at home and nowhere strangers," often identified language as both product and sign of their inferiority.[67]

For Wagner, music is inseparable from language as both define "German."[68] In the realm of music, as with language, the Jew's lack of understanding will similarly reveal itself. For the Jew, according to Wagner, "the most external accident on our domain of music life must pass for its very essence." For this reason, "Judaic works of music often produce on us the impression as though a poem of Goethe's was being rendered in the Jewish jargon." Wagner depicts the Jew as capable neither of passion nor of calm, and in Jewish music-works one finds "nothing but ... prickling unrest ... [or] soulless, feelingless inertia." The Jews' art is thus all "coldness and indifference ... triviality and absurdity."[69] In his 1869 essay *On*

---

[64]   Wagner, *Judentum*, p. 85: "ein zischender, schrillender, summsender und murksender Lautausdruck."

[65]   Wagner, *Judentum*, pp. 84–5.

[66]   Wagner, *Judentum*, p. 84.

[67]   Cited in Paul Lawrence Rose, *German Question/Jewish Question*, p. 36; on language in general as a marker of difference, see Gilman, *Jewish Self-hatred*. Deleuze and Guattari, of course, identify "major" and "minor" languages in their book *A Thousand Plateaus: Capitalism and Schizophrenia* (Minneapolis, 1987). They claim that "the German of Prague, Black English, and Québecois" exemplify minor languages. Minor authors (whom they consider "in fact the greatest, the only greats") are those who "find the minor language, the dialect or rather idiolect, on the basis of which one can make one's own major language minor" (p. 105). Their main example is Kafka who as "a Czechoslovakian Jew writing in German, submits German to creative treatment as a minor language" (p. 104). They go on to claim that "Minor authors are foreigners in their own tongue" (p. 105). While this is no doubt inspiring for those who would bring back Yiddish (a worthy pursuit), it unfortunately only flips the binary, it does not uncouple it. Merely placing German in the place of Yiddish does not move the argument forward.

[68]   Wagner, *What is German?*, pp. 147–69, in particular pp. 159 and 163.

[69]   Wagner, *Judentum*, pp. 92 and 93.

Conducting Wagner harshly criticized Mendelssohn, who, he claimed, advocated "getting over the ground quickly" as a way to disguise any shortcomings of the orchestra.[70] Wagner's position was that the ability of a conductor to choose the correct tempo indicated how well he understood the piece. Wagner relates trying to convince Mendelssohn to take the third movement of Beethoven's Eighth in a true *tempo di menuetto*, as marked. When Mendelssohn not only fails to correct the tempo but turns to Wagner smiling as if all is fine, Wagner writes, "Mendelssohn's indifference ... raised doubts in my mind as to whether he saw any distinction and difference ... at all. I fancied myself standing before an abyss of superficiality, a veritable void."[71] Mendelssohn has thus made Beethoven's Eighth "Jewish" by taking a tempo that creates "prickling unrest." While "true" (read: German) language and art reveal depth, Jewish products reveal only a trivial surface; in place of feeling, they reveal thinking; as a substitute for serenity, only nervousness. Wagner's own language constructs a binary opposition in which Jewish inferiority is antithetical to German superiority.

Cultural Acceptance

As already observed in Chapter 2, Mann identifies neither of his main characters in "The Blood of the Walsungs" explicitly as Jews, but rather, through a variety of physical signs he signals this information to the reader. These features are referred to later as the "mark of [Siegmund's] race."[72] The original final line of the story, after the twins consummate their incestuous passion, would have left no doubt as to the "race" of the twins: Siegmund tells his twin: "We robbed [*beganeft*] the non-Jew [*goy*]." Incest itself would have been recognized as particularly "Jewish"—indeed, it was thought to be the cause of their susceptibility to nervous diseases[73]—but the inclusion of the Yiddishisms was a particularly overt

---

[70] Richard Wagner, *Wagner on Conducting*, trans. Edward Dannreuther (New York, 1989; rpt London, 1887), pp. 22–3. According to Natalie Bauer-Lechner, the criticism that he "lacked calm" upset Mahler the most (quoted in DLG II, pp. 325–6).

[71] Wagner, *On Conducting*, pp. 20 and 28.

[72] Mann, "Walsungs," pp. 290 and 314.

[73] Richard von Krafft-Ebing, *Text-Book of Insanity, Based on Clinical Observations: For Practitioners and Students of Medicine*, trans. Charles Gilbert Chaddock, M.D. (Philadelphia, 1905; orig. German edn *Lehrbuch der Psychiatrie auf klinischer Grundlage für practische Ärzte und Studirende*, 3 vols in 1 [Stuttgart, 1879–80]), p. 143: "statistics have been collected with great care to show the percentage of insanity in the various religious sects, and it has been shown that among the Jews and certain sects the percentage is decidedly higher." The reason for this, according to Krafft–Ebing, is "insufficient crossing of the race and increased inbreeding." All citations from the English translation. Gilman further discusses incest in *Love + Marriage = Death: And Other Essays on Representing Difference* (Stanford, 1998), pp. 134–55.

gesture. Mann later edited these out, at the instance of his father-in-law, Alfred Pringsheim.[74] Gilman comments that the story "echoed the sense of the corruption of both 'modern life' as typified by the Wagner cult and the Jews. The Jews, through their lack of redemption, are morally weak, and this manifests itself in the most primitive manner, through incest."[75] Thus, the inability to produce art, the lack of creativity, the idea that culture can simply be "bought and paid for," and the juxtaposition of the lifeless surface with a soul-stirring depth all appear in Mann's short story. Since, beyond the physical stereotypes, Mann had betrayed the "race" of his protagonists in a draft of the story, there can be no doubt that Wagner's essay—or at least the ideas addressed therein—had been absorbed by the culture at large as "signs" of the Jew.

Yet despite its acceptance from high to low culture, the image, even the musical one, had no fixed meaning. For example, Weininger accuses Wagner himself of writing "Jewish" music. Weininger believes that "aggressive Antisemites … nearly always display certain Jewish characters, sometimes apparent in their faces, although they may have no real admixture of Jewish blood."[76] From this definition of antisemitism as self-hatred, Weininger then moves to Wagner, who, although "the bitterest anti-Semite," can nevertheless not "be held free from an accretion of Jewishness even in his art," despite the fact that "his Siegfried is the most un-Jewish type imaginable."[77] Weininger points to Wagner's "extreme instrumentation" as evidence of Wagner's "Jewishness," because it was through these means that Wagner "tried to gain coherence." Likewise, his works "cannot be declared free from the obtrusiveness, loudness, and lack of distinction."[78] Although it may seem contradictory that Weininger accuses Wagner of all people of writing Jewish music, it is nonetheless characteristic of antisemitic discourse. The concept of the "Jew" was always used as representative of the "Other," in whatever context it happened to occur. Like any binary opposition it could be inverted, but the structure always implied a value judgment regardless of which pole was considered to be positive. Noteworthy in any case is Weininger's insistence on the characteristics of Jewish music—it is obtrusive, loud, and lacking in distinction. Dressing up the surface—in Wagner's case, with instrumentation—can serve to create the illusion of "coherence." These characteristics, despite the fact that they have been turned on their author, are consistent with Wagner's own descriptions of Jewish music.

---

[74]   Gilman, *Love + Marriage*, p. 142.

[75]   Gilman, *Jewish Self-hatred*, p. 292. Regarding the Mann short story, see Marie Walter, "Concerning the Affair Wälsungenblut," *Book Collector* 13 (1964), 463–72; on the reception of the story, see Hans Rudolf Vaget, "*Sang réservé* in Deutschland: Zur Rezeption von Thomas Manns Wälsungenblut," *German Quarterly* 57 (1984), pp. 367–75.

[76]   Weininger, *Sex and Character*, p. 304.

[77]   Ibid., p. 305.

[78]   Ibid., p. 305.

Potter's claim that Wagner's essay is a "useless model" thus has validity only if one is seeking a detailed catalog of musical examples or traits. But providing that was never Wagner's aim, and such a catalog would serve to negate the strategic utility of the essay by virtue of its very specificity. Wagner was concerned only with being able to criticize Jewish composers generally. To point out specific musical traits (such as use of certain keys or instrumental combinations, or specific instances of formal problems) would have limited the applicability of the essay *and* provided the Jewish composers with a handbook to correct their "mistakes." Far more powerful are Wagner's metaphors, as they could be used universally— and in changing contexts that ensured their almost absolute applicability. Potter's view, that such musical traits can in fact be identified, may be a more dangerous position—and certainly more specious today—than the one that Wagner ultimately took.

The language of the early critics, with its the invocations of categories such as banality, triviality, incomprehensibility, eclecticism, and overwhelming orchestration may not have been antisemitic in itself. But when their discussions imply that Mahler's music was all surface; that it lacked depth and thus true feeling; that he was incapable of true creativity and tried to hide that lack with elaborate orchestration; that he had to steal from other composers; or that his melodies themselves revealed their inadequateness with their forced naïveté or simplicity, then the critics were indeed reacting—consciously or unconsciously—to the idea of Mahler's Jewishness. And those beliefs—that Jewish music lacks depth; that Jewish composers cannot be creative; that they do not have a true voice and cannot express true feelings; that they must attempt to hide their insufficiencies; that they can only mimic the music or styles of others—are very clearly articulated in Wagner's essay *Das Judentum in der Musik*.

Chapter 4
Die Wiener Kritiker

Mahler in Vienna—and Beyond

As Table 4.1 indicates, Mahler's symphonies received their premieres in Vienna out of order and, in most cases, a year or more after their initial performances. The first of Mahler's symphonies to be performed in Vienna was the Second, followed by the First, Fourth, Third, Fifth, and Sixth. Critics were often quick to complain that Mahler tried out his symphonies on others before bringing them back to Vienna. Each Viennese performance received at most two reviews in each newspaper: one main review of the concert, often in the form of a feuilleton (see Chapter 1); and occasionally an earlier review of an open rehearsal. Particularly early in Mahler's tenure in Vienna, concerts were often lumped together, so that it was not remarkable for a review to appear days or even weeks after its premiere.

Table 4.1   Mahler Symphony Premieres, 1899–1907 (Mahler conducting)

Symphony	Vienna	World Premiere	Notes
First	18 Nov. 1900	Berlin, 16 Mar. 1896	Earlier versions performed in Budapest, Hamburg, and Weimar
Second	9 Apr. 1899	Berlin, 13 Dec. 1895	3 mvts perf. in Berlin, 4 Mar. 1895; 2nd mvt perf. in Vienna, 7 Mar. 1899
Third	14 Dec. 1904	Krefeld, 9 June 1902	Mvts 2, 3, and 6 perf. in Berlin, 9 Mar. 1897
Fourth	12 Jan. 1902	Munich, 25 Nov. 1901	
Fifth	7 Dec. 1905	Cologne, 19 Oct. 1904	
Sixth	8 Jan. 1907	Essen, 27 May 1906	

Between Mahler's departure from Vienna and his death in 1911, however, only the Seventh was given there (by Ferdinand Löwe). Despite the drop in the number of significant performances, the number of newspaper reviews actually increased. In preparation for both the Seventh and Eighth Symphony premieres, many of the Viennese daily papers sent correspondents to Prague and Munich respectively, and reports were filed within days of the performances. At the premiere of the Eighth Symphony, the *Neue freie Presse* ran articles for four days, beginning on 11 September 1910, which was an open rehearsal, culminating on the 14th with a feuilleton devoted solely to the performance. The first performances of *Das Lied von der Erde* and the Ninth Symphony, which took place after Mahler's death, were similarly covered.

Table 4.2   Mahler Symphony Premieres, 1908–1912 (Mahler conducting, unless noted)

Symphony	Vienna	World Premiere	Notes
Seventh	3 Nov. 1909	Prague, 19 Sept. 1908	Dir. Ferdinand Löwe (Vienna) w/3rd
Eighth	—	Munich, 12 Sept. 1910	
Das Lied	—	Munich, 20 Nov. 1911	Dir. Bruno Walter
Ninth	26 June 1912	Vienna	Dir. Bruno Walter

In the late twentieth century, it is hard to imagine the place that music—"classical" or serious music, as we would call it today—held in Viennese public imagination. As Stefan Zweig noted in his memoir, *The World of Yesterday*, about his Viennese childhood:

> It was not difficult to mock this "theatromania" of the Viennese, and their following up to the most minute details of the lives of their darlings often was more than grotesque. Our Austrian indolence in political matters, and our backwardness in economics as compared with our resolute German neighbor, may actually be ascribed to our epicurean excesses ... In the Vienna Opera and in the Burgtheater, nothing was overlooked; every flat note was remarked, every incorrect intonation and every cut were censured; and this control was exercised at premières not by the professional critics alone, but day after day by the entire audience, whose attentive ears had been sharpened by constant comparison. Whereas in politics, in administration, or in morals, everything went on rather comfortably and one was affably tolerant of all that was slovenly, and overlooked many an infringement, in artistic matters there was no pardon; here the honor of the city was at stake.[1]

---

[1]   Stefan Zweig, *The World of Yesterday*, no trans. given (Lincoln, 1964; rpt New York, 1943), pp. 18–19.

Mahler's place within the city was supreme: everyone knew who he was, and his position at the Hofoper made him the most important person in Vienna after the emperor. As Zweig notes, "To have seen Gustav Mahler on the street was an event that we proudly reported to our comrades the next morning as a personal triumph."[2] Bruno Walter, Mahler's conducting protégé, reports that cab drivers would stop and mutter "Der Mahler!"[3]

In this chapter, I am concerned with the language of Viennese reviews of Symphonies 1–6 that imports a lack of creativity to Mahler, utilizing five themes[4]: 1. program music vs. absolute music; 2. formal difficulties (incomprehensibility); 3. originality (reminiscences or quotations); 4. banality or quality of themes; and 5. orchestration. I stress here once more that my claim is *not* that the language of these reviews can be understood only in terms of antisemitism; nor do I claim to have looked at every paper or found every review for every symphony. Neither do I claim that these reviews cannot reveal other things about Mahler, or about Viennese culture at the turn of the century. What interests me are the resonances that I hear in these reviews with the language of the Jewish stereotype as compiled in Wagner's *Judentum* essay. I have selected quotes that I consider the most symptomatic in this regard: it would be trivial to find both more inconsequential and more overtly antisemitic language if that were indeed the goal. As emphasized in Chapter 3, Wagner's essay provides metaphors, not a laundry list. What I propose is that we listen for those metaphors at work in the language of the earliest Viennese who discussed the music of Gustav Mahler, and in order to do that we need to read their language. While it might be tempting to skip the quotes, my analyses are not nearly as important as the voices of the critics themselves.

Program Music vs. Absolute Music

Although program music is defined as any instrumental music that has an external referent, or so-called "extramusical" content, its position within musical history is hardly this straightforward.[5] Music claiming to be "about something" quickly

---

[2]   Zweig, *World of Yesterday*, p. 41.

[3]   Bruno Walter, *Gustav Mahler*, trans. James Galston (London, 1937), p. 35; cited in Norman Lebrecht, *Mahler Remembered* (New York, 1987), p. xxiii.

[4]   For identification of reviews with a four-digit number, see "Appendix I: Mahler Reviews Consulted and Appendix II: Strauss Reviews Consulted.

[5]   Examples of program music include Hector Berlioz's *Symphonie Fantastique*, where the composer uses a five-movement symphonic structure to narrate a story of a young musician unlucky in love, or a single movement symphonic poem, such as Franz Liszt's *Hamlet*. In most cases, the composer of program music attempts to guide the listener's orientation through the piece by providing an idea or narrative (*always* given to the audience) that he then claims the music to "be about." The listener is then left to put together the story and the music together, following the "program."

became politicized as the bastion of the "New German School" of composers, and soon there was an all-out war between those who advocated program music as the future of the symphony, and those who believed that programmatic music was inferior and thus to be avoided:

> The dispute between the "New Germans" and the "formalists" over the legitimacy or illegitimacy of program music, which hardened into a partisan battle of musical politics around 1860, can be viewed as an attempt by each group to deny the other's right to the concept of the "spiritual in music." Whereas Franz Brendel, the ideologue of the New Germans, maintained that, by going from "indeterminate" expression of feeling to "determinate" characterization and programmatic content, modern instrumental music had progressed from the level of "sentiment" to that of "spirit," the [Eduard] Hanslickian esthetic of the "specifically musical" was based on just the opposite theory: that spirit in music was form, and form spirit. Musical form was not a mere manifestation that formed the shell or vessel for a content that, as idea, subject, or feeling, comprised the true essence of music; instead, as spiritual formation of sounding matter, it was itself "essence" or "idea."[6]

Perhaps ironically, given the position of the New Germans, even Richard Wagner (who coined the term "absolute music" in 1846 in reference to Beethoven's Ninth Symphony) was convinced of the idea's fundamental validity, even as he polemicized against it.[7]

Sanna Pederson has argued that the definitions of program music and absolute music cannot be separated from the definition of "German":

> Dahlhaus, for instance, has observed that "the idea of absolute music—gradually and against resistance—became the esthetic paradigm of German musical culture in the nineteenth century." I would like to suggest the reverse: it was the idea of a German musical culture that—gradually and against resistance—became the paradigm of absolute music in the nineteenth century. My premise is that "the idea of absolute music" arises primarily out of the correlation of two systems of differences: one of function (music for its own sake as opposed to other kinds of music); the other of nation (German music as opposed to that of other countries). Absolute music is distinguished not so much by intrinsic properties but on the

---

[6]   Carl Dahlhaus, *The Idea of Absolute Music*, trans. Roger Lustig (Chicago, 1989; orig. German pub. 1978), p. 129.

[7]   Wagner made up the term in "Beethoven's Choral Symphony at Dresden, 1846," *Richard Wagner's Prose Works*, trans. William Ashton Ellis (8 vols, New York and London, 1966; rpt. 1894), vol. 7, p. 252; his use of the term is negative—that is, Beethoven, in the fourth movement, makes the words a necessity, "almost breaking the bonds of absolute music already" with the instrumental recitative. For more on the history of the term, see Dahlhaus, *Absolute Music*.

basis of what it (presumably) is not. Therefore the absence of non-Germanic music in the realm of "absolute" music is hardly an accident; rather, this very concept was shaped by a new, exclusionary ideology directed at other nations.[8]

As Pederson notes, it was the symphonic genre that came to be the most fraught with German nationalistic baggage. After all, the symphony was Beethoven par excellence, and therefore was held up to higher standards than other genres.

More recently, Daniel Chua has interrogated the term "absolute music," and suggested that far from being an emancipation of music, absolute music was "a reconstruction of it."[9] Absolute music was not so much music about music as it was "a transcendental sign of absence that enabled the German Idealists and the early Romantics to make instrumental music mean nothing in order that it might mean everything."

> Having been constructed by a semiotics of zero, instrumental music was raised to a higher power by the Romantics, to become in turn a 'meta-sign' for their system of philosophy as the *absolute zero* that both participates within the system and organises it from the outside ... The problem for the Romantics was that they had two absolutes in their hands—'God' in terms of totality (the world), and 'God' in terms of autonomy (the self) ... Thus music, as *the* sign of zero, was used to balance the books.[10]

"Absolute Music" therefore became a weapon in the hands of anyone who would use it: there was no way to fight back. An "empty sign" or a "blank flag" (Chua uses both these terms) can be manipulated for use against all comers: against so-called "inadequate" composers, "foreign" composers, New Germans, Old Germans, anyone against whom the critic in question has a grudge.

Mahler, by choosing to write symphonies, headed right into the storm. No other genre he could have chosen, I believe, would have provoked quite the same enraged reaction. As Pederson has argued, it was precisely the symphony where themes of Germanness, absolute music, and national fervor came together. Wagner's linking of language and music had a long history, and music, in the form of Beethoven

---

[8] Sanna Pederson, "A.B. Marx, Berlin Concert Life, and German National Identity," *19th-Century Music* 18 (1994), pp. 87–107; quote is p. 89. The essays in *Music and National Identity* (ed. Celia Applegate and Pamela Potter [Chicago, 2002]) often ignore or disparage Pederson's work. For a short but useful discussion of German nationalism, see Hagen Schulze, *Der Weg zum Nationalstaat: die deutsche Nationalbewegung vom 18. Jahrhundert bis zur Reichsgründung* (Munich, 1985); trans. Sara Hanbury-Tenison as *The Course of German Nationalism: From Fredrick the Great to Bismarck*, 1763–1867 (Cambridge, 1991).

[9] Daniel K.L. Chua, *Absolute Music and the Construction of Meaning* (Cambridge, 1999), p. 168.

[10] Chua, *Absolute Music*, pp. 168 and pp. 160–70; orig. italics.

symphonies, were the works held up to emphasize nationalism and the prestige of German absolute music.[11] That the criticism of Mahler was often couched in the duality of absolute versus program music is therefore understandable: if it could be shown that Mahler was not writing real symphonies, then danger could be averted. And certainly a real symphony could never be programmatic.

Especially in the reviews of Mahler's first three symphonies, but in reviews of 4–6 as well, Mahler was accused of writing symphonies that were symphonies in name only. In a review of Mahler's First, Eduard Hanslick wrote that Mahler's "new symphony belongs to that musical genre, which for me is no genre at all."[12] A similar sentiment was expressed by Theodor Helm, who, calling the First Symphony "a stylistic absurdity," claimed it failed both as absolute and as program music.[13] For Hans Geisler, the Second Symphony was program music, even if Mahler did not acknowledge it: "Mahler's work, which calls itself a symphony, is however program music without a program up to the second half, where the text comes in to help us."[14] The Second Symphony, even for the extremely sympathetic Ludwig Karpath, was "no symphony in the usual sense of the word," although he does believe that it is in fact a symphony.[15] Robert Hirschfeld went so far as to refer, in regard to the Fifth, to "the people, who cheer a Mahler-symphony as a symphony because they have never by chance previously heard or tried to judge another symphony." Hirschfeld likens such listeners to those who do not know wine and therefore drink "artificial wine," getting from it regular headaches, and soon they "will come to believe that the wine must produce headaches."[16] Julius Korngold acknowledged that the Fifth

---

[11]   Sanna Pederson, "On the Task of the Music Historian: The Myth of the Symphony after Beethoven," *repercussions* 2/2 (1993), pp. 5–30, see esp. pp. 12–22.

[12]   Eduard Hanslick (2799), pp. 7–8; quote is p. 7: "die neue Symphonie zu jener Gattung Musik gehört, die für mich keine ist."

[13]   Theodor Helm (2802), p. 7: "ein stilistisches Unding."

[14]   Hans Geisler (2883), pp. 5–6; quote is p. 5: "Mahler's Werk nennt sich Symphonie, ist jedoch Programmmusik ohne Programm bis zur zweiten Hälfte, wo das Wort uns zu Hilfe kommt."

[15]   Ludwig Karpath (2882), pp. 1–2; quote is p. 1: "Der knappe Raum, der uns zur Verfügung steht, zwingt uns, über das Werk weit weniger zu sagen, als diesem mit Fug und Recht zukommen würde. Zunächst sei die Frage aufgeworfen, ob die Mahler'sche Composition auch wirklich eine Symphonie sei? Darauf ist mit einem entschiedenen Ja! zu antworten. Allerdings keine Symphonie im landläufigen Sinne des Wortes."

[16]   Robert Hirschfeld (3229), pp. 1–2; quote is p. 1: "Leute, die einst nichts Neues neben Brahms gelten ließen, um Brahms und sich selbst einen engen, undurchdringlichen Stachelzaun errichteten, werfen nun alle Erfahrung, alle Beziehungen zur tiefen Brahmschen Kunst, alle Erinnerung von sich und stellen sich willig zu den Leuten, die eine Mahler-Sinfonie als Sinfonie bejubeln, weil sie zufällig vorher nie eine andere Sinfonie gehört oder zu beurteilen versucht haben. Wer zufällig keinen echten Wein kennt, Kunstwein trinkt und davon regelmäßig Kopfschmerzen bekommt, wird mit einigem Recht behaupten, daß der Wein Kopfschmerzen erzeugen muß." Sandra McColl ("Max Kalbeck and Gustav Mahler,"

"looks at first glance more normal than the ones that preceded it," by which he means that it contained "no explicit and no concealed program." However, he nevertheless stated that, "a puzzling something prevails behind these unusual tone formations."[17]

As many commentators noted, some of Mahler's symphonies did originally carry programs. As Hanslick explained about the First: "At its first performance in Weimar, the symphony was called 'Titan' and was accompanied by a comprehensive program. The critics found it 'abstruse' and so the composer suppressed the title as well as the explanation."[18] Accordingly, in his review of the Viennese premiere of the First, Theodor Helm faulted Mahler for trying to pass off program music as absolute music:

> Mahler wanted this completely unknown Opus to appeal to the Viennese public only as absolute music, and he supposed, the impression would form much more directly and more considerably through simply hearing alone, without any help for the critically examining eye. In this regard, however, the clever composer has decidedly overestimated the receptivity of the majority of the visitors to the Philharmonic Concerts. He also forgot that what originally was thought of as program music can never become fully satisfying absolute music, that, in any case, it really loses poetic charm through the simple cancellation of the programmatic explanation.[19]

Critics saw in Mahler's actions an attempt actually to deceive the listener. Korngold referred to this tendency in his review of the Third Symphony where he informed the reader that Mahler "based his symphony on a program, only to

---

19th-Century Music 20 [1996], pp. 167–8) suggests that this statement was directed at a specific person, David Josef Bach, although she does not explain why.

[17] Julius Korngold (3227), p. 1: "Und gerade sie sieht auf den ersten Blick normaler aus, als die vorangegangenen. Kein ausdrückliches und kein verschwiegenes Programm ... Ein rätselhaftes Etwas waltet hinter diesen ungewöhnlichen Tongebilden."

[18] Hanslick (2799), pp. 7–8: "Bei ihrer ersten Aufführung in Weimar hieß die Symphonie 'Titan' und war von einem ausführichen Programm begleitet. Die Kritiker fanden es 'abstrus,' und so tilgte der Componist sowol den Titel als die Erklärung."

[19] Theodor Helm (2804), pp. 204–5; quote is p. 204: "Mahler wollte, das dem Wiener Publicum gänzlich unbekannte Opus solle auf dasselbe nur als absolute Musik wirken, und er vermeinte, der Eindruck würde sich durch das blosse Hören allein, ohne jede Nachhilfe für das kritisch prüfende Auge, viel unmittelbarer und bedeutender gestaten. In dieser Hinsicht hat aber der geistreiche Componist die Aufnahmsfähigkeit der Mehrzahl der Besucher der Philharmonischen Concerte entschieden überschätzt. Auch vergass er dass, was ursprünglich als Programmmusik gedacht, nimmer mehr vollbefriedigende absolute Musik werden kann, jedenfalls durch einfaches Wegstreichen der programmatischen Erläuterung an poetischem Reiz sehr verliert."

suppress it later."[20] Hirschfeld implied that Mahler's deceit was all the worse for being unnecessary:

> Program music is in itself a difficult problem. It is above board with Berlioz and Liszt, who are not ashamed and place their poetic program in the front of the score. Gustav Mahler is, however, a bashful writer of program music. The Third Symphony, which was already given twice by the Gesellschaft der Musikfreunde, is like the First [Symphony] based on a program. Suddenly, however, Gustav Mahler simply dismissed the program like a troublesome tenor or alto; his program-symphonies are served to us now as absolute music.[21]

Critics equated Mahler's dependence on the program with his weakness as a composer: if he were truly inspired, or had real ideas to convey, so the argument went, he would not need to rely on something as tangible as a program. In his review of the Fourth, Richard Heuberger complained that its "theatrical effects" were difficult to understand and that perhaps—as in the first three symphonies—Mahler was concealing an underlying program. Although Heuberger confessed that he was "not crazy about program music," he nevertheless suggested a new name for Mahler's "genre": "the newly discovered [genre of] program music with secret program!"[22]

Even as late as the Sixth Symphony—which many commentators agreed was "normal" and without a program—Max Vancsa asserted that, "This much trickles through from the program, upon which this symphony, like every other one of Mahler's, is based (although intentionally concealed): that this symphony and especially the finale should be 'tragic' and that the rumbling hammer blows mean 'blows of fate.'"[23] In the case of the Sixth, it was the orchestration that raised

---

[20]   Julius Korngold (3029), pp. 1–3; quote is p. 1: "Mahler hat seinen Symphonien Programme zu Grunde gelegt, um sie hinterher zu unterdrücken."

[21]   Robert Hirschfeld (3034a), p. 1: "Die Programmusik ist an sich ein schwieriges Problem. Sie ist ehrlich bei Berlioz und Liszt, die sich ihrer nicht schämten und das dichterische Programm der Partitur voransetzten. Gustav Mahler ist aber ein verschämter Programmusiker. Der dritten Sinfonie, die nun zweimal von der Gesellschaft der Musikfreunde aufgeführt wurde, liegt wie der ersten ein Programm zu Grunde. Plötzlich hat aber Gustav Mahler die Programmusik wie einen lästigen Tenor oder eine Altisten einfach entlassen; seine Programm-Sinfonien werden uns jetzt als absolute Musik serviert."

[22]   Richard Heuberger (3130), p. 4: "Vielleicht hängt das mit dem der Symphonie angeblich unterlegten 'Programm' zusammen. Ich schwärme nicht für Programm-Musik. Für die bedenklichste Form dieser bedenklichen Kunstgattung halte ich aber die neuerfundene Programm-Musik mit verschwiegenem Programm!"

[23]   Max Vancsa (3321), pp. 37–8; quote is p. 38: "So viel sickert aus dem Programme, das dieser Sinfonie wie einer jeden Mahlerschen zugrunde liegt, aber geflissentlich verschwiegen wird, durch, daß diese Sinfonie und besonders das Finale 'tragisch' sein sollen und daß die dröhnenden Hammerschläge die 'Schicksalsschläge' bedeuten."

suspicions of a program. The use of a hammer in the final movement provoked Vancsa to ask if such a thing could truly be heard as lacking extramusical ideas.

Although it was already considered a problem that Mahler both wrote program music and then attempted to deceive his listeners about it, a secondary concern was the music's lack of cohesiveness. Critics claimed that sense could not be made of Mahler's music without reference to the hidden program, because the music was either too disparate, too disunified, or simply too confusing to be followed on its own terms. This raises another aesthetic issue in regard to program music, namely the paradoxical requirement that it had to be able to stand on its own. Thus Theodor Helm faulted Mahler first for writing program music, and then for taking away any hope that the listener might follow his musical ideas:

> Since [the Weimar premiere] Mr Mahler himself has backed away from this incomprehensible, supremely motley program and wants his First Symphony, from which he canceled all titles and otherwise explanatory remarks, to be understood simply as absolute music. That is not quite right, however: in its absentmindedness, specifically in the middle between the first two movements and the last two movements [which] structurally fall apart, the curious thing really cries out for a program.[24]

Despite the fact that the program itself—based in part on Jean Paul's novel *Titan*—never made much sense (Helm dismissing the symphony as "eccentric program music with detailed titles"), Mahler committed yet a larger sin by canceling the titles altogether. The work thus could not communicate musically in any way. Max Kalbeck echoed the same sentiment when he wrote of the same work that it should have been able to express itself, without the help of outside forces. Kalbeck suspected that Mahler deliberately programmed the other works on the concert—Beethoven's Prometheus Overture and Schumann's Manfred Overture—to help explain his own work's basic elements: "the cheerful optimism, carefreely indulging in life [=Beethoven], and the world-negating pessimism, despairing of mankind [=Schumann]."[25] But Mahler's work was unable to pass this dangerous

---

[24] Theodor Helm (2802), p. 7: "Seither scheint Herr Mahler selbst von diesem unbegreiflichen, höchst buntscheckigen Programm zurückgekommen und will seine erste Symphonie, aus welcher er alle Überschriften und sonst erklärenden Bemerkungen wegstrich, einfach als absolute Musik aufgefaßt wissen. Das geht aber erst recht nicht: in seiner Zerfahrenheit, ja in der Mitte zwischen den beiden ersten und beiden letzten Sätzen förmlich auseinander fallend, schreit das curiose Ding geradezu nach einem Programm."

[25] Max Kalbeck (2801), pp. 1–3; quote is p. 1: "der Dirigent wollte ihnen auch in anschaulichen Gegenbildern die beide Grundelemente seiner Symphonie zeigen: den heiteren, dem Leben sich sorglos hingebenden Optimismus und den an der Menschheit verzweifelnden, weltverneinenden Pessimismus."

test, in fact "could not pass it, because it urgently needed, more than another of its kind, the explanatory program."[26]

Although both Helm and Kalbeck implied that Mahler should have made the program available to the public, some critics believed that not even that could have made the work intelligible. Hanslick, no fan of such music himself, conceded only that the existence of the program might have made the composer's intentions more clear:

> Mahler's symphony would have hardly pleased us with a program any more than without. But we would not be uninterested to learn what a spiritual man like Mahler imagined for each of these movements and how he would have explained their puzzling connection to us. And so we lacked a leader who could lead the way in this darkness. What does this suddenly intruding End-of-the-World-Finale mean, what of the funeral march on the old student canon "Brother Martin [Frère Jacques]," what about the interruption of the same [funeral march] marked with "parody"? The music itself would have neither won nor lost charm with a program, certainly, but the intentions of the composer would have become clearer to us and the work more understandable.[27]

Geisler also contended that no program would have been able to solve the musical problems of the bedeviling the symphony:

> No logical thread connects the music: it flutters, dances like a will-o'-the-wisp, confuses, fools, and jeers. Once it was called "Titan" and borrowed titles from Jean Paul, for the first movement "From the days of the youth, flowers-, fruit- and thorn pieces," the third movement was called "The huntsman's funeral" and the last "Dall' inferno al paradiso." Later Mahler deletes all this that could make the opinions of the composer halfway comprehensible to the listener, he wanted to approach him in an absolute-musical manner and left the pitiable [listeners] to stand perplexed and helpless. Certainly a program would have not been able

---

[26] Kalbeck (2801), p. 1: "Aber die Symphonie sollte sich selbst erklären, Mahler glaubte sie auf die Probe stellen zu können. Das Werk bestand diese gefährliche Probe nicht, konnte sie nicht bestehen, weil es, mehr als ein anderes seiner Art, des erläuternden Programms dringend bedarf."

[27] Hanslick (2799), p. 8: "Schwerlich hätte auch Mahlers Symphonie uns mehr erfreut mit einem Programm, als ohne solches. Aber gleichgiltig war es uns nicht, zu erfahren, was ein geistreicher Mann wie Mahler sich bei jedem dieser Sätze vorgestellt und wie er ihren uns räthselhaften Zusammenhang erklärt hätte. Und so fehlte uns doch ein Führer, der in diesem Dunkel den rechten Weg weisen könnte. Was hat dieses plötzlich einbrechende Weltuntergangs-Finale zu bedeuten, was der Trauermarsch mit dem alten Studentencanon 'Bruder Martin,' was die mit 'Parodie' bezeichnete Unterbrechung desselben? Die Musik selbst hätte mit einem Programm an Reiz weder gewonnen noch verloren, gewiß, aber die Absichten des Componisten wären uns deutlicher und damit das Werk verständlicher geworden."

to move the listener willing to follow the unprecedented, the instrumental forced musical remarks.[28]

Korngold likewise asserted in his review of the Third Symphony that, "no program can justify the march-potpourri of the first movement."[29] Mahler's tendency to write program music was always cited as a weakness, a sign that he was not a true composer. His reliance on extramusical sources for his inspiration served as evidence that Mahler—"like all Jews" remains unspoken—lacked the creative spark. The critics' belief that Mahler then suppressed the program, or that it remained hidden, can also be linked to the common stereotype that Jews are deceitful, conniving liars. As in the original end of Mann's short story "Blood of the Walsungs," here Mahler has "beganeft" the "goy": he has passed off his (inferior) program music as (superior) absolute music. The music, in any event, cannot exist on its own because its origin has tied it to the world of the real, and it will betray its origins by its incomprehensibility and its incoherence.

An interesting sidelight on this issue can be found in the reactions to Alban Berg's Lyric Suite. Although critics had long suspected that the Lyric Suite was programmatic, with titles of the movements like "Trio estatico" or "Scherzo desolato," it was not until 1976 that Douglass Greene reported the existence of a score of the work in which the Largo had been underlaid by the composer with the text of Charles Baudelaire's poem *De profundis camari* in Stefan Georg's translation. Subsequently, George Perle found that practically every aspect of the work had been dictated by a program which tracked the course of a love affair between the (married) composer and Hanna Fuchs-Robettin. Far from destroying the work's attraction, the discovery of the secret program seemed instead to heighten critics' admiration for Berg's ingenuity. Perhaps because the piece existed as absolute music for so long, and Berg was so successful at hiding the program, or perhaps because the program explained so many things about the work, critics were so intrigued that they rushed to find more hidden programs in Berg's later works. In any event, this comparison shows that it was not simply the focus on a particular aspect—programs, orchestration, triviality—that served as evidence of

---

[28] Geisler, *Neue musikalische Presse* 9 (25 Nov. 1900), pp. 351–2: "Kein logischer Faden führt durch die Musik, sie flattert, tänzelt wie ein Irrlicht herum, verwirrt, narrt und höhnt. Einst nannte sie sich 'Titan' und entlehnte Ueberschriften von Jean Paul, für den ersten Satz 'Aus den Tagen der Jugend, Blumen-, Frucht- und Dornenstücke,' der dritte Satz hiess 'Des Jägers Leichenbegängnis' und der letzte 'Dall' inferno al paradiso.' Später löscht Mahler alles weg, was dem Zuhörer die Meinung des Componisten halbwegs fasslich machen konnte, er wollte ihm absolut musikalisch kommen und liess den Bedauernswerthen rath- und hilflos dastehen. Doch auch ein Programm hätte den Zuhörer nicht bewegen können, den unerhörten, den Instrumenten aufgenöthigten musikalischen Äusserungen willig zu folgen."

[29] Korngold (3029), p. 2: "Auch kein Programm vermag das Marschpotpourri zu rechtfertigen, das in den ersten Satz Mahlers geraten ist."

Mahler's Jewishness, but rather the way in which such aspects were treated within the critical discourse.[30]

Incomprehensibility, Eclecticism, and Formal Problems

In the comments of both Hanslick and Geisler, the underlying problem is not really that Mahler's music may or may not be program music, but rather that it fails to communicate some message in a coherent way. I propose equating problems of form with problems of comprehension because I see them as being the same problem described from complementary perspectives. In the absence of a program, which would indicate a specific message the delivery of which could therefore be judged as either a success or a failure, absolute music needs to follow some type of internal logic. If the listener can follow the internal logic—or (to put it another way) Mahler's intentions—then the work is a success. Critics find problems with Mahler's internal logic on all levels from the motivic, to the formal, to the larger generic level in the way (or whether) the separate movements of the symphony form some coherent whole. The critic's position is often inconsistent with common assumptions: Mahler is blamed both for attempts to unify movements motivically and for failures to do so. These contradictions are important, for I believe they indicate that the real problem for his critics was not Mahler's actual compositional technique, but rather the fact that he was composing at all.

Perhaps the most often cited problem was Mahler's failure to unify the moods of his works. In a review of the First Symphony, Max Graf asserted that the extreme contrasts could only be justified by an underlying programmatic idea:

> Gustav Mahler's First Symphony (in D major), which has incited the audience of the philharmonic concert to indiscretions of the worst kind, is—like the Symphonie fantastique [of Berlioz]—copied from storms, crises, and emotional disasters of youth and may be counted on to be understood and felt by the young generation of our time. Only from this the composer may claim that it integrates the crass mood changes between poetry, parody, and pathos—owing to their own internal agitation and mobility—and that the work feels unified despite all the contrasts.[31]

---

[30] On Berg's programs, see Douglas Jarman, "Secret Programs," in *The Cambridge Companion to Berg*, ed. Anthony Pople (Cambridge, 1997), pp. 167–79.

[31] Max Graf (2803), p. 415: "Gustav Mahlers Erste Symphony (in D-dur), welche das Publicum der philharmonischen Concerte zu Taktlosigkeiten ärgster Art aufgereizt hat, ist—gleich der Symphonie phantastique—aus Stürmen, Krisen und seelischen Katastrophen der Jugend heraus geschrieben und darf darauf rechnen, von der jungen Generation unserer Zeit empfunden und verstanden zu werden. Nur von dieser darf der Componist verlangen, dass sie die crassen Stimmungswechsel zwischen Lyrik, Parodie und Pathos—dank ihrer

In other words, such contrasts could not be justified in musical terms. Helm cites the same problem with the Third—its lack of a uniform mood or style, and especially the blatant contrasts in the first movement—and again blames this on the lack of a program: "Considered from this standpoint [as absolute music], the style of the 'Third' appears, even more than that of the 'First'—despite the many interesting details and the commanding knowledge of the orchestra—on the whole too motley, not adequately logical and uniform."[32]

A lack of coherence can stem from causes other than the suppression of a program. Vancsa locates the problem of the Third both in Mahler's stylistic contrasts—which he here suggests might stem from the movements being composed over a period of time—and in his inability to create thematic unity:

> Altogether flagrantly it diverges into two parts: against the first movement, which alone lasts about three-quarters of an hour, stand five further movements, of which indeed the three last join directly together and claim together about an hour. But this outward length of time would not yet mean much, if it were not an internal moment of separation, above all the bringing to light of a clear style difference. The two parts appear to have emerged as from two different creative periods of the composer. In the first part we still see completely the manner that prevails in most movements of other Mahler symphonies, the stringing together of small motives, small orchestral ideas and jokes, although here it has been driven too far: every moment another instrument comes forward with a small solo, among which especially empty noises, small and large drums, timpani, cymbals, triangles, bells are special favorites. So the movement looks like a stringing together of loud color specks and color spots, like a pointillist painting by Rysselberghe. Completely different, or at least in large part completely different is the second part! Here this manner emerges mainly in the third movement, in the Scherzo, and there only sporadically; all others strive for organic development of the themes flowing uniformly, yes the second and last movement generally carry, if we forgo the instrumentation, no other character, than what we were familiar with in the old-style symphony.[33]

---

eigenen inneren Bewegtheit und Beweglichkeit—zusammenfasse und das Werk trotz aller Contraste einheitlich empfinde."

[32] Helm (3037), p. 12: "Von diesem Standpunkt betrachtet, erscheint aber der Stil der 'Dritten' noch weit mehr als jener der 'Ersten' trotz der vielen interessanten Einzelheiten und der souveränen Beherrschung des Orchesters im ganzen zu buntscheckig, zu wenig logisch und einheitlich."

[33] Max Vancsa (3035), pagination unclear: "Ganz offenkundig klafft sie in zwei Theile auseinander: dem ersten Satz, der allein etwa dreiviertel Stunden währt, stehen fünf weitere Sätze gegenüber, von denen allerdings die drei letzten sich unmittelbar aneinander anschließen und die zusammen etwa eine Stunde beanspruchen. Aber dieser äußerliche Moment der Zeitdauer würde noch nicht viel bedeuten, wenn nicht noch ein innerer Moment der Trennung, nämlich ein deutlicher Stilunterschied zu Tage treten würde. Die beiden

Vancsa identifies Mahler's typical manner as lacking unity, although in the Third Symphony—in particular the second and sixth movements—he finds much to praise in this same regard. Despite his praise, however, the piece still fails as a whole, precisely because of its internal contradictions. Toward the end of the review, Vancsa reiterates his basic point:

> Let us sum up once more the aforesaid into a general judgment, so that no one can deny that Mahler's Third Symphony is an altogether important achievement, the work of an ingenious performer full of spirit and humor with perfect mastery of all technical means presently available. What the large work of art lacks is the force of a distinctively genuine artistic conviction.[34]

So despite mastery of "technical means," Mahler's work still fails as a totality. Mahler's work may resemble a real work of art, but only on the surface, and the perfection of technical means are an indication that the music is only surface. Korngold also believed Mahler's Third to be all surface. He maintained that it was not that Mahler lacked thematic or melodic ideas—in fact overflowed with ideas—but that "the stock of themes for this movement appear frequently to lack a keynote" that would make sense out of the abundance.[35]

Theile erscheinen wie aus zwei verschiedenen Perioden des Komponisten hervorgegangen. Im ersten Theile sehen wir noch ganz die Manier, die in den meisten Sätzen der andern Mahler'schen Symphonien vorherrscht, das Aneinanderreihen kleiner Motivchen, kleiner Orchestereinfälle und -witze, ja sie ist hier gerade auf die Spitze getrieben: jeden Augenblick tritt ein anderes Instrument mit einem kleinen Solo hervor, wobei insbesondere leere Geräusche, kleine und große Trommeln, Pauken, Becken, Triangeln, Glocken beliebt sind. So nimmt sich der Satz wie eine Aneinanderreihung lauter Farbenfleckchen und Farbentüpfelchen aus, wie ein pointillistisches Gemälde von Rysselberghe. Ganz anders, oder doch größtenteils ganz anders der zweite Theil! Hier taucht diese Manier höchstens im 3. Satz, im Scherzo, und da nur stellenweise auf, alles andere strebt organische Entwicklung der Themen, einheitlichen Fluß an, ja der zweite und letzte Satz trägt überhaupt, wenn wir von der Instrumentierung absehen, kein anderes Gepräge, als wir in der älteren Symphonie gewohnt waren."

[34] Vancsa (3035), pagination unclear: "Fassen wir noch einmal das Gesagte zu einem allgemeinen Urteil zusammen, so wird man nicht leugnen können, daß Mahlers dritte Symphonie eine ganz bedeutende Leistung ist, das Werk eines genialen Artisten voll Geist und Witz mit vollendeter Beherrschung aller gegenwärtig sich darbietenden technischen Mittel. Was ihr zum großen Kunstwerk fehlt, ist die Macht der eigenen ehrlichen, künstlerischen Überzeugung."

[35] Korngold (3029), p. 2: "Nicht als ob es an thematischem und melodischem Material fehlte; ganz im Gegenteil … Dem Themenbestande dieses Satzes scheint uns vielfach die Eigennote zu fehlen, und zum Teile, wie der zweiten Themengruppe, auch der echte symphonische Charakter."

Yet it was not the music to which these critics reacted so much as it was to the composer. Hirschfeld's review of Mahler's First recognizes its motivic unity, but even this is cast in a negative light:

> Among the innovators, masters such as Johannes Brahms have tried to fashion a whole symphonic movement from one motive. Mahler's parodistic symphony illustrates for the listener how easily such a fashioning can be misunderstood, can even become comic. He allows the interval of a fourth to be heard during the introduction of his symphony. The ingenious satirist industriously positions this leap of a fourth throughout the whole symphony, like buttons on a Swabian skirt. Wherever a place is free, in leaps the fourth; all instruments from the contrabass up to the piccolo make the effort to sprinkle the score with fourths. In these parodistic games of Mahler, one would like to send the mocked fourth finally "to the cuckoo" [i.e., get rid of them], if a mischievous remark in the score did not advise us that these fourths are actually the cuckoo in person ... I also understand this satire; it is directed at the ossification of art. For almost a millennium the minor third has served the cuckoo for the musical expression of his soul. Now he has had enough. To the age its cuckoo, to the cuckoo its freedom.[36]

The phrase "Der Zeit ihren Kuckuck" etc. is a parody of the motto of the Vienna Secession: "Die Zeit ihre Kunst, der Kunst ihre Freiheit" [To the age its art, to art its freedom]. Hirschfeld thus drew a direct line between Mahler and the modernist (read: decadent) art culture in Vienna. Helm also noted that, with the cuckoo call of the Fourth, Mahler had invented the "Über-Kuckuck."[37] Far from praising Mahler for writing a unified piece, Hirschfeld refuses to take him seriously. He proposes that Mahler is writing a satire and that the motivic unity is simply part of that

---

[36] Hirschfeld (2800), p. 2: "Meister wie Johannes Brahms unter den Neueren haben es versucht, aus einem Motiv ganze symphonische Sätze zu gestalten. Mahlers parodistische Symphonie erklärt dem Hörer, wie leicht solches Gestalten mißverstanden, ja ins Komische verkehrt werden könne. Er läßt im Eingange seiner Symphonie das Intervall der Quart ertönen. Diesen Quartsprung setzt der kunstreiche Satiriker die ganze Symphonie hindurch fleißig an, wie Knöpfe auf einen Schwabenrock. Wo ein Plätzchen frei wird, springt die Quart ein; alle Instrumente von Contrabaß bis zur Piccolo-Flöte bemühen sich, die Partitur mit Quarten zu bestreuen. Man möchte in diesem parodistischen Spiele Mahlers die von ihm verhöhnte Quart endlich zum Kuckuck wünschen, wenn eine schalkhafte Bemerkung in der Partitur uns nicht belehrte, daß diese Quart der Kuckuck in persona sei ... Auch diese Satire verstehe ich; sie ist gegen die Verknöcherung der Kunst gerichtet. Fast ein Jahrtausend hat der Kuckuck zum musikalischen Ausdruck seines Seelenlebens sich der kleinen Terz bedient. Nun hat er's satt. Der Zeit ihren Kuckuck, dem Kuckuck seine Freiheit ..." See 2802, p. 7 and 2804, p. 204 regarding the "Über-Kuckuck."

[37] The inability of Mahler to get his Kuckuck right may be a subtle reference to Wagner's parrots who "reel off human words" with "little real feeling and expression." Richard Wagner, "Judentum in der Musik," *Richard Wagner's Prose Works*, trans. William Ashton Ellis (8 vols, New York and London, 1966; rpt 1894), vol. 3, p. 89.

satire. The critic refuses to grant Mahler an artistic conception and by dwelling on the ridiculous "cuckoo call" underscores the impression that, no matter what Mahler might have written, the reaction still would have been negative.[38] Another example of contradiction lies in the form of the symphony itself. As we have seen, Mahler was roundly criticized for his mixing of the programmatic into the symphony. In critiques of Mahler's symphonies Five and Six, however, where Mahler adhered more closely to traditional symphonic form, critics were forced to suggest other reasons why Mahler's work failed. One strategy was to suggest, with Korngold, that Mahler's music lacked "a keynote," or a fundamental, underlying *something* that ensures unity. Liebstöckl does this in his review of the Sixth, but that something is hard to identify:

> Every advance of sound technology, of colors, I feel an embarrassing impoverishment of the invention, an impotence in inspiration, in the true musical moment. The mood is missing, sensitive, happy tenderness, the quiet of creation. All these things lived and shined for the last time in Johannes Brahms, as if in eternal memorial so to speak. After him begins the circus of the modern.[39]

Liebstöckl's vagueness is typical of critics attempting to locate the perceived lack in Mahler's music, but it echoes Wagner's assertion that art and civilization "remained to the Jew a foreign tongue," and, as in his speech, the Jew will betray himself "by the entire want of human expression."[40] It is this lack of true feeling that characterizes Jewish art in Wagner's opinion:

---

[38]   The continual insistence that Mahler's music is "ironic" would certainly bear closer scrutiny. I believe that it may provide for the critics a way to praise aspects of the work while condemning—or not taking seriously—the whole. The issue of irony itself in relation to the Jewish stereotype is also important, as Jews (like women) were thought to lack a sense of humor (Weininger makes this point). According to Sander Gilman, "The Jews' supposed predilection for mockery became a leitmotif in the fin de siècle, one that was related to the very nature of the Jewish body." *The Jew's Body* (New York, 1991), p. 135. A collection of essays, *Gustav Mahler et l'ironie dans la culture viennoise au tournant du siècle: Actes du colloque de Montpellier 16–18 juillet 1996*, ed. André Castagne, Michel Chalon, and Patrick Florençon (n.p., 2001), parts of which specifically discuss musical irony, does not take the Jewish stereotype into account but rather treats "irony" as a neutral category for exploration.

[39]   Hans Liebstöckl (3320), p. 3: "Aber bei allem Fortschritt der Klangtechnik, der Farben, fühle ich eine beschämende Verarmung der Erfindung, eine Impotenz im Einfall, im wirklich musikalischen Augenblick. Die Laune fehlt, die Zartheit, die glückliche Innigkeit, die Ruhe des Schaffens. Alle diese Dinge lebten und leuchteten zum letzten Mal in Johannes Brahms, gleichsam zum ewigen Gedächtniß. Hinter ihm beginnt der Circus der Moderne."

[40]   Wagner, *Judentum*, pp. 84 and 85.

... the Jew ... has no true passion [*Leidenschaft*], and least of all a passion that might thrust him on the art-creation. But where this passion is not forthcoming, there neither is true calm [*Ruhe*]: true, noble Calm is nothing else than Passion mollified through Resignation. Where the calm has not been ushering in by passion, we perceive naught but sluggishness [*Trägheit*]: the opposite of sluggishness, however, is nothing but that prickling unrest which we observe in Jewish music works from one end to the other, saving where it makes place for that soulless, feelingless inertia. What issues from the Jews' attempts at making Art, must necessarily therefore bear the attributes of coldness and indifference, even to triviality and absurdity.[41]

Liebstöckl's idea of the "quiet of creation" seems to echo to Wagner's "true calm."

A similar move on the critics' part was to suggest that even where Mahler's music followed the traditional plan, his work nevertheless failed as a totality. Korngold reveals this in the opening discussion of Mahler's Fifth:

Not lacking in strangenesses beside new and rich beauties, Gustav Mahler's Fourth Symphony has received in his Fifth an excessively genial sister. And at first glance it looks more normal than its predecessors. No explicit and no concealed program; nothing which would have to be suppressed afterwards. Nowhere is the mood assisted by the sung word; no choir, no soloist on the podium. If the symphony did not begin with the slow movement—everything would be apparently in the best classic order. Apparently. The more precisely Mahler captures outwardly the classical form, the—we do not continue this sentence ... Not least, a work like this symphony carries uneasiness in the soul of the critic. A mysterious Something rules behind these unusual tone formations.[42]

Korngold's inability or unwillingness to complete his "je desto ... desto" (the more ... the more) construction is telling because it suggests that he can not

---

[41] Wagner, *Judentum*, pp. 92–3.

[42] Korngold (3227), p. 1: "Nicht arm an Seltsamkeiten neben neuen und reichen Schönheiten, hat Gustav Mahlers 4. Symphonie in seiner 5. eine ausschweifend genialische Schwester erhalten. Und gerade sie sieht auf den ersten Blick normaler aus, als die vorangegangenen. Kein ausdrückliches und kein verschwiegenes Programm; keines, das hinterher unterdrückt werden müßte. Nirgends nimmt die Stimmung das gesungene Wort zu Hilfe; kein Chor, keine Solosängerin auf dem Podium. Führte die Symphonie nicht den langsamen Satz an der Spitze—alles wäre scheinbar in bester klassischer Ordnung. Scheinbar. Je mehr nämlich Mahler äußerlich die klassische Grundform festhält, desto—wir setzen dieses desto nicht fort ... Ein Werk, wie diese Symphonie trägt nicht zuletzt Unruhe in die Seele des Kritikers. Ein rätselhaftes Etwas waltet hinter diesen ungewöhnlichen Tongebilden ..."

articulate what the problem actually is. He comments that Mahler's themes lack "the classic cut," and complains about the contrapuntal complexity of the symphony, but otherwise offers no specific details to justify the hanging sentence. Korngold raises the same issue in his review of the Sixth, where he again begins by pointing out how normal the symphony is:

> Mahler builds in his new work self-contained symphonic movements. The classic diagram is not broken, the traditional number of movements kept, as are their traditional designations. And the Allegro is really an allegro, the Andante an andante, the Scherzo a scherzo, the Finale a finale. In the first movement the first part is even repeated: a ceremonious demonstration of the classic form. An innovation is found apparently only in the instrumental means: the percussion is assembled in a completeness never before heard, an organized intrusion of rhythmic noises into the symphony.[43]

This time, Korngold is better able to identify the reasons for his unease:

> On the whole one can say that the new symphony exceeds the unity of the symphonic structure of the earlier [symphonies], but unfortunately also their realism, which heightens the nerve-churning tensions. It also appears to us that it lags behind the works recently heard, the Third and Fifth symphonies, in variety and vigor of invention. The unusual musical shaping power, the bold natural explorer, the unusual ability of Mahler are unmistakably attested to by this new, weaker work. There is warm and cold music, said [Hans von] Bülow. Certainly the music of Mahler is not cold, and it makes us all warm.[44]

Yet Korngold still gives the impression of not really knowing what it is he is trying to say, or what problems he really finds with the music. His praise of the unity

---

[43]   Julius Korngold (3314), p. 1: "Mahler baut in seinem neuen Werke, baut geschlossene Symphoniesätze. Das klassische Schema ist nicht durchbrochen, die herkömmliche Zahl der Sätze beibehalten, wie deren herkömmliche Bezeichnung. Und das Allegro ist wirklich ein Allegro, das Andante ein Andante, das Scherzo ein Scherzo, das Finale ein Finale. Im ersten Satze wird sogar der erste Teil wiederholt: eine förmliche Demonstration für die klassische Form. Eine Neuerung findet sich scheinbar nur in den instrumentalen Mitteln: das Schlagwerk ist in einer bisher nicht erhörten Vollständigkeit herangezogen, ein organisierter Einbruch rhythmisierier Geräusche in die Symphonie."

[44]   Korngold (3314), p. 2: "Im ganzen kann man sagen, daß die neue Symphonie in der Geschlossenheit des Symphonischen Aufbaues die vorangegangenen übertrifft, aber leider auch deren Realismen, die nervenaufwühlenden Spannungen steigert. Auch scheint sie uns in der Mannigfaltigkeit und Frische der Erfindung hinter den letztgehörten Werken, der dritten und fünften Symphonie, zurückzustehen. Die ungewöhnliche musikbildene Kraft, das kühne Entdeckernaturell, das außerordentliche Können Mahlers bezeugt untrüglich auch dieses neue, schwächere Werk. Es gibt warme und kalte Musik, sagte Bülow. Kalt ist die Musik Mahlers gewiß nicht, und sie macht uns allen warm."

of the work, in relationship to the earlier symphonies, must be countered by an equally negative statement: that the work lacks "invention" and is "weaker."

As noted above, Wagner's real anger at Meyerbeer stemmed not just from Meyerbeer's popularity but from Meyerbeer's supposed catering to public whims and tastes. Meyerbeer, so Wagner believed, sets out to dupe his audience, passing his Jewish "jargon" off "as the modern-piquant utterance." As mentioned in Chapter 3, the audience was not blameless:

> [Meyerbeer] has addressed himself and products to a section of our public whose total confusion of musical taste was less to be first caused by him, than worked out to his profit. The places in our halls of entertainment are mostly filled by nothing but that section of our citizen society whose only ground for change of occupation is utter 'boredom' [*Langweile*]: the disease of boredom, however, is not remediable by sips of Art; for it can never be distracted of a set purpose, but merely duped into another form of boredom.[45]

Wagner's anxiety stemmed from the apparent ease with which Meyerbeer mimicked the surface of true art, and the inability of the audience to tell the difference. A similar distaste for the audience and dismissal of apparent success can be seen in the reviews of Mahler's Viennese premieres. It was de rigueur to point out—usually toward the end of the review—that Mahler had a fanatical faction in the audience that insisted upon applauding every movement and calling him back to the podium again and again. The implication was both that Mahler's successes were such on the surface only, and that the audience was easily fooled by Mahler's "modern-piquant utterance."

As early as 1899, the year the Second Symphony was premiered, the Viennese critics were commenting on the audience. Richard Heuberger wrote:

> The outer success of the symphony was several glorious minutes of ringing thunderous applause. Mahler has just become a favorite of the Viennese, and he is at each possible occasion given proof of their appreciation. Several hissers were also at hand with their discords. I want to employ no comparison between Mahler and our great masters, but I believe, however, that the unknowing members of the opposition of today, if they lived one hundred years ago, would have also hissed at Haydn.[46]

---

[45] Wagner, *Judentum*, pp. 96–7.

[46] Richard Heuberger (2880), p. 1: "Der äußere Erfolg der Symphonie war ein glänzenden Minutenlang erscholl stürmischer Beifall. Mahler ist eben ein Liebling der Wiener geworden, dem man bei jedem möglichen Anlasse Sympathie-Bewurfe gibt. Einige Zischer waren auch mit ihren Mißtönen bei der Hand. Ich will keinen Vergleich zwischen Mahler und unseren grössen Meistern anstellen, glaube aber, daß die factlosen Oppositionellen von heute, wenn sie vor hundert Jahren gelebt, auch Haydn ausgezischt hätten."

Note that he refers to the "outer" success, and implies that the audience would have reacted in the same way no matter what had been performed. At the premiere of the Fifth, Helm commented on the overwhelming—which, as he says, was obligatory—reception of the work, and then speculated on whether this same work would have been so well received had it been by another author.[47] Maximilian Muntz called Mahler "the musical Messiah" whose "unconditional followers" praised the Fifth Symphony.[48]

As a summary of critical concerns relating to unity, comprehensibility, and effective communication, consider the review of the Sixth Symphony by Vancsa. Here are the first four paragraphs, as published in 1907 in the magazine *Die Wage*:

> Mahler symphonies are created in a cold way. Works of the mind, of jokes, of clever refinement, [but] not dithyrambic enthusiasm, thus the regularity of their emerging amid the troubles of a stressful profession. Each season a new symphony and the public really burns with impatience for this sensation, that we Viennese, to increase the tension even more, always enjoy at least a year after its creation. Even now the Seventh Symphony has seen the light of day and almost simultaneously the first performance of the Sixth follows in the "Wiener Konzertverein," naturally under the composer's own direction.
>
> In the few years since our public was offered these new narcotics, it has already been demoralized under their influence. It visits these performances no longer to experience artistic revelations, in order to raise or cheer themselves up, but rather it waits only for the latest pranks, for the latest madness and is disappointed when these fail to appear.
>
> In his Sixth Symphony in A minor Gustav Mahler wanted to appear formally quite moderate, quite serene; already in his Fifth he had turned back. It is not only that the classic four-movement structure is relatively normal, almost understandably clear. But just as this sought-for simplicity comes out, certainly more than in any of the earlier works, how slight is the creativity, how insignificant, even banal are the themes, many of which originate second hand no less. In the first movement, which is dominated by march themes of rather stubborn sharp accents, only a couple of bizarrenesses occur, and the middle

---

[47]   Helm (3232), pp. 34–5: "... entfesselte jene dröhnenden Applaussalven und überschwenglichen Ovationen, welche in Wien bei jeder Mahler-Premiere obligat geworden sind. Ob das Publikum auch so begeistert applaudiert hätte, wenn diese merkwürdige Cis moll/D dur -Symphonie einen anderen Autor zum Verfasser hätte, bliebe dahin gestellt."

[48]   Maximilian Muntz, *Deutsche Zeitung*, 14 Dec. 1905, p. 1: "Im ersten außerordentliches Gesellschaftskonzert kam unter der Leitung des Komponisten Gustav Mahlers fünfte Symphonie zur Erstaufführung in Wien. Die unbedingten Anhänger des musikalischen Messias priesen sie als neue Offenbarung, das Modepublikum erheuchelte, vermutlich um seine geistige Verlegenheit zu verbergen durch enthusiastische Beifallskundegebungen Verständnisinnigkeit, aber hinter dem Sensationserfolg, der daraus erwuchs, stand doch das Gespenst einer allgemeinen Enttäuschung."

movements are missing even these. The sentimental cantilena of the Andante has a likewise cordially insignificant effect, as do the Ländler tunes of the Scherzo. The last is really ballet music. One really misses the dance pantomime, which, as you know, Mahler loves so very much.

In the finale one realizes immediately why the composer in three preceding movements has been so tame and restrained. It was in order to achieve an amazing contrast. Already in its dimensions this movement is nearly as long as the first three combined. But also all bizarreness, all madness, all monstrosity, which were so long held back against the grain, are now unleashed. He who has not yet lost patience is compensated now with sensations aplenty.[49]

First, probably with reference to Mahler's conducting schedule which allowed him time to compose only during the summers, Vancsa states that Mahler's symphonies are "cold"; they are produced on a regular timetable and have nothing of the spontaneity of true creative endeavors. They are works of the mind, not of

---

[49] Vancsa (3321), pp. 37–8: "Mahlers Sinfonien sind auf kaltem Wege erzeugt. Werke des Verstandes, des Witzes, des ausgeklügelten Raffinements, nicht der dithyrambischen Begeisterung, daher die Regelmäßigkeit ihres Entstehens mitten in den Mühen eines aufreibenden Berufes. Jede Saison eine neue Sinfonie und das Publikum brennt ordentlich auf diese Sensation, die wir Wiener, um die Spannung noch zu erhöhen, immer erst ein Jahr nach dem Entstehen zu genießen bekommen. Eben hat die Siebente Sinfonie das Licht der Welt erblickt und fast gleichzeitig erfolgte die erste Aufführung der Sechsten im 'Wiener Konzertverein,' selbstverständlich unter des Komponisten eigener Leitung.

In den wenigen Jahren, seit unserem Publikum diese neuen Narkotika kredenzt werden, ist es bereits unter ihrem Einflusse demoralisiert worden. Es besucht diese Aufführungen nicht mehr, um künstlerische Offenbarungen zu erleben, um sich zu erheben, zu erfreuen, sondern es wartet nur noch auf die neuen Witze, auf die neuen Verrücktheiten und ist enttäuscht, wo sich diese nicht einstellen wollen.

In seiner Sechsten Sinfonie in A-moll wollte Gustav Mahler formell recht gemäßigt, recht abgeklärt erscheinen; schon in seiner Fünften hatte er ja zurückgelenkt. Nicht nur daß die klassische Vierzahl der Sätze ist verhältnismäßig normal, fast verständlich klar. Aber gerade bei dieser gesuchten Einfachheit kommt es mehr noch als bei einem der früheren Werke heraus, wie gering die Erfindungsgabe ist, wie unbedeutend, ja banal diese Themen sind, die sogar noch dazu vielfach aus zweiter Hand stammen. Im ersten Satze, der ziemlich hartnäckig von scharfakzentuierten Marschthemen beherrscht wird, gibt es noch ein paar Bizarrerien, in den Mittelsätzen fehlen auch diese. Die sentimentale Kantilene des Andante wirkt ebenso herzlich unbedeutend, wie die Ländlerweisen des Scherzos. Letzteres ist ganz ausgesprochene Ballettmusik. Man vermißt ordentlich die Tanzpantomime, die Mahler bekanntlich so sehr liebt.

Beim Finale merkt man sofort, warum der Komponist in drei vorhergehenden Sätzen so zahm und zurückhaltend gewesen ist. Es soll eine verblüffende Kontrastwirkung erzielt werden. Schon seinen Dimensionen nach ist dieser Satz nahezu so ausgedehnt, wie die drei ersten zusammengenommen. Aber auch alle Bizarrerie, alle Verrücktheit, alle Monstrosität, die so lange wider die Natur zurückgehalten wurde, wird nun losgelassen. Wem vordem nicht die Geduld ausgegangen, wird nun durch reichliche Sensationen entschädigt."

the spirit. (Mahler is a Thinker and not a Poet.) Next, Vancsa turns to the public, who eagerly await each new offering, although he chides Mahler for holding back his works from the Viennese by introducing them elsewhere. These works are to the public a narcotic, which destroys their ability to attend to performances by offering only isolated moments and not an organic whole. (Mahler, like Meyerbeer, offers "sips of Art" to allay boredom and the audience exhibits "total confusion" and is easily "duped.") Not only is Mahler's music bad, but it is also like a disease, eating away the audience's ability to appreciate true or real art.[50]

Vancsa then confronts the Sixth Symphony itself, making note of how normal it appears: it retains the four-movement structure and is "almost understandably clear." But this simplicity is not real because it is searched for, and its inferiority is revealed in the lack of quality, the banal themes, and the absence of originality. (Mahler listens only to the "barest surface of art, and not to its life-bestowing inner organism.") But even the relative calm and serenity of the first three movements proves to be an illusion: with the finale, Mahler's true nature, long held in check, breaks forth. (Mahler can know no true calm.) Here Mahler's stylistic disjunctions become apparent, creating a lack of unity across the whole symphony. (Mahler "hurls together … diverse forms and styles.") Vancsa goes on to discuss the orchestration and to show how Mahler, as Wagner maintained of Jewish composers, offers "at each instant a new summons to attention, through a change in outer expressional means." The abrupt contrast between the "calm" first three movements and the disruptive finale recalls the end of Oskar Panizza's story "The Operated Jew," where Itzig Faitel Stern, after much time and effort spent on trying to become a German, reverts to his natural (Jewish) self:

> Everyone scattered. The terrifying visage drove the young ladies from the room. Those people who remained behind watched with horror as Faitel's blond strands of hair began to turn from red to dirty brown to blue-black. The entire glowing and sweaty head with tight gaunt features was once again covered with curly locks. In the meantime it appeared that Faitel had peculiar difficulties and struggled with his exalted movements. His arms and legs, which had been stretched and bent in numerous operations, could no longer perform the recently learned movements, nor the old ones . Everyone saw that this was a catastrophe which could no longer be prevented. The beautiful Othilia sought refuge in the

---

[50]   Nietzsche famously calls Wagner's music a "narcotic"; see *Ecce Homo: How One Becomes What One Is*, trans. R. J. Hollingdale (New York, 1992), p. 62: "Such people desire Wagner as an *opiate*—they forget themselves, they are free of themselves for a moment … What am I saying? *for five or six hours!*—" Eduard Hanslick states a similar sentiment in his *On the Musically Beautiful: A Contribution Towards the Revision of the Aesthetics of Music*, trans. and ed. Geoffrey Payzand from the 8th edn (1891) (Indianapolis, 1986), p. 59: "Incidentally, for people who want the kind of effortless suppression of awareness they get from music, there is a wonderful recent discovery which far surpasses that of art. We refer to ether and chloroform."

arms of her mother. Everyone looked with dread at the crazy circular movements of the Jew ... And finally ... [Faitel] lay before him crumpled and quivering, a convoluted Asiatic image in wedding dress, a counterfeit of human flesh, Itzig Faitel Stern.[51]

The "moral" of Panizza's tale is that the Jew will reveal himself, no matter how hard he tries to disguise himself or to change. Wagner also noted that although the Jew "takes pains to strip off [the peculiarities of speech] ... they nevertheless shew an impertinent obstinacy in cleaving to him."[52] The "moral" of Vancsa's review is similar: Mahler will reveal himself eventually as a Jew—by writing banal or second-hand melodies, with orchestration—no matter how hard he may try to write a "normal" symphony.

Originality: Melodic Reminiscences

Wagner had stated that in both speech and art, "the Jew can only after-speak and after-patch—not truly make a poem of his words or an artwork of his doings."[53] As a Thinker and not a Poet, having no community to draw upon for inspiration, the Jew has no choice but to imitate what he hears, but cannot truly understand. The image of imitation or borrowing—or even stealing—culture is the manifestation of the supposed Jewish lack of creativity. Anatole Leroy-Beaulieu's book *Israel among the Nations: A Study of Jews and Antisemitism*, although written in defense of the Jews, contains the following statement: if the Jew has no "distinctive genius and is capable of imitating, of borrowing, of transmitting to some what it has received from others, how can this slim remnant of Judah, thinned by intermixture with a hundred peoples, endanger our national genius?"[54] Mahler is likewise accused both of using the themes of other composers verbatim, and of depending on the works of others for inspiration. Either way, he is denied any possibility of being a creative or original composer.

Helm, in a passage cited above from his review of the First Symphony, claimed that the work really "cries out for a program," especially to explain the disjunction between the first two movements and the last two. But Mahler does not stop at simply canceling the program:

---

[51]   Jack Zipes, "The Operated Jew," in *The Operated Jew: Two Tales of Anti-Semitism* (New York, 1991), pp. 73–4.

[52]   Wagner, *Judentum*, p. 89.

[53]   Ibid., p. 85.

[54]   Anatole Leroy-Beaulieu, *Israel among the Nations: A Study of Jews and Antisemitism*, trans. Frances Hellman (New York, 1895), p. 249; orig. pub. *Juifs et l'antisémitisme: Israél chez les nations* (Paris, 1893); cited in Gilman, *Smart Jews: The Construction of the Image of Jewish Superior Intelligence* (Lincoln and London, 1996), pp. 50–51.

... In the self-denial of his own earlier artistic intents Mahler now went so
far that he had directly forbidden the otherwise usual technical analysis in the
program book of the Philharmonic—according to statements from the publisher
himself!!

Why suddenly this secret fuss? Did Mr Mahler worry perhaps, that one
would discover only too quickly through the musical examples that everything
in this symphony by him—is not? It almost appears so. For indeed the work
offers one an almost humorous wealth of citations from Beethoven, Wagner,
Bruckner, Mendelssohn, Weber etc. We could see this before the concert from
playing through the four-hand piano arrangement kindly made available to us by
the publisher Mr C. Weinberger in Vienna.[55]

Helm uses the term "Citatenschatz," which seems to imply that he believes that
Mahler was using the themes consciously rather than inadvertently. In this case,
however, the quotes are so obvious—and so exact?—that Helm has no trouble
finding them simply by playing through the arrangement. A similar point, as we
saw in Chapter 1, is made in a cartoon from around 1900: Mahler is shown dressed
up as Wagner, Liszt, Meyerbeer, Schubert, Beethoven, and finally in peasant garb,
"orchestrating a folk song" (see Figure 1.1). The title of the cartoon is "Mahler's
Metamorphoses," and it ridicules the melodic reminiscences and borrowings in a
recent Mahler symphony (perhaps the Fifth). Although on the surface it appears
relatively benign, it can also be seen as illustrating Wagner's assertion that Jews
hurl together diverse forms and styles from every age and every master. Read in
the context of this and the earlier statements regarding Jewish imitation, its status
as a straightforward reaction to Mahler's music becomes suspect.

Although both Helm and the cartoon indict entire Mahler works as derivative,
many critics simply note similarities between particular themes. For example,
Korngold hears a similarity between the first theme in the finale of the Fifth and
the finale of Brahms's Second in D major.[56] Also in the Fifth, Hirschfeld calls
the theme in the funeral march a "reshaping of the Allegretto theme from the

---

[55]   Helm (2802), p. 7: "... In der Selbstverleugnung seiner eigenen früheren
künstlerischen Absichten ging nun aber Mahler gar so weit, daß er sich die sonst übliche
technische Analyse in Programmbuch der Philharmoniker—nach ausdrücklicher Erklärung
der Herausgeber desselben—diesmal direct verboten hatte!!

Wozu auf einmal diese Geheimthuerei? Fürchtete vielleicht Herr Mahler, daß man
durch die abgedruckten Notenbeispiele nur zu rasch dahinterkommen würde, was in dieser
Symphonie alles von ihm—nicht ist? Es scheint fast so. Denn in der That bietet das Werk
einen fast ergötzlichen Citatenschatz aus Beethoven, Wagner, Bruckner, Mendelssohn,
Weber u.s.w. Wir konnten uns noch vor dem Concert davon überzeugen beim Durchspielen
des uns von dem Verleger Hernn C. Weinberger in Wien freundlichst zur Verfügung
gestellten vierhändigen Clavierauszuges."

[56]   Korngold (3227), p. 2: "Das erste Thema hat etwas vom Charakter des Finales von
Brahms' D-dur-Symphonie."

Third [Symphony] of Brahms." With regard to the finale of the same symphony, Hirschfeld writes:

> The finale, however, bubbles in boisterous cheer. All sources of musical pleasure from Haydn to Humperdinck trickle through the voices. Quotations, which may be conscious or unconscious, buzz through the score. The finale-theme of the Symphonic Etudes of Schumann flashes by note for note. Is it homage or mockery? We do not ask.[57]

Hirschfeld implies that Mahler is not capable of writing music that is truly "cheerful," and so must depend on quotations from other composers to get the idea across. He wonders whether these are conscious or unconscious, although Mahler appears in a bad light regardless. Either way, Mahler is not in control of his music. The question, "homage or mockery?" by definition implies the latter, especially when Hirschfeld does not even do Mahler the favor of attempting to discover which it is. In his review of the Second Symphony, Liebstöckl finds similarities to the music of Schubert, Wagner, Tchaikovsky, Humperdinck, Dvořák, von Weber, and Mozart.[58]

Even where Mahler did not quote exactly, critics found similarities in his works to those of other composers, again denying Mahler any possibility of creativity. Hirschfeld suggests in his review of the Sixth that Mahler kept the symphonies of Brahms, Liszt, and Bruckner handy to provide ideas if he could not come up with adequate themes on his own:

> One does injustice to the symphonist Gustav Mahler to reproach him for all the strange percussion—the cow bells, the hammer, the small wooden rods which hit the drum rim, the switch. They are artistic necessities, which belong to his innermost nature. One does not believe that the composer Gustav Mahler wants only to startle with strange sounds and poundings. No, he is under an artistic pressure. When he finds nothing other than inadequate, meaningless themes, he turns immediately to the first movements of Brahms, Liszt, and Bruckner, to steal motives, which he can then only dress up with drum and switch in order to create new effects. If he were capable of expressing tragic feelings through the power of tones, he would gladly renounce the hammer and its blows of fate. However, he lacks inner, true creative power. So at the supreme point of the excitement in

---

57   Hirschfeld (3229), p. 2: "Das Finale aber sprudelt in ausgelassener Heiterkeit. Alle Quellen musikalischer Lust von Haydn bis Humperdinck rieseln durch die Stimmen. Zitate, die bewußt oder unbewußt aufgenommen sind, schwirren durch die Partitur. Das Finale Thema der sinfonischen Etüden von Schumann blitzt Note für Note auf. Ist das Huldigung oder Spott? Wir fragen nicht." Earlier quote pp. 1–2: "Das Thema des Trauermarsches, mit dem die Sinfonie beginnt— eine Sinfonie *muß* doch auch einmal mit einem Trauermarsch beginnen—ist eine Umbildung des Allegretto-Themas aus der Dritten von Brahms."

58   Liebstöckl (2885), p. 5.

the tragic symphony he grabs the hammer. He cannot do otherwise. If the tones refuse, so falls a blow. That is completely natural. Speakers, for whom words fail at the decisive moment, hit the table with their fists.[59]

"Artistic pressure" (to produce? to be original?) causes Mahler to search for themes to replace the meaningless ones he comes up with. As we shall see, orchestration is intimately bound up with issues of creativity or the lack of it, and Hirschfeld sees the percussion in the Sixth as compensation for an inability to be truly expressive. Nonetheless, he believes that Mahler must mine the works of others to provide themes for his own works, and then attempt to disguise his pillaging with orchestration. Heuberger accuses Mahler of literal plagiarism in the Fourth, where he "disguises himself as Haydn and plays under the intentional application of certain old formulae, no longer workable in our new tone language."[60]

Other critics who implied that Mahler used the work of others as a model included Korngold, who in a review of the Third related the form of the second movement to the third movement of Brahms' D major Symphony.[61] According to Vancsa, the same movement achieved a "harmlessness à la Haydn."[62] Helm on the other hand suggests that, for the main part of the second movement, Mahler "very happily copied a Mozartian or Gluckian Rococo."[63] In all cases, Mahler lacked the ability to create a certain effect, and so the effect that Mahler does achieve is unreal, insofar as it is copied.

---

[59]   Robert Hirschfeld (3317), p. 1: "Man tut Unrecht, dem Sinfoniker Gustav Mahler die Herdenglocken, den Hammer, die Holzstäbchen, die an den Trommelrand schlagen, die Ruten, all das sonderbare Schlagwerk vorzuhalten. Es sind künstlerische Notwendigkeiten, die zu seinem innersten Wesen gehören. Man glaube nicht, daß der Tonsetzer Gustav Mahler durch seltsame Klänge und Schlager nur verblüffen will. Nein, er steht unter einem künstlerischen Zwang. Wenn er nichts anderes als dürftige, nichtssagende Themen findet und gleich im ersten Satze zu Brahms, Liszt und Bruckner sich wendet, um ihnen Motive abzunehmen, so kann er schließlich nur mit Trommeln und Ruten noch neue Wirkungen erzielen. Wäre er imstande, tragische Gefühle durch die Macht der Töne auszudrücken, so wollte er gern auf den Hammer und dessen Schicksalsschläge verzichten. Ihm mangelt aber die innere, wahre schöpferische Kraft. So greift er denn in der tragischen Sinfonie auf dem höchsten Punkte der Erregung zum Hammer. Er kann nicht anders. Versagen die Töne, so fällt ein Schlag. Das ist ganz natürlich. Redner, denen im entscheidenden Momente die Worte fehlen, schlagen mit der Faust auf dem Tisch ..."

[60]   Heuberger (3130), p. 4: "Mahler verkleidet sich als Haydn und spielt unter absichtlicher Verwendung bestimmter alter, in unserer neuesten Tonsprache nicht mehr gangbarer Formeln ..."

[61]   Korngold (3029), p. 2.

[62]   Vancsa (3035), pagination unclear.

[63]   Helm (3037), p. 12

Triviality and Absurdity

According to Wagner, the Jewish artwork will "bear the attributes of coldness and indifference, even to triviality and absurdity."[64] Mahler's melodies were often described as banal or trivial. Such a designation functioned in criticism in one of two ways: either as an indication of "mass production" (and thus, again, a sign that it is the work of a Thinker and not a Poet), or as one of insincerity masquerading as "naïveté"—perhaps a sign of coldness and indifference, or perhaps a sign that Mahler has mistaken the "external accidents" as the essence, thus missing "the life bestowing inner organism."

In the hierarchy of musical forms and styles, if the symphony is considered (by the Germans at least) to be the pinnacle, then rock bottom is salon music. This genre was denigrated in part because it was created solely for entertainment, but also because it was the domain of women, both as consumers and as performers. The implication is that such music is rolled off the assembly line, so to speak, without thought to its quality, meaning, or value. Implied, too, is that it is music written for money. Hirschfeld conjures up all of these images in his description of the Adagietto in the Fifth:

> In the following Adagietto, however, the composer satirizes himself. A longing motive from the Kindertotenlieder: "Nun seh ich wohl, warum so dunkle Flammen," is turned—through simplified harmonization and through sweet suspensions, or rather long appoggiaturas which close each bar phrase—into the trivial and is continued in the handkerchief style of the salon composers, who stop at Opus 700. The style portrait of dreadful banality is extremely successful and mockingly prepares the witty Rondo-finale. A soft cushion from the harp and string quartet completes this entrance into a musical garden bower.[65]

Hirschfeld affects to assume that Mahler is writing satire, and notes the way that a melodic fragment—by indicating that it comes from another Mahler work he implies that in and of itself it is not to blame—can be consciously manipulated and made into music of the drawing room. The emotional effect here is calculated—much like the actions of Panizza's Stern, who carefully observes and then imitates the gestures and expressions of the Germans and therefore deceives them into

---

[64]   Wagner, *Judentum*, p. 93

[65]   Hirschfeld (3229), p. 2: "In dem folgenden Adagietto persifliert aber der Komponist sich selbst. Ein Sehnsuchtsmotiv aus den Kindertotenliedern: 'Nun seh ich wohl, warum so dunkle Flammen,' wird durch vereinfachte Harmonisierung und durch süßliche Vorhalte, beziehungsweise lange Vorschläge, die jede Taktphrase abschließen, ins Triviale gewendet und im Schmachtlappenstile der Salonkomponisten, die bei Opus 700 halten, fortgeführt. Das Stilporträt entsetzlicher Banalität ist überaus gelungen und das witzige Rondo-Finale spöttisch vorbereitet. Eine weiche Rasenunterlage von Harfe und Streichquartett vervollständigt diesen Eingang in eine musikalische Gartenlaube."

believing that his emotions are sincere. Panizza, it will be recalled, states that this took place "in the social gatherings of the ladies' salons." The calculation results in "triviality" and "dreadful banality" precisely because it is not—cannot—be real.

Hirschfeld uses the same image when describing the Andante of the Sixth, but here he locates the calculation more minutely:

> Here, too, internal constraint drives the incessant change, because the trivial, banal themes want to achieve a symphonic bearing. Who would even consider them if they appeared naturally? Let us take the Andante of the Sixth! One would like to attribute the theme to a drawing-room piece or a Sonatina of Fritz Spindler op. 389 (or some other number in the region of mass production), if in E flat a little note did not slide down from F to F flat and from G to G flat. Thus the triviality instantly takes on an interesting mien, and we feel we are in the presence of a personality. The real creativity in Mahler's nature, if we want to ignore the percussion, rests in that F flat or G flat. What follows next gets lost in incoherent formula stuff. Everything pertaining to the material essence of sound in this movement is technically perfect and holds itself up to the height of modern Kapellmeisterkultur. Thus a small motive—a sixth, and later fourth— spread throughout the Andante is a completely ordinary, insignificant speech-particle that has been heard a thousand times. In a speech that motive would correspond to the phrase "Highly esteemed!" [*"Hochverehrte!"*] Split by a 16th-note rest, however, the motive will become immediately interesting as if one in his speech would continually say "Highly e-steemed!" [*"Hochver-ehrte!"*] Once again the creative idea of Mahler lies in a mere 16th-note rest.[66]

According to Hirschfeld, it is these chromatic pitches that dress up an otherwise banal theme in symphonic clothing. To locate Mahler's creativity in a half-step—

---

[66] Hirschfeld (3317), p. 2: "Auch hier treibt innere Nötigung den unablässigen Wechsel hervor, denn die gehaltlosen, banalen Themen wollen sich sinfonisch gebärden. Wer würde sie beachten, wenn sie natürlich erschienen? Nehmen wir das Andante der Sechsten vor! Das Thema möchte man einem Salonstück oder einer Sonatine von Fritz Spindler op. 389 (oder sonst einer Nummer in der Region der Massenproduktion) zuschrieben, wenn in dem Es-dur ein Nötlein nicht von f aus fes und eines von g auf ges herabgerutscht wäre. So aber macht die Trivialität, plötzlich zuckend, eine interessante Miene, und wir werden auf eine Individualität gewiesen. Das eigentlich Schöpferische in der Mahlerschen Natur, wenn wir vom Schlagwerk absehen wollen, beruht in jenem fes oder ges. Was dann folgt, verliert sich in zusammenhanglosem Formelkram. Alles materielle Klangwesen in diesem Satze ist technisch vollkommen und hält sich auf der Höhe der modernen Kapellmeisterkultur. So ist das kleine, in das Andante fleißig eingestreute Sexten- und später Quartenmotiv eine ganz gewöhnliche, unbedeutende Redefloskel, die tausendmal gehört wurde. In einer Rede würde jenes Motiv etwa dem Worte 'Hochverehrte!' entsprechen. Durch eine Sechzehntelpause aber gespalten, wird das Motiv sofort interessant als ob einer in seiner Rede beständig 'Hochver-ehrte!' sagen wollte. Diesmal also liegt die schöpferische Idee Mahlers wieder nur in einer Sechzehntelpause."

or later, in a 16th-note rest—on the surface may seem complimentary. After all, he is taking a trivial theme and making it interesting. However, not only does Mahler start with inferior goods, but he tries to disguise them with carefully thought-out chromaticism as something other than what they are. Note that Hirschfeld is not citing Mahler's creativity, but rather pointing out how he exploits this trivial melody in order to create—as Wagner claimed of Meyerbeer—an *Effekt*. Hirschfeld shows that Mahler's gift is as Wagner said: the ability to offer "at each instant a new summons to attention, through a change in outer expressional means."

The Fourth Symphony, when it received its Vienna premiere in 1902, was accused of a kind of studied simplicity. Geisler called the thematic material "supremely simple, often the motives strike one as quite childlike, not to say trivial."[67] He averred that "Gustav Mahler had a penchant for folk art and liked to weave the *Urnaive* of the folk as an essential element into the complicated, nervous, reflective products of his imagination—see [for example] the 'Klagende Lied,' the First Symphony, the 'Lieder eines fahrenden Gesellen' among other works."[68] For Helm, there is a contradiction between the simplicity of the melodies and their use in the symphony:

> Indeed, however, a supremely curious thing, this Fourth Symphony of our ultra-secessionist clever Opera director! Apparently he wanted to make a point of working with the simplest possible folk-like (or at least intended to be folk-like), old-fashioned, even childlike melodies, which he then sets however in such strangely complicated combinations, so that without knowledge of the score one loses the thread only too often, and occasionally, especially in the first movement—where one occasionally thinks one hears even animal voices or something like that—[one] receives the impression of the most colorful confusion.[69]

---

[67] Geisler, *Neue musikalische Presse* 11 (19 Jan. 1902), p. 37: "Das thematische Material der neuen Symphonie ist höchst einfach, oft muthen die Motive recht kindlich, um nicht zu sagen trivial an."

[68] Ibid., p. 37: "Gustav Mahler hielt sich von je mit Vorliebe an die Volkskunst und webte das Urnaive derselben als ein wesentliches Element gerne den complicirten, nervösen, reflectirten Erzeugnissen seiner Phantasie ein—siehe das 'Klagende Lied,' die erste Symphonie, die 'Lieder eines fahrenden Gesellen' und Anderes."

[69] Helm (3136), p. 69: "In der That aber auch ein höchst curioses Ding, diese vierte Symphonie unseres hypersecessionistisch geistreichen Operndirectors! Anscheinend hat er sich diesmal angelegen sein lassen, mit möglichst einfachen volksthümlichen (oder doch volksthümlich gemeinten), altväterischen, selbst kindlichen Melodien zu arbeiten, die er aber dann in so sonderbar verzwickte Combinationen setzt, dass man ohne Kenntniss der Partitur nur zu oft den Faden verliert und mitunter, namentlich im ersten Satz—wo man zuweilen selbst Thierstimmen oder Aehnliches zu vernehmen glaubt—den Eindruck des buntesten Durcheinander empfängt."

For both Helm and Geisler, Mahler makes a conscious choice to use "folk-like" or simple melodies, which makes them immediately suspect. Both also disparage the themes—Geisler calling them trivial and Helm suggesting that they are not folk-like at all, really—and both think that Mahler then ruins the effect with his complicated treatment. Wagner had claimed that the Jew had no folk from which to draw inspiration and therefore Mahler's use of folk-like themes could only be a bastardization.

In Hirschfeld's review of the Fourth he conjures up images of the modern world:

> ... I lack a sympathetic sensitivity for Mahler's affected folkiness, prepared naïveté, artificial childishness. It calls up visions of father Haydn bumping along in an automobile with a cloud of gasoline fumes. The form of the first "sleigh bell" movement would be clear, but the development is tiring through incessant application of wit. It is a swarm of motives, sound effects, rushings, spots, lights, accents, musical jokes. Wherever a space opened up, a witty combination is tried.[70]

The virtual equation of the modern and the urban with "Jewish" certainly calls into question Hirschfeld's metaphor of Haydn in the driver's seat. Mahler's folkiness is not only affected but overdone and the result is confusion: in attempting to dress up the surface of his work, Mahler loses the trust of his listeners.

Muntz notices a similar situation in the second movement of the Fifth Symphony, where Mahler again seems to be working against his own purposes:

> In the second movement of the symphony, the Scherzo, artistic cynicism again comes to light in a completely different way. Mahler tries here a doubtful experiment, to stylize Heuriger [tavern] music. Waltz and Ländler motives, robbed of their naive innocence, impudently made up with modern orchestral colors, whirl a contrapuntal cancan, which occasionally goes seriously awry, since sounds of popular songs are also mixed in and threaten a violent quarrel.[71]

---

[70]   Hirschfeld (3132), p. 2: "... Für Mahlers affectirte Volksthümlichkeit, zubereitete Naivetät, künstliche Kindlichkeit fehlt mir die sympathische Empfindung. Man meint Vater Haydn im Automobil mit brenzlichen Benzindämpfen vorüberholpern zu sehen. Die Form des ersten Schellensatzes wäre klar, aber die Durchführung ermüdet durch unausgesetzte Anwendung von Witz. Es ist ein Gewimmel von Motiven, Klangeffecten, Schnellern, Tupfern, Lichtern, Accenten, Tonspässen. Wo nur ein Plätzchen frei scheint, wird eine geistreiche Combination versucht."

[71]   Muntz, *Deutsche Zeitung*, 14 Dec. 1905, p. 1: "Im zweiten Satze der Symphonie, dem Scherzo, tritt der künstlerische Zynismus wieder in einer ganz anderen Art zutage. Mahler führt hier das bedenkliche Experiment aus, Heurigenmusik zu stilisieren. Walzer- und Ländlermotive, ihrer naiven Unschuld beraubt, frech geschminkt mit modernen Orchesterfarben, wirbeln einen kontrapunktischen Cancan, der mitunter bedenklich ausartet,

Mahler throws together an odd assortment of common styles and "robs" them of their innocence. Muntz sees this as cynicism on Mahler's part, rather than actual deception, but in any case, he does not think it successful.

It is noteworthy that much of the criticism of Mahler's "banal" or "trivial" themes or his would-be folk songs occurs in the discussion of scherzo movements. As Kalbeck suggests, the Scherzo of the First "would perhaps work more fascinatingly as a ballet."[72] Korngold likens the third movement of the Third Symphony to beer hall music.[73] Graf calls the post-horn melody of the same movement not simply a folk song, but "a flaxen-haired, blue-eyed melody." The use of such physical features—of course in stark contrast to the features of the melody's composer—leave no doubt that Graf perceives Mahler again to be disguising himself. Graf is careful to state that although one is stirred a little by this melody, it is in fact the memories (of "first love") that the melody recalls which are moving, not the melody itself.[74] Vancsa finds this same third movement "somewhat intrusive and bizarre," and uncovers "good and bad jokes, grotesque humor, and trivialities."[75]

Mahler's themes betray an outsider. Critics see his use of folk material as disingenuous or deceitful, and none of his themes have the power to communicate. Any attempt at emotion is either satire or irony; use of folk song is faux naiveté or studied simplicity. Rarely do critics grant Mahler the ability to produce moving, beautiful music. Heuberger does find the slow movement of the Fourth Symphony to be "completely without joking disguise" and regards it as the most beautiful movement because it is "*without* mask, without pigtail and powdered wig."[76] However, the critic had begun his review by expressing the belief that Mahler had decided to write his "Pastorale" Symphony and wanted to show "how sociable and *gemütlich*" he could be, suggesting that Mahler not only continued to be derivative

---

da auch einige Gassenhaueranklänge sich an dem Treiben beteiligen und mit tätlichem Streit drohen." A *Heurige* is a new wine and also the designation of the (specifically Austrian) taverns that serve them. In Vienna, most are in the suburbs and are self-consciously "rustic."

[72]   Kalbeck (2801), p. 2: "Im Theater würde das geniale Stück als Ballet vielleichte noch hinreißender wirken als im Concertsaal, obwohl auch hier Alles elektrisirte."

[73]   Korngold (3029), p. 3: "Er hat auch gewiß an einem schönen Sommerabend bei einer Biergartenmusik die gefühlvolle 'Post im Walde' gehört."

[74]   Graf (3033), p. 6: "Auf dem Posthorn wird eine Volksliedmelodie geblasen, eine semmelblonde, blauäugige Melodie, eines jener Lieder, das man anstimmt, wenn man recht eselhaft verliebt ist, zwischen fünfzehn und zwanzig Jahren, in der Zeit der ersten Liebe. Wir fangen an, gerade ein wenig gerührt zu werden—nicht durch die Melodie, sondern durch Erinnerungen—da verspottet uns der Komponist durch ein keckes Militärsignal: 'Abgeblasen.'"

[75]   Vancsa (3035), pagination unclear.

[76]   Heuberger (3130), p. 4: "Dies, *ohne* Maske, ohne Zopf und Perrücke. Ganz ohne Verkleidungsscherz gibt sich das 'Poco adagio,' der schönste Satz der Symphonie."

of Beethoven, but that he was putting on yet another costume.[77] Mahler simply cannot write an entire work "without disguise."

Orchestration

In *Opera and Drama*, Wagner charged that "not one departure is [Meyerbeer's] own, but each he has eavesdropped from his forerunner, exploiting it with monstrous ostentation."[78] As noted in Chapter 3, orchestration was not explicitly identified by Wagner as "Effect," but could be seen in the context of Wagner's essay as representing the impoverished surface, and the Jew's orchestration will ultimately reveal itself in its dishonesty or subterfuge, attempting to hide, ornament, or make enticing its utter lack of true expressive power.

"Orchestration" might seem out of place here, as many of the early Viennese critics praised Mahler for it. I would like to suggest, however, that these early comments on and interest in Mahler's orchestration techniques do not necessarily represent neutral observations; rather, these critiques, too, may reveal ingrained beliefs regarding Jewish inferiority and difference.

Wagner had asserted that the Jew's foreignness will reveal itself in the "repulsive *how*." Just as the Jew's German is unfamiliar and strange sounding, so do Mahler's instruments sound foreign. According to Robert Hirschfeld, writing after the premiere of the First Symphony in Vienna, "The parodistic treatment of the instruments in the D major Symphony seeks to take the individual instruments through unfamiliar registers and manipulations of all types of their natural sounds; the violins (col legno) must rattle, the trumpets [must] flute, the horn may not sound like a horn, nor the cello like a cello."[79] Mahler is then accused of mustering huge means for one small, fussy effect—one which ultimately does not even sound particularly pleasant: "[In the opening of the first movement] [t]he whole string orchestra, with the cellos and contrabasses themselves triply divided, must hold an A harmonic in all achievable octaves for 50 bars, ultimately in order to achieve the effect of a creaking door."[80]

---

[77]   Heuberger (3130), p. 4: "Mahler ging diesmal offenbar darauf aus, seine 'Pastorale' zu schreiben und zu zeigen, wie umgänglich, wie gemüthlich er sein könne."

[78]   Wagner, *Oper und Drama, Prose Works*, vol. 2, pp. 88–9.

[79]   Hirschfeld (2800), p. 2: "Die parodistische Behandlung der Instrumente in der D-dur-Symphonie geht darauf aus, den einselnen Instrumenten durch ungewonte Lage und Manipulationen aller Art ihren natürlichen Klang zu nehmen, die Geigen (col legno) müssen klappern, die Trompeten flöten, das Horn darf nicht wie Horn, das Cello nicht wie Cello klingen."

[80]   Hirschfeld (2800), p. 2: "Das ganze Streichorchester muß mit je dreifach getheilten Celli und Contrabässen über fünfzig Takte ein Flageolet-A durch alle erreichbaren Octaven halten, um schließlich den Effect einer knarrenden Thür zu erzielen."

None of Mahler's instruments are thought to sound as they should. According to Geissler, also writing about the Viennese premiere of the First Symphony, "the most unusual is intentionally demanded of the instruments." Geissler offers what he calls "a single example from the countless bizarre effects":

> The winds are chased into the highest and lowest registers, must sound from a far or muted; the violins squander themselves on harmonics, pizzicati, col legno. A beautiful melody in the first movement will whimper forth from the violoncellos with miserable tone, as if the players have pulled a flannel glove over the left hand—perhaps they had to place the fingers of the left hand only loosely, without pressure, and draw the bow over the fingerboard.[81]

Here, although the original idea may have been beautiful, Mahler's performance directions purportedly make it ugly. Geissler comments that not even the program, although it would have been helpful, would allow the listener "to follow the unprecedented, forced musical remarks."[82] In some reviews, the instruments are said not only to speak in ways foreign to their nature, but to become animated as well, almost as if they were out of control. Note especially the verbs used in the following passage, taken from a review of the Fourth Symphony by Hans Liebstöckl:

> Suddenly the clarinets whimper for help, without anyone knowing what ails them, then secretive 16th notes scamper like scared mice over the contrabasses; in one place, four flutes call out a trivial "theme" "flowing, but without haste," while the cellos virtually trill themselves to death and the contrabasses hop without tiring from tonic to dominant. Timpani growl, bells play, triangles shrill, and the tam-tam strikes mercilessly in between, until finally everything is united in trivial carnival music and after a short reflection, "still slow and somewhat hesitatingly," joins in with the tavern celebration.[83]

---

[81] Geissler, *Neue musikalische Presse* 9 (25 Nov. 1900), p. 352: "Die Bläser werden in die höchsten und tiefsten Lagen gejagt, müssen aus der Ferne blasen oder stopfen, die Geigen prassen mit flageolets, pizzicati, col legno. Ein schöner Gesang im ersten Satze wird von den Violoncellen mit jämmerlichem Tone hervorgewinselt, als hätten die Spieler einen Flanell-Handschuh über die Linke gezogen—vielleicht mussten sie die Finger der Linken nur lose ohne Druck aufsetzen und den Bogen nahe daran über dem Griffbrett führen."

[82] Ibid., p. 352, cited above.

[83] Liebstöckl (3135), p. 2: "Bald wimmern die Clarinetten um Hilfe, ohne daß man wüßte, was ihnen fehlt, bald laufen geheimnißvolle Sechzehntel wie aufgescheuchte Mäuse über die Contrabässe; an einer Stelle raufen sich vier Flöten 'fließend, aber ohne Hast,' um ein triviales 'Thema,' während sich die Celli vor Vergnügen schier zertrillern und die Contrabässe unverdrossen von der Tonica zur Dominante hüpfen. Pauken brummen, Glocken spielen, Triangelgebimmel gellt hervor und das Tamtam schlägt unbarmherzig dazwischen, bis sich endlich Alles auf einem trivialen Pratergesang vereinigt und nach kurzer Einkehr 'noch langsam und etwas zögernd' beim Heurigen einfällt."

Whereas Liebstöckl grants that Mahler is an "outrageously bold master of instrumentation," Richard Heuberger, in a review of the Second Symphony's Viennese premiere, denies Mahler even that skill. He claims that several startled concert-goers thought that the "merciless dissonances" in the finale "could be achieved without printed music of any kind, if each orchestral player were allowed to rage ad libitum fortissimo on his instrument."[84] In each of these cases, it is implied, if not stated outright, that the awkward use of instruments undermines whatever it is that Mahler is trying to say. The unaesthetic nature of the surface draws the attention to the *how* rather than to the *what*.

Far more common than the implication that Mahler's orchestral language reveals his inability to speak any musical language as a native, is the charge that Mahler's surface betrays his lack of ideas. Geissler, for example, compares the first two symphonies, claiming that a sharper contrast cannot be imagined. He notes that in both, however, "we observe the same art of clothing and the same defect in real invention."[85] Maximilian Muntz suggests that even if Mahler had possibly succeeded in four previous symphonies, "the highest decibel levels could ultimately not drown out the knowledge that his inventive power—even considering the bizarrenesses and absurdities, and despite the most unprecedented mental effort in his Fifth Symphony—had overstepped its bounds, and that his art—could go no further."[86] According to Max Kalbeck, Mahler may have ideas in the First Symphony, but something is still missing: the ideas in both the Scherzo and the Adagio "betray more the master of technique, the shrewd orchestral-thinker, rather than the musical inventor and writer of musical themes."[87] It is important to stress that both Kalbeck and Muntz emphasize mental effort, and it is thus strongly implied that Mahler lacks the ability or possibility to be anything more than a mere thinker—never a poet.

Others grant that even if Mahler does have ideas, they are too insignificant to merit such colossal means. Liebstöckl describes the enormous number of people

---

[84]   Heuberger (2880), p. 1: "Einzelne darüber erschreckte Concertbesucher meinten, die Wirkung solcher Stellen wäre auch ohne Noten zu erreichen, wenn man jeden Orchesterspieler ad libitum Fortissimo auf seinem Instrumente toben ließe."

[85]   Geissler, *Neue musikalische Presse* 9 (25 Nov. 1900), p. 351: "Ein schärferer Contrast, wie zwischen der tragischen C-moll Symphonie Mahler's und der ironischen Ersten lässt sich nicht denken. In beiden aber merken wir dieselbe Kunst des Kleidens und denselben Mangel an wirklicher Erfindung."

[86]   Muntz, *Deutsche Zeitung*, 14 Dec. 1905, p. 1: "Die größten Klangexzesse vermochten schließlich die Erkenntnis nicht zu übertönen, daß die Erfindungskraft Mahlers, selbst was Bizarrerien und Absurditäten anbelangt, und trotz der unerhörtesten geistigen Anstrengung in seiner fünften Symphonie, ihren Höhepunkt überschritten habe, und daß seine — Kunst nun nicht mehr weiter könne."

[87]   Kalbeck (2801), p. 2: "Beide Sätze [Scherzo und Adagio] sind mit Geist geladen und wimmeln von Einfällen, die mehr den Meister der Technik, den scharfsinnigen Orchester-Denker, als musikalischen Erfinder und Thematiker verrathen."

required to perform the Second Symphony, and then questions the result, which he calls "music of the fourth dimension":

> Mr Mahler makes music of the fourth dimension, he discovers this dimension for the orchestra, he engages an unbelievable number of people for his feelings and thoughts, his music comes from the right and the left, from above and below. He doubles the power of the orchestra, positions a strengthened wind section, his polyphony and discord break out sporadically in choirs, and the breathlessness of his creation lines itself up very attractively at a distance. In invention the C minor Symphony is not terribly rich, but in the awful racket with which it lashes out, even this invention appears sumptuous. Mr Mahler's music is already full of lightning and thunder when he has little to say, so it is no wonder that an entire Last Judgment closes in when he wants to say a lot. And in the C minor Symphony he has—a lot he wants to say! The musicians of our valiant Philharmonic have blown their souls from their bodies for him yesterday and sprained their hands.[88]

The idea that the means outweigh the message is perhaps the most common complaint about Mahler's music. Kalbeck writes that "the problem from which Mahler's orchestral art in general and in his Sixth Symphony in particular suffers, lies in the waste of instrumental means, which stand ... in an inverse relationship to the power of his invention and the agility of his thematic work."[89] Richard Wallaschek states that while the first movement of the First Symphony is the most successful, even that movement betrays its lack of content suitable to justify its resources:

> What Mahler in this work lures out in unusual sounds from the orchestra is really admirable, especially at a time which in this respect appears to have arrived at the boundary of the possible. The unusual skill for sound mixture would qualify

---

[88] Liebstöckl (2885), p. 4: "Herr Mahler macht Musik der vierten Dimension, er entdeckt diese Dimension für das Orchester, er beschäftigt unglaublich viele Leute mit seinen Gefühlen und Gedanken, seine Musik kommt von rechts und links, von oben und unten. Er verdoppelt die Kräfte des Orchesters, postirt verstärkte Bläser, seine gährende Poln- und Disphonie bricht stellenweise in Chöre aus, und die Athemlosigkeit seines Schaffens steht sich von Weitem sehr interessant an. An Erfindung ist die C-moll-Symphonie nicht überaus reich, aber in dem Höllenlärm, den sie darum schlägt, erscheint selbst diese Erfindung üppig. In Herrn Mahler's Musik blitzt und donnert es schon, wenn er wenig zu sagen hat, kein Wunder, daß ein ganzes jüngstes Gericht hereinbricht, wenn er viel sagen will. Und in der C-moll-Symphonie hat er—sehr viel sagen wollen! Unseren wackeren Philharmoniker haben sich gestern für ihn die Seele aus dem Leibe geblasen und die Hände verrenkt."

[89] Max Kalbeck (3318), p. 1: "... das Uebel, an welchem Mahlers Orchesterkunst im allgemeinen und seine sechste Symphonie im besonderen krankt, liegt in der Verschwendung instrumentaler Mittel, die teils im umgekehrten Verhältnisse zu der Kraft seiner Erfindung und der Gewandtheit seiner thematischer Arbeit stehen, teils die Konzeption und Ausführung eines geordneten Planes überhaupt illusorisch machen."

him for the art of mood painting in the highest degree, if the listener were not torn from each poetic mood through the helplessness of the invention and through recherché *Klangeffecte*, which serve no higher purpose and as a result appear to be only showing themselves off. The most successful appears to me to be the first movement, a kind of Pastoral, with fine harmonies and many lovely, graceful turns, which appear to lie nearest to the composer. Unfortunately this character ultimately gets lost in an instrumental extravagance not justified by the original fundamental mood, and the more the piece of music wants to stretch its modest content toward large dimensions, the smaller it appears to us.[90]

Mahler does not have the inventive power to justify such extravagance, and ultimately defeats his own purpose by his inability to sustain any particular mood and his tendency to use orchestration simply for its own sake. Wallaschek believes that Mahler's skill is actually a detriment to his art. After hearing the Fifth Symphony, Theodor Helm admits that:

> Now first of all as far as my personal feelings go concerning this peculiar Fifth (which I studied very carefully before the orchestral performance from the score and the four-hand piano arrangement), although the work has recently demanded of me the highest respect for Mahler's famed virtuosity of orchestral technique, at the same time the melodic invention appeared to me again quite modest, even inadequate, as in the four earlier symphonies of the composer, and in any case not standing in correct relationship to the tremendous expense of polyphonic art and instrumental means.[91]

---

[90]   Wallaschek, *Die Zeit*, 24 Nov. 1900, p. 125: "Was Mahler in diesem Werke an ungewöhnlichen Klängen aus dem Orchester hervorlockt, ist wirklich bewunderungswürdig, zumal in einer Zeit, die in dieser Beziehung an der Grenze des Möglichen angelangt zu sein scheint. Das außerordentliche Geschick für Klangmischung würde ihn zur Kunst der Stimmungsmalerei in hohem Grade befähigen, wenn der Hörer nicht durch die Unselbständigkeit der Erfindung und durch gesuchte Klangeffecte, die keinem höheren Zweck dienen und nur ihrer selbst wegen angebracht zu sein scheinen, aus jeder poetischen Stimmung herausgerissen würde. Am gelungensten scheint mir der erste Satz zu sein, eine Art Pastorale, mit feinen Harmonien und vielen lieblichen, graziösen Wendungen, die dem Componisten am nächsten zu liegen schienen. Leider geht dieser Charakter schließlich in einem durch die ursprüngliche Grundstimmung nicht gerechtfertigten instrumentalen Aufwand verloren, und je mehr das Tonstück seinen bescheidenen Inhalt nach großen Dimensionen strecken will, desto kleiner erscheint es uns."

[91]   Helm (3232), p. 34: "Nun was zunächst mein persönliches Empfinden gegenüber dieser eigenartigen 'Fünften' anbelangt (die ich vor der Orchesteraufführung aus der Partitur und dem vier-händigen Klavierauszug sehr genau studiert), so hat mir das Werk neuerdings höchsten Respekt vor Mahler's fabelhafter Virtuosität der Orchestertechnik abgenötigt, während mir die melodische Erfindung wieder recht bescheiden, ja beinahe noch dürftiger erschien, als bei den vier früheren Symphonien des Komponisten, jedenfalls

Some critics believed that Mahler used orchestration to dress up the surface of his works and hide their limitations. As we know, Wagner believed that Jewish composers will attempt to make the surface of their music appealing "by offering at each instant a new summons to attention, through a change of outer expressional means." In some cases, this is merely distracting to the listener. Hirschfeld, in a review of the Fifth Symphony, calls Mahler "a virtuoso of the orchestra," who:

> has placed in this movement an immense series of sound effects which change almost with every bar. The lighting changes continually—a counterpoint of colors. The sound pictures are so amusing that one certainly does not feel at all obliged to think about a symphony or to long for symphonic themes; one would especially like to know, when the trembling pizzicato-triads of the violins unite with the triads of the flutes—this effect alone is worth an entire symphonic movement, and one sees on the astonished faces of the listeners, that they would like to know how it is done. Hardly has one become contemplative in this way, however, than the composer once again places another "Columbus egg" of instrumentation on its end. Art? Yes, it is an art, to symphonize in such a way.[92]

The designation "Columbus egg" could be regarded as slightly derogatory, recalling as it does Christopher Columbus's challenge to make an egg to stand on its end. After everyone had attempted it, Columbus himself tapped the egg lightly on its end, creating a flat place for it to stand. Columbus's point was that anything was easy once you had been shown how to accomplish it—that it was easy now to say that the New World was no great discovery in itself. Hirschfeld thus demeans Mahler's art by suggesting it was remarkable not for what it was but only for how it was done.

In a review of the Sixth Symphony, Hirschfeld again took Mahler to task for his constantly changing surfaces. Hirschfeld first accused Mahler of stealing his themes from first movements of Brahms, Liszt, and Bruckner, which he could then only dress up with "drum and switch" in order to create "new workings." He then turns to Mahler's own themes:

---

zu dem enormen Aufwand von polyphoner Kunst und instrumentalen Mitteln durchaus nicht in rechtem Verhältnisse stehend."

[92]   Hirschfeld (3229), p. 2: "… hat unübersehbare Reihen von Klangeffekten, die fast mit jedem Takte wechseln, auch in diesen Satz gestellt. Unaufhörlich wechselt die Beleuchtung—ein Kontrapunkt der Farben. Die Klangbilder sind so amüsant daß man sich gar nicht bemüßigt fühlt, an eine Sinfonie zu denken oder sinfonische Themen herbeizuwünschen; man ist besonders gut gelaunt, wenn die Pizzikato-Dreiklänge der Geigen sich bebend mit den Drieklängen der Flöten vereinigen—dieser Effekt allein ist einen ganzen Sinfoniesatz wert, und man sieht an den erstaunten Gesichtern der Hörer, daß diese wissen möchten, wie das gemacht wird. Kaum ist man aber in dieser Art nachdenklich geworden, so stellt der Komponist gleich wieder ein anderes Columbus Ei der Instrumentation auf die Spitze. Kunst? Ja, es ist eine Kunst, so zu sinfonisieren."

Where Gustav Mahler actually decided to contribute a whole theme of his own for his Sixth Symphony, he allowed the theme no organic development. Immediately the sound colors change; the rhythmic character shifts, before it has been fully understood; as in a bad theatrical production, the lighting flickers. Hardly eight bars go by consistently. Immediately the sound is thickened, sharpened, or exaggerated, and if the outer lines seem to move away quietly, certain individual motives scramble between them or there are instrumental effects lashed to them without respite that emerge from the unnatural application of the sound characters.[93]

Elsewhere in the same review, Hirschfeld describes a single bar of the Sixth Symphony:

Who would want to maintain that Gustav Mahler arbitrarily or lightly distorts Brucknerian thoughts? If a composer has absolutely no symphonic themes to go to and he must nevertheless write symphonies from an internal spur, he will unconsciously reach for the treasures of Brucknerian melody. The countless performance indications then bring on the peculiarities that would allow a Mahler score to swell into a thick novel, even if it contained not a single note. In a single bar of the Sixth Symphony the following instructions are found over an insignificant, inadequate march motive: fortissimo, decrescendo, piano, four horns "open," four horns "muted," the first violins (triply divided) *sempre pizzicato*, the second violins *col legno*, that is to say with the wood of the bow, the violas, violoncellos and basses however "arco" [with the bow], and then the very next bar: two trumpets "open," two trumpets "with mutes." To it add triangle, small drum, and tambourine.[94]

---

[93]   Hirschfeld (3317), p. 2: "Wo sich Gustav Mahler wirklich entschlossen hat, ein ganzes Thema aus eigenem für seine Sechste Sinfonie beizusteuern, gestattet er dem Thema keine organische Entwicklung. Sofort wechselt die Klangfarbe; der rhythmische Charakter verschiebt sich, bevor er noch sicher erfaßt wurde; wie bei einer schlechten Theaterbeleuchtung wechselt ruckweise das Licht. Kaum acht Takte fließen gleichmäßig fort. Augenblicklich wird der Klang verdickt, geschärft oder zugespitzt, und wenn die äußeren Linien sich auch scheinbar ruhig fortbewegen, so klettern doch einzelne Motive dazwischen hinauf oder es werden instrumentale Effekte, die aus der widernatürlichen Verwendung der Klangcharaktere entstehen, ohne Unterlaß herzugepeitscht."

[94]   Hirschfeld (3317), p. 1: "Wer wollte auch behaupten, daß Gustav Mahler willkürlich oder leichtfertig Brucknersche Gedanken verzerrt? Wenn einem Tonsetzer durchaus keine sinfonischen Themen zufließen und er dennoch aus innerem Drange Sinfonien schrieben muß, so wird er unbewußt nach den Schätzen Brucknerscher Melodik greifen. Das Eigene bringen dann die zahllosen Vortragszeichen hinzu, die eine Mahlersche Partitur auch dann zu einem dicken Novellenbande anschwellen ließen, wenn bei ihnen keine einzige Note stünde. In einem Takte der sechsten Sinfonie finden sich bei einem belanglosen, dürftigen Marschmotiv folgende Vorschriften: Fortissimo, decrescendo, piano, vier Hörner 'offen,' vier Hörner 'gestopft,' die ersten Violinen (dreifach geteilt) *sempre pizzicato*, die zweiten

Hirschfeld adds sarcastically that with Mahler's influence, in order to evoke a painful feeling—prior to this a sad melody had sufficed—soon "the score will simply specify that an orchestral musician will break a valuable vase or a water bottle."[95]

So dependent was Mahler's music upon orchestration that his critics claimed his themes would disappear entirely if heard on their own. The finale of the Sixth Symphony, according to Vancsa, proves that "Mahler, despite all the force of deceit, is missing true greatness of expression." He calls the increase in the percussion section a "technical trick" and states that "if one removes the giant apparatus there remains nothing at all of the tragic, and only a minimum of invention." Vancsa, like Hirschfeld, believes that this orchestration only masks inadequacies: Mahler again must "feign" tragic expression with "desolate noise." Despite the increase in the sheer numbers of performers, Vancsa nonetheless considers this movement to be the weakest that Mahler has written.[96] A more sinister image is presented in Liebstöckl's review of the Sixth Symphony where he claims that Mahler's themes "have a constructed face, behind which machinery is hidden. They have no life of their own, and they collapse if removed from their orchestral environment."[97] Muntz writes about the Fifth that, "The monstrous array of technical devices and shrill instrumental color effects, unavoidable due to Mahler's complicated affectation, only aggravate the impression of inner distractedness of the symphony to an unbearable degree." Mahler thus increases the emptiness of his works by

---

Violinen *col legno*, das heißt mit dem Holzrücken des Bogens, die Violen, die Violoncelle und Bässe aber 'arco,' dann noch zum nächsten Takte überleitend: zwei Trompeten 'offen,' zwei Trompeten 'mit Dämpfer.' Dazu Triangel, kleine Trommel und Tamburin."

[95] Hirschfeld (3317), p. 1: "Dieses Prinzip des kleinsten Kraftmaßes wird nach Mahlers Vorgang das sinfonische Schaffen einmal gänzlich umgestalten. Um schmerzliche Gefühle wachzurufen (was früher durch eine dolorose Melodie geschah), wird die Partitur einfach vorschreiben, daß ein Orchestermusiker eine kostbare Vase oder eine Wasserflasche zertrümmere." Earlier quote cited above.

[96] Vancsa (3321), p. 38: "Die Technische Trick dieser Sinfonie im allgemeinen und dieses Finales im besonderen besteht in der rücksichtslosen Ausnützung aller Möglichkeiten der Schlaginstrumente ... Entfernt man aber den Riesenapparat, so bleibt rein gar nichts von tragischer Empfindung und ein Minimum von Erfindung über. In wüstem Lärm und uferlosen Monstrositäten muß sich der Komponist ergehen, um den tragischen Ausdruck vorzutäuschen! Diese scheinbar stärkste Steigerung des tondichterischen Wesens ist zugleich der schwächste Sinfoniesatz, den Mahler geschrieben."

[97] Liebstöckl (3320), p. 3: "Das liegt in den Themen, die Alle ein construirtes Gesicht haben, hinter denen eine Maschinerie steckt. Sie haben kein eigenes Leben, sie fallen um, wenn man sie aus der orchestralen Umgebung loslöst."

attempting to disguise it.[98] Liebstöckl echoes this sentiment, proclaiming that in the Fourth Symphony, "empty nuts are brilliantly arranged."[99]

Thus as with the language of the Jew, Mahler's musical surfaces are deemed ugly, forced, unnatural, and bizarre—surfaces that distract attention from the message of the music. But there is no message: orchestration, for Mahler's critics, becomes the composer's way of either deliberately or resignedly compensating for his lack of musical depth. It is not important whether the critics are actually impressed by Mahler's orchestrational technique—many of them are—but rather that they focus on orchestration as a divorceable aspect of the music, a superfluous effect that hides a lack of ideas.

As a final example, I offer a cartoon, published in 1907 after the premiere of Mahler's Sixth in Vienna (Figure 4.1). Titled "Tragic Symphony," the cartoon is ostensibly harmless, poking fun at the Sixth's enormous percussion section: depicted are the famous hammer and cowbells, and also timpani, switch, another bell, and even a big stick for good measure. The artist's inclusion of the sleigh bells from the Fourth Symphony and the caption both suggest that Mahler has found still another percussion instrument to add to his odd collection: "My goodness, I have forgotten the motor horn! Now I can write yet *another* symphony." Clearly, this hypothetical, motor horn–inspired work, like all Mahler's music before it, will lack any message and exist solely to showcase its exotic and excessive orchestration. And that orchestration—given the battery of unpitched percussion—guarantees a surface that will be anything but pleasing. The image of the motor horn, itself an emblem of the modern age, serves to emphasize not just Mahler's lack of creativity, but to suggest that in fact all his music is just as trivial and absurd. The cartoon thus presents a collection of Jewish stereotypes: both the physical (note the gaze, the crooked body, overlong arms, and big feet) and the musical. The juxtaposition of surface versus depth, the implication that Mahler has nothing to say, and the emphasis on noise and novelty rather than music or ideas can all be traced to beliefs about the inferiority of Jewish music, as articulated by Richard Wagner.

---

[98] Munz, *Deutsche Zeitung*, 14 Dec. 1905, p. 1: "Das bei der komplizierten Unnatur Mahlers unvermeidliche Riesenaufgebot an technischen Mitteln und grellen instrumentalen Farbeneffekten steigert noch den Eindruck der inneren Zerfahrenheit der Symphonie bis zur Unerträglichkeit."

[99] Liebesöckl (3135), p. 2: "taube Nüsse sind glänzend arrangirt."

Figure 4.1   "Tragische Sinfonie." *Die Muskete: Humoristische Wochenschrift*,
            19 January 1907, cover. Source: Gilbert Kaplan, *The Mahler
            Album* (New York: Abrams, 1995), plate 300, image owned by the
            Internationale Gustav Mahler Gesellschaft Wien, used with kind
            permission.[100]

---

[100]   "Herrgott, daß ich die Huppe vergessen habe! Jetzt kann ich *noch* eine Sinfonie
schreiben." Italics in original.

Chapter 5
Das Problem Richard Strauss

"Two Miners"

On 12 January 1907 Mahler wrote to Alma from Berlin where he was to conduct his Third Symphony and where he was spending considerable time with Richard Strauss and his wife, Pauline. Having just heard Strauss's opera on the 10th, Mahler wrote: "today to *Salome* again, and I will have another try to see to the bottom of the problem of Strauss." Mahler was probably referring primarily to Strauss's personality: his nonchalance, his unbelievable egotism, his overweening confidence, aspects that made Mahler ask, "are other men made of different clay?"[1] Mahler seemed troubled both by Strauss's personality and his music, and his famous paraphrase of Schopenhauer that they were "two miners who dig a tunnel from opposite sides and then meet on their subterranean ways,"[2] has often been invoked to emphasize the distance—musical, personal, professional—between the two men.

Even so, they were almost exact contemporaries, Mahler born in 1860, Strauss in 1864; both made names for themselves as the premier conductors—particularly of opera—of their age while simultaneously advancing their careers as composers. They even both held both the prestigious positions as director of the Wiener Hofoper and Wiener Philharmoniker, albeit in different eras.[3] They actively promoted each other's works, although it is to be doubted that they were ever friends. Even Carl Dahlhaus, who otherwise does not concern himself with a connection between the two composers, nevertheless writes in his *Nineteenth-century Music* that "For

---

[1] Alma Mahler, *Gustav Mahler: Memories and Letters*, ed. Donald Mitchell and Knut Martner, trans. Basil Creighton, 4th English edn, with additional notes and commentaries (London, 1990), p. 284.

[2] In a letter to Arthur Seidl, Feb. 1897; cited in Stephen E. Hefling, "Miners Digging from Opposite Sides: Mahler, Strauss, and the Problem of Program Music," in *Richard Strauss: New Perspectives on the Composer and His Work*, ed. Bryan Gilliam (Durham and London, 1992), pp. 41–53. While Mahler may have been implying that he and Strauss did have much in common, he was being disingenuous. As Hefling notes, Mahler was furious when Seidl made the letter public only three years later, complaining to Natalie Bauer-Lechner that it made him "appear to be an advocate of Strauss and program music." Mahler told Natalie that "program music was 'the greatest musical and artistic error.'" Hefling, p. 41.

[3] After World War I, Strauss shared the directorship of the now Wiener Staatsoper with Franz Schalk; he was one of the guest directors with the Wiener Philharmoniker; Kurt Wilhelm, *Richard Strauss Persönlich: Eine Bildbiographie* (Berlin, 1999), pp. 207–11.

the music historian, no matter how much or how little significance he attaches to chronological simultaneity, the year 1889, by witnessing such works as Mahler's First Symphony and Strauss's *Don Juan*, stands out from the continuum of history as the dawning of 'musical modernism'."[4] Dahlhaus implies that we cannot help but link the name of Gustav Mahler with that of Richard Strauss, even if only as an accident of timing.

Yet for all the very real similarity between them, the differences between Strauss and Mahler do make any straightforward attempt to compare either their careers or their music difficult. Whereas Strauss was even as an 18-year-old being advanced as the heir to German music—called "Richard III" by Hans von Bülow[5]—Mahler's claims as a composer took much longer to solidify. Strauss's name for himself came primarily from his early tone poems, works of program music, music ideologically opposed to Mahler's dedication to the absolute musical status of the symphony. (And whatever one thinks of Mahler's own troubled history regarding program music, he did publish his works as "symphonies.") By the time Mahler's music was getting performed regularly, Strauss himself had switched to writing operas. Finally, of course, Strauss outlived Mahler by almost 40 years, and, with *Der Rosenkavalier*, abandoned the high-modernist style of *Salome* and *Elektra* to embrace a neoclassic or nostalgic style—depending on your point of view—that seemed to disown his earlier progressive stance.[6]

Nevertheless, whatever Mahler may have meant by the "problem of Strauss," it is no secret that Strauss's music was criticized in much the same way as Mahler's, particularly in regard to the overwhelming size of the orchestras. In 1892, when Strauss's *Don Juan* was heard for the first time in Vienna, critics claimed, as they later would do with Mahler, that Strauss's orchestras hid his lack of ideas:

> In the fifth philharmonic concert an outstanding member of the young school, Richard Strauss, was called upon to speak. Strauss, presently Kapellmeister at the Hoftheater in Weimar, is an excellent conductor and admirable musician. Despite a personal, friendly relationship, the writer of these lines can feel no pure joy about the Strauss tone poem "Don Juan," performed at the fifth philharmonic concert. The orchestration is brilliant, and it is certainly no slight praise to say that Richard Strauss has found new tone colors. However, the musical invention is insignificant, flat. The themes, particularly the more broadly executed melodic

---

[4]   Carl Dahlhaus, *Nineteenth-century Music*, trans. J. Bradford Robinson (Berkeley and London, 1989), p. 330.

[5]   Von Bülow was claiming that Wagner could have no direct successor. In 1885 Strauss became von Bülow's assistant conductor in Meiningen. Bryan Gilliam, "Strauss, Richard (Georg)," in *The New Grove Dictionary of Music and Musicians*, ed. John Tyrell, 2nd edn (29 vols, London and New York, 2001), vol. 24, p. 497.

[6]   Dahlhaus claims that "Strauss irrevocably parted company with the musical modernism which he ... had represented for two decades," with *Frau ohne Schatten*, not *Rosenkavalier*; *Nineteenth-century Music*, p. 337.

motif, sung by the oboe, have little to say to us and one almost regrets that so many powers are set in motion for so little content. [7]

Strauss's "Don Juan" is a coloristic masterpiece, a musical Makart of the first rank, but nothing more. In the brilliant mastery of the dazzling and splendid orchestra colors of Liszt and Berlioz, Mr Richard Strauss has no worthy rival among the younger German composers save perhaps Jean Nicodé, the musical controller of the sea—will not the reader still recall last year's sensational concert of the Männergesangverein? But in neither of these two excellent musical colorists could we discover a capacity for melodic invention, for a wholly individual tonal language, in the examples offered up to now.[8]

In particular, Theodor Helm's harsh dismissal of Strauss's work—the comparison to Hans Makart is not a compliment—is confusing, to say the least.[9] Why would Helm

---

[7]   dr. h. p., "Feuilleton. Musik. Concerte," *Wiener Abendpost*, 28 Jan. 1892, p. 6: "Im fünften philharmonischen Concerte war einem hervorragenden Mitgliede der jungen Schule, Richard Strauß, das Wort ertheilt worden. Strauß, gegenwärtig Capellmeister am Hoftheater in Weimar, ist ein ausgezeichneter Dirigent und vortrefflicher Musiker. Trotz persönlicher, freundlicher Beziehungen kann Schreiber dieser Zeilen über die im fünften philharmonischen Concerte aufgeführte Strauß'sche Tondichtung 'Don Juan' keine reine Freude empfinden. Die Orchestration ist glänzend, und es ist gewiß kein geringes Lob, wenn man sagen muß, daß Richard Strauß neue Farbentöne gefunden hat. Doch ist die musikalische Erfindung unbedeutend, flach. Die Themen, insbesondere das breiter ausgeführte, von Oboe gesungene melodische Motiv, sagen uns blutwenig, und man bedauert es beinahe, daß so viele Kräfte wegen so wenig Inhalt in Bewegung gesetzt werden."

[8]   Theodor Helm, "Concerte," *Deutsche Zeitung*, 16 Jan. 1892, pp. 1–3; quote p. 1: "Strauß' 'Don Juan,' ist ein coloristisches Meisterstück, ein musikalischer Makart ersten Ranges, aber nicht mehr. An glänzender Beherrschung der blendenden und prächtigen Liszt-Berlioz'schen Orchesterfarben hat Herr Richard Strauß unter der jüngeren deutschen Tonsetzern vielleicht nur an Jean Nicodé, den musikalischen Beherrlicher des Meeres--die Leser erinnern sich doch noch an das vorjährige sensationelle Concert des Männergesangvereins?—einen ebenbürtigen Rivalen. Aber das Vermögen selbständiger melodischer Erfindung, völlig eigenartiger Tonsprache konnten wir nach den bisher gebotenen Proben weder bei dem einen, noch dem anderen der beiden ausgezeichneten musikalischen Coloristen entdecken." Jean Louis Nicodé (1853–1919) was a German pianist, composer, and conductor; *Das Meer* (1889) was an enormous work for large orchestra and chorus in six movements whose performance lasted an entire evening.

[9]   Hans Makart (1840–84) was probably late nineteenth-century Vienna's most famous painter; he was in great demand as a portraitist. Emperor Franz Joseph summoned him to Vienna in 1869 where he was supported by the court and given a splendid atelier. "His lavish historicist aesthetic now determined fashion, decoration, and all aspects of bourgeois artistic preference. Despite his Imperial patronage, most of Makart's work was done for the *Geld-Baronen* who were building houses along the Ringstrasse." Erika Esau, "Artists' Biographies Vienna 1848–1898," in *Pre-Modern Art of Vienna, 1848–1898*, ed. Leon Botstein and Linda Weintraub (Annendale-on-Hudson, 1987), p. 147. Helm alludes

criticize Strauss in the first place, let alone criticize him in the same language he would later use to vilify Mahler? Both reviews raise interesting questions about the role of the orchestra, its relation to the conception of musical ideas, and the extent to which these could be—and obviously were—often treated as separate entities.

I would not deny the challenge presented by the language of Strauss criticism, but I do want to emphasize that in this—as in all reception history—the goal is not to create binary oppositions ("favorable"/"unfavorable") but rather to explore how the critics' language reveals the context within which they write. The "Strauss"/ "Mahler" dichotomy has likewise always been oversimplified, as if all that were at stake were whether any given critic liked either's music or not. What must be taken into account is the respective positions that Strauss and Mahler held within the musical world of Vienna—and, to an even greater degree, their very different career paths. Vienna was never a particularly easy town in which to make a musical career, but in 1892, when these reviews were written, Mahler was still exiled in Hamburg and had yet to become a major player on the Viennese stage (or on any stage as an orchestral composer, for that matter). Nor had Strauss, not even 30, as yet failed to live up to his early promise.

The similarities in critical language reveal shifting political and cultural forces that need to be identified and contextualized in order to ascertain the reasons for the coincidence. The problem of Richard Strauss also shows vividly how dichotomies such as German/Jew, insider/outsider, or absolute music/program music must always be evaluated with due account of the context in which they are presented. What must be emphasized is not the similarity of language itself but its shifting meaning. Unsatisfying though it may be, it is not possible simply to define a given label as "positive" or "negative"—antisemitic or not—without some context in which to evaluate the author's use of language. Yet precisely because the labels had no fixed meaning, I hope to emphasize that, in a critical sense, anyone could be a Jew.

Richard Strauss in Vienna

Focusing for the moment on the tone poems, as can be seen from Table 5.1, the story of the Viennese introduction to Strauss's music is not straightforward. Particularly striking is the order in which the tone poems were first brought to Vienna—first came *Don Juan*, performed by Richter and the Philharmonic in 1892, which was actually the second in order of composition. *Macbeth*, Strauss's first tone poem, was not heard in Vienna until 1905 under Felix Mottl, and the slightly earlier *Aus Italien* (a programmatic *symphonische Phantasie* rather than strictly a tone poem) was not performed in Vienna until 1899, under Mahler with the Philharmonic. Equally significant is Strauss's own absence as a conductor of his own work,

---

to Makart's use of "ornate decorative settings," and the whiff of bourgeois taste that surrounded the painter.

until he brought *Ein Heldenleben* to Vienna in 1901. It should also be noted that between the years 1892 and 1897, Richter performed with the Philharmonic the works that many would agree are Strauss's strongest in the genre: *Don Juan, Tod und Verklärung, Till Eulenspiegel,* and *Also sprach Zarathustra.* The order in which Strauss's works entered the Viennese consciousness therefore inadvertently suggests a falling off in quality as the earlier works, *Aus Italien* and *Macbeth,* were only heard in 1899 and 1905 respectively, interspersed with works with which many critics found fault, and not just in Vienna: *Don Quixote, Ein Heldenleben,* and *Sinfonia domestica.*

Table 5.1   Strauss's Viennese Premieres (Vienna Philharmonic, unless noted)

Title	Vienna	Conductor	Notes	Composed
Don Juan	10 Jan. 1892	Hans Richter		3
Tod und Verklärung	15 Jan. 1893	H. Richter	25 & 28 June 1902, in Vienna with Strauss, Tonkünstler Orch	4
Till Eulenspiegel	5 Jan. 1896	H. Richter	1 Dec. 1896, Richter	5
Also sprach Zarathustra	21 Mar. 1897	H. Richter		6
Aus Italien	19 Nov. 1899	Gustav Mahler	2nd season	[1]
Ein Heldenleben	23 Jan. 1901	Strauss	Munich Kaim Orchestra; 19 Dec. 1904, F. Mottl	8
Don Quixote	17 & 19 Dec. 1904	Ferdinand Löwe	Orch of the Vienna Konzertverein	7
Sinfonia domestica	23 Nov. 1904	G. Mahler	Schoenberg's 1st Vereinigung Concert	9
Macbeth	17 Dec. 1905	Felix Mottl	2nd version	2

Theodor Helm noted as much in the above-cited review where he complained that by hearing *Don Juan* first, the conservative Viennese audiences were not first given the opportunity to hear Strauss "der absolute Musiker" ["the absolute musician"] or even to hear *Aus Italien*, the first work to be composed after Strauss had "renounced his old gods and with bag and baggage gone over to the camp of program-musicians":[10]

Whether it was in the interest of the already highly esteemed composer to introduce him to the essentially conservatively sensibilities of the majority of our Philharmonic public with, of all things, the most recent and boldest of his works may well be doubted. Had the way been paved earlier for the absolute musician Richard Strauss with, for example, the much-praised F minor Symphony, then the reception of the artist who paints and writes poetry in sound would probably have been warmer, more suited to his technical ability. If, however, one had to choose one of his more recent creations, then the great poetic fantasy "Aus Italien," described most enticingly from the professional viewpoint of the Leipzig *Musikalisches Wochenblatt*, would likely have been preferable.[11]

Even though Helm does go on to call *Don Juan* "a musical Makart of the first rank," he seemed to regard its excesses as those of youth:

Admittedly, even as an illustration of the aforementioned program, Strauss's music falls short of the chosen: how differently Wagner in his Parisian "Venusberg" understood the frenzy of unleashed sensuousness, Berlioz in the "Roman carnival" to lend fascinating tone to the bacchanalian joy of life! Against such orchestral fashion, sparklingly spirited and at the same time dominated by a great melodic thought, that of Richard Strauss seems merely wittily contrived,

---

[10] Theodor Helm, "Concerte," *Deutsche Zeitung*, 16 Jan. 1892, p. 1: "Mit einer zweiten großen Symphonie (in F-moll) erwarb er sich neuen Ruhm in den Kreisen der absoluten Musiker, von einigen Seiten wurde die contrapunktische Arbeit in diesem Werke, besonders im Finale, der Brahms'schen an Meisterschaft zur Seite gestellt. Umsomehr überraschte es, als plötzlich verlautete, Richard Strauß habe seine alten Götter abgeschworen und sei mit Sack und Pack ins Lager der Programm-Musiker übergegangen."

[11] Ibid., p. 1: "Ob es im Interesse des jedenfalls hochachtbaren Componisten war, ihn gerade mit dem letztgenannten kühnsten seiner Werke bei der wesentlich conservativ empfindenden Mehrheit unseres philharmonischen Publicums einzuführen, muß wohl bezweifelt werden. Hätte man etwa durch die so viel gerühmte F-moll-Symphonie dem absoluten Musiker Richard Strauß früher die Bahn geebnet, die Aufnahme des in Tönen dichtenden und malenden Künstlers wäre wahrscheinlich eine wärmere, seinem technischen Können entsprechendere gewesen. Wählte man aber schon einer seiner letzten Schöpfungen, so wäre die große, im Leipziger 'Musikalischen Wochenblatt' von fachmännischer Seite äußerst verlockend geschilderte poetische Phantasie 'Aus Italien' wohl vorzuziehen gewesen."

even if, on the other hand, one must cite as admirable his refined combinations of the most manifold instrumental colors and highlights, the audacity and certainty with which the whole is made. Most surprising to those listeners not familiar with Lenau's poem may have been the rather persistent sound of the glockenspiel alongside the highest violin tones, probably a joking allusion to the dubious cloister scene, which interrupt the desolate orgies with their chiming of the hour.[12]

Helm ended his review with a reference to Franz Strauss's well-known antipathy toward modern music, claiming that Strauss *père* felt "every bold harp glissando, trombone blast, or cymbal crash in the heart as a moral patricide: 'You, too—my son Brutus?!!'"[13]

Not surprisingly, Eduard Hanslick believed that Richard Strauss and all of his contemporaries were on the wrong path:

… the tendency is the same: to use purely instrumental music merely as a means of describing certain things; in short, not to make music, but to write poetry and to paint. Hector Berlioz is the common father of this ever-multiplying younger generation of tone poets. With Liszt and Wagner he makes up the triumvirate to which one may attribute essentially all that these youngsters can, and will, do. In the one-sided study of these three orchestral geniuses, the younger generation has developed a virtuosity in the creation of sound effects beyond which it is hardly possible to go. Color is everything, musical thought nothing. What I said about

---

[12]   Ibid., pp. 1–2: "Freilich bleibt Strauß' Musik selbst als Illustration vorstehenden Programms hinter der gewählten Aufgabe zurück: wie anders wußte Wagner in seinem Pariser 'Venusberg' dem Taumel entfesselter Sinnlichkeit, Berlioz im 'Römischen Carneval' bacchantischer Lebensfreude die rechten fascinirenden Töne zu leihen! solcher sprühend temperamentvoller und dabei von einem großen melodischen Zuge beherrschten Orchesterweise gegenüber erscheint die von Richard Strauß mehr nur geistreich ausgeklügelt, so bewunderungswürdig andererseits auch die raffinirt seine Combination der mannigfaltigsten instrumentalen Farben und Schlaglichter, die Keckheit und Sicherheit, mit der das Ganze gemacht ist, genannt werden muß. Am wunderlichsten mag den mit Lenau's Dichtung nicht vertrauten Hörern das neben den höchsten Violintönen ziemlich lange vernehmbare Glockenspiel vorgekommen sein, wahrscheinlich eine witzige Anspielung auf die bedenkliche Klosterscene, in deren wüsten Orgien das Horaglöckchen hineinklingt."

[13]   Ibid., p. 2: "Die Aufnahme der jedenfalls ungewöhnlich interessanten, von unseren Philharmonikern virtuos gespielten Neuheit war eine sehr getheilte, während dieselbe, nach uns vorliegenden Berichten, in München einhellig stürmischen Beifall erzielte. Auch der noch immer lebende alte Kammermusikus Strauß hatte damals Gelegenheit, die ihm dargebrachten Glückwünsche über das 'Talent' und die 'Meisterschaft' seines so sehr aus der Art geschlagenen Sprößlings mit süßsaurer Miene entgegenzunehmen, während er als hartgesottener Reactionär wohl jeden etwas kühneren Harfengriff, Posaunenstoß oder Beckenschlag im Herzen wie einen moralischen Vatermord empfand: 'Auch du—mein Sohn Brutus?!!'"

Nicodé's *Das Meer* goes double for Richard Strauss: "Virtuosity in orchestration
has become a vampire sapping the creative power of our composers."[14]

By linking Liszt and Wagner to Berlioz, Hanslick positioned them as outsiders to
German culture—and therefore dangerous role models for the young. Like Helm,
Hanslick appears to blame not Strauss himself but rather his youth: "The tragedy
is that most of our younger composers think in a foreign language (philosophy,
poetry, painting) and then translate the thought in to the mother tongue (music).
People like Richard Strauss, moreover, translate badly, unintelligibly, tastelessly,
with exaggeration." Moreover, the problem is not necessarily Strauss himself,
but the pull of orchestration: if the vampire could be resisted, then perhaps the
situation would right itself. That the situation might change—or at least that there
may be hope for change—seems to be reinforced by Hanslick's final sentence, in
which he states that "we are not so sanguine as to expect the reaction against this
emancipated naturalism in music to come immediately—but come it must."[15] Only
one year later, however, his reaction to *Tod und Verklärung* seemed less optimistic:
"The composer of *Don Juan* has again proved himself a brilliant virtuoso of the
orchestra, lacking only musical ideas."[16]

Strauss's youth was likewise emphasized in a review of *Tod und Verklärung* by
the critic for the *Wiener Abendpost*, who began his discussion with a brief history
of program music, from the Pastorale Symphony, to Berlioz, to Liszt. It is no
surprise that genius threatens the status quo:

> Certainly the conventional form always became too narrow for the truly great
> geniuses—in his Ninth, Beethoven had far overflowed the dams of the Mozart–
> Haydn symphony; Wagner, in his music dramas, broke the fetters of the old
> opera. It was, however, always an enormous content, an immense greatness of
> personality, a colossal wealth of feeling (which for the genius is the same as
> invention), which found no more place in the old form and created for itself a
> new form. The situation was quite different with symphonic program music.
> The melodic capacity and the real musical invention of Berlioz were much too
> inadequate to build therewith a symphony in Beethoven's style. The wealth of
> instrumentation, with all the blended new orchestral colors and the printed word
> had to come to the aid of the—for the most part—short, empty motives ... It
> is often said that it is a pity when a talent goes in the wrong direction. That is
> fundamentally wrong. Genuine talents never—or at most, only temporarily—
> go down the wrong paths. By contrast, program music offers an exquisite gift

---

[14]   Eduard Hanslick, "Richard Strauss's 'Don Juan' [1892]," *Vienna's Golden Years
of Music, 1850–1900*, trans. Henry Pleasants III (New York, 1950), pp. 308–10; quote is
pp. 308–9.

[15]   Ibid., p. 310.

[16]   Hanslick, "Richard Strauss's 'Tod und Verklärung' ('Death and Transfiguration')
[1893]," in *Vienna's Golden Years*, pp. 311–14; quote is p. 311.

like Strauss's refined talent the proper arena. With an entirely special art of color—Strauss's orchestration is multicolored and always sounds beautiful—it is now painted, mood is supposed to follow on mood, yet this never quite materializes for the listener. There is indisputably much of interest in Strauss's tone poem *Tod und Verklärung*. The best is indeed the beginning; heavy string chords brood in the depths, flute and oboe tread softly under harp chords as well—the one fatally ill is sunk in exhausted sleep. By comparison, the fight of death with life is a desolate orchestral spectacle, and the conclusion ("But he hears mightily resounding from heaven that which he longingly sought here: world-redemption, world-transfiguration!") a completely everyday and not at all transfigured triumphal march. Even so, Hofcapellmeister Hans Richter was much to be praised for having performed the Strauss tone poem in such a consummate fashion. Richard Strauss counts as one of the most important representatives of the younger school, and it is the duty of our concert enterprises to be fair to every direction and every talent. Incidentally, Strauss's work enjoyed an unquestionable *succès d'estime* with the public.[17]

---

[17] dr. h. p., "Feuilleton. Musik. Concerte." *Wiener Abendpost*, 20 Feb. 1893, pp. 1–2: "Gewiß ist die üblich gewesene Form stets zu enge geworden für die ganz großen Genien—Beethoven hat in seiner Neunten die Dämme der Mozart-Haydn'schen Symphonie weit überflutet, Wagner in seinen Musikdramen die Fessel der alten Oper gebrochen. Immer war es aber ein ungeheurer Inhalt, eine immense Größe der Individualität, ein kolossaler Reichthum der Empfindung (die beim Genius zugleich Erfindung ist), welcher in der alten Form nicht mehr Platz fand und sich die neue schuf. Da lagen nun die Dinge bei der symphonischen Programmusik ganz anders. Der melodische Gehalt und die eigentlich musikalische Erfindung Berlioz' waren viel zu dürftig, um damit eine Symphonie Beethoven'schen Styles aufzubauen. Den zumeist kurzen phrasenhaften Motiven mußte der Reichthum der Instrumentation mit allen blendenden neuen orchestralen Farben und das gedruckte Wort zu Hilfe kommen … Man pflegt häufig zu sagen, daß um ein Talent schade sei, wenn es in eine falsche Richtung geräth. Das ist grundfalsch. Echte Talente kommen nie oder höchstens ganz vorübergehend auf falsche Bahnen. Die Programmusik aber bietet im Gegentheile der raffinirten Begabung, wie sich auch Richard Strauß besitzt, den rechten Spielraum. Mit einer ganz besonderen Farbenkunst—Strauß instrumentirt … vielfärbig und stets klangschön—wird nun gemalt, Stimmung soll auf Stimmung folgen, und doch will sich dieselbe beim Hörer nicht einstellen. Es giebt unstreitig manches des Interessanten in der Strauß'schen Tondichtung 'Tod und Verklärung.' Das beste ist wohl der Anfang; schwere Accorde der Streicher brüten in der Tiefe, Flöte und Oboe treten sanft unter Harfenaccorden dazu—der Todkranke ist erschöpft in Schlaf gesunken. Hingegen ist der Kampf des Todes mit dem Leben ein wüster Orchesterspectakel und der Schluß ('Aber mächtig tönet ihm aus dem Himmelsraum entgegen, was er sehnend hier gesucht: Welterlösung, Weltverklärung') ein ganz gewöhnlicher und gar nicht verklärter Triumphmarsch. Immerhin war es von Hofcapellmeister Hans Richter sehr zu loben, die Strauß'sche Tondichtung, noch dazu in so vollendeter Art zur Aufführung gebracht zu haben. Richard Strauß gilt für einen der bedeutendsten Vertreter der jüngeren Schule, und es ist Pflicht unserer Concertunternehmungen, jeder Richtung und jedem Talente gerecht

In none of the reviews sampled thus far is there evidence of special pleading. Even Helm, whose later reviews reveal a more sympathetic outlook, does not go to any great lengths to "save" Strauss from the charges of over-refinement or excessive interest in orchestration. In other words, in these reviews it does not seem that orchestration per se has become contested space; the argument seems to be centered on the legitimacy—or not—of program music as a genre rather than on the use or misuse of the orchestra. Likewise, Gustav Schoenaich's review of the Viennese premiere of *Till Eulenspiegel* takes pains to portray Strauss's piece as "program music only in the sense in which it always has been and probably always will be considered permissible"—that is:

> the firm structure [of an expanded rondo form] allows us to absorb and enjoy the underlying mood of the whole, as it is laid out in the themes and fully exploited by variations, undisturbed by programmatic suppositions. We do not know if the piece had been sent out into the world without the title, whether the name Eulenspiegel would have been attached to it by someone from among the circle of listeners; but [its] fundamental character, oscillating between humor, sarcasm, and irony, radiates from every measure, here and there perhaps even too garishly. The piece is dazzlingly clever, does not break down into its individual parts, and captivates the intellect of the listener perhaps more than his sensibility.[18]

The defense of program music undertaken here is in line with Hanslick's criticisms of it: the piece works as absolute music, without its program—that is, it is unified via legitimately musical, not programmatic, means. Schoenaich is not damning Strauss for writing music that is cold and lacks sentiment, but rather praising him for writing program music that behaves, sounds, and makes the same demands on the listener as absolute music. More interesting insofar as Strauss criticism is concerned are Schoenaich's attempts to place *Till Eulenspiegel* within the context of Strauss's larger output:

> Among the young composers, most of whom have already been crushed under the weight of the phenomenon of Richard Wagner and can only stammer out their own sounds if they bring forth anything at all, Richard Strauss occupies a prominent place. Everything of his that has come to the attention of the public until now, even the unfortunate things, reveals a personal element, unmistakable attempts at an individual language. The great confidence that Hans von Bülow, who hated every epigonal art, placed in the talent of this young man—he is now in his thirty-first year—seems entirely justified to us. Richard Strauss's musical

---

zu werden. Uebrigens hat das Strauß'sche Werk einen zweifellosen Achtungserfolg beim Publicum gefunden."

[18]   Gustav Schoenaich, "Opera and Opera Concerts," *Neue Musikalische Presse* 2 (1 Dec. 1896), trans. Susan Gillespie, in *Richard Strauss and His World*, ed. Bryan Gilliam (Princeton, 1992), pp. 321–3; quote is p. 322.

education is profoundly thorough. Not until he had acquired quite astonishing knowledge in the center of music making, in all the technical matters did he begin to become eccentric. But the solid connection, which he can never lose, with this good foundation, prevents him from flying off completely.[19]

Schoenaich is careful to acknowledge the huge burden of chronological fate that any young composer must face, even without attempting to follow the master's footsteps: many would-be composers had been silenced by this unbearable anxiety. Strauss thus earns respect by refusing to be defeated. His success depends on his possessing an individual language, one that is unmistakably his even if it fails; he reveals one aspect of true genius, the unique voice. The dropping of von Bülow's name serves to reinforce Strauss's credentials with the conservative element, for von Bülow was not only a consummate performer and conductor in his own right, but of course, by necessity if rather ambivalently, an anti-Wagnerian. Schoenaich goes on to emphasize Strauss's musical education in order to confirm that his "eccentricity" was nonetheless a choice, not a fate. It is as if Strauss, having assimilated all musical knowledge and finding himself bored, then sought a different path. The thorough understanding of "all technical matters" is what ultimately grounds him, justifies his subsequent choices. Even if you do not agree with his eccentricities, Schoenaich seems to say, you must acknowledge that it was done by design and not by accident, and therefore has to be respected as a choice.

Schoenaich does not shy away from the fact that "the means that are used are, admittedly, very opulent," but he does not blame Strauss:

> When one considers that from the death of Gluck until the creation of the *Symphonie fantastique* of Berlioz not even 50 years went by, one might, for a change, express a certain satisfaction with the fact that the means of musical expression have undergone so little intensification, relatively speaking, in the longer period that has elapsed since then.[20]

Things may be bad, Schoenaich acknowledges, but they could have been worse. The blame is clearly Berlioz's, and thus a "French" problem—as further implied by the mention of Gluck, a composer who, although German-surnamed, spent "the best years of his life" in France. Deflecting the problem of "opulent means" onto the French allows Schoenaich to leave Strauss blameless—indeed to praise him for not contributing further to the problem. A subsequent charge that "the effect [of Strauss's works] aims more at the intellect than at the heart" is countered by the vague, and less convincing, assertion that it could not be otherwise during a period "when every 'truth' gives birth, as though through self-generation, to the worm of the question mark." Nevertheless, Strauss is not someone who "should be taken lightly," and his work is decidedly not "a cheap effect, based for example on a few

---

[19] Ibid., p. 321.
[20] Ibid., p. 322.

cleverly thought-out tonal effects." Such a statement seems an attempt to shield
Strauss from Wagner's diatribe against "an effect without a cause." *Eulenspiegel* is
"a very personal piece and a stroke of genius," one that "has that drastic and plastic
quality that is one of the indispensable characteristics of every significant piece of
music." Schoenaich ends his discussion by comparing the "flaming sword of the
aesthetician" to "the schoolmaster's cane,"[21] which, while it could be directed at
Hanslick's well-known conservatism, also seems designed to defend the younger
composer's choices in attempting to deal with Wagner's legacy.

Vienna 1904

My thesis, that Mahler's music was evaluated, more often than not, from the
standpoint of his Jewishness, might seem problematic when read in the context
of Strauss's own early Viennese reviews: the same criticisms leveled at Mahler,
particularly those of overwhelming orchestral means versus paltry musical
invention and mistrust of program music, were also leveled at Strauss. Yet given the
complicated overlapping allegiances and prejudices among the musical community
and that of Vienna in particular—the presence of the powerful and vehemently
conservative Hanslick; the existence of an antisemitic government; myriad
newspapers, each with its own political allegiance; and, in 1897, the appointment
of Gustav Mahler to arguably the most important musical post in all of Europe—a
surface comparison between reviews of Strauss and those of Mahler tells us little
beyond the fact that that they were both understood as "modernists." The context
in which such criticisms were made is the crucial factor in evaluating the language
used, and by context I mean something beyond simply knowing who the critic
was or what the political leanings of his paper were. When Strauss's first four
tone poems were performed in Vienna, Mahler was not on the scene. Even when
Mahler finally took over the directorship of the Hofoper, he was slow to introduce
his own music in Vienna, waiting until 1899 to perform one of his symphonies
(the Second). When Mahler conducted *Aus Italien* on 19 November 1899 with the
Vienna Philharmonic, reviewers did not take the opportunity to compare Strauss's
earliest work with any composition by Mahler, who is mentioned only as the
conductor. Thus, in the 1890s, Mahler did not provide the backdrop to Strauss's
output, as the reviews cited above make clear with their repeated references to
Berlioz, Liszt, and Wagner. It was only *after* Mahler had established himself as a
composer in Vienna that direct comparisons with Strauss began. And only when
an author explicitly compares Mahler and Strauss does it become possible to
attempt an analysis of the ideological undercurrents that affected the reception
of their works. While the reviews already cited are interesting in so far as they
establish some of the vocabulary that would become characteristic in the Viennese

---

[21]   Ibid., pp. 321–2.

context, it is not possible to deduce the critics' positions on Mahler and Strauss or to evaluate whether any given criticism is in fact coded "antisemitic."

In 1904, however, a confluence of events made it possible to see for the first time how critics positioned themselves vis-à-vis Strauss and Mahler as a pair. Over the course of November and December 1904, a series of performances of three of Strauss's tone poems coincided with the Viennese premiere of Mahler's Third Symphony.

Table 5.2   Strauss and Mahler Concerts in Vienna, November–December 1904

Sunday	Monday	Tuesday	Wednesday	Thursday	Friday	Saturday
Nov. 20	21	22	23 Strauss, *Sinfonia domestica*	24	25	26
27	28	29	30	Dec. 1	2	3
4	5	6	7	8	9	10
11	12	13	14 Mahler, Third Symphony	15	16	17 Strauss, *Don Quixote*
18 Strauss, *Ein Heldenleben*	19 Strauss, *Don Quixote* repetition	20	21	22 Mahler, Third Symphony repetition	23	24
25	26	27	28	29	30	31

This amazing period began with Mahler conducting the *Sinfonia domestica* on 23 November in the first of Schoenberg's Vereinigung concerts[22] and ended with a repetition of Mahler's Third on 22 December. Many of the critics took the opportunity to compare the two composers, and it is here that it becomes possible to evaluate the critical responses to Strauss as they relate to Mahler.

---

[22]   Strauss himself had originally planned to conduct the *Sinfonia domestica* but changed his mind at the last minute. According to de La Grange, Schoenberg wanted to program "the latest work by the head of the neu-deutsch school" in order to turn the concert "into a great event." The *Sinfonia domestica* had its premiere on 31 March in New York and thus its performance in Vienna followed more quickly on the heels of its premiere than any other of Strauss's tone poems. DLG III: 57–8.

Julius Korngold's feuilleton on Mahler's Third appeared on 17 December, one of the first of several articles to invoke both composers. Korngold opened his review by joking about the difficulty that Mahler's symphonies have experienced in Vienna, comparing them to "a gruesome monster" that was pictured in the most recent exhibit of the Secession—a "half sphinx, half sea serpent" that was titled *The Symphony*. (The drawing, by Alfred Kubin, dates from 1901/02 and was exhibited at the 17th Exhibition of the Secession, March to May 1903.[23]) Referring to the recent success that the Third had experienced at the *Allgemeiner Deutscher Musikverein* concert in Crefeld, Korngold suggested that, since this was the work that "disarmed the opposition to Mahler in Germany as well," maybe, as in a fairy tale, the monster had transformed itself into a prince.[24] Then came a rhetorical question:

Why does Mahler have it so much harder than Richard Strauss? The two composers are juxtaposed often enough as the peaks of the "musically modern." But up to now, only Strauss was not merely modern but also in fashion. Is Mahler not also a brilliant technician, a virtuoso of orchestral serpentine dances, a shining exponent of the "musical=ingenious"? Certainly, but in this he is entirely different from Richard Strauss. One can say: he is both more conservative and more progressive at the same time. Strauss is at base just the "new German musician" raised to a higher degree. He was able to stride down the paths that Wagner and Liszt made passable 50 years ago. The symphonic poem, which derives its form from extramusical content, had taken its place alongside the classical symphony. Mahler does not break fully with the old formalistic rules of style. Rather, he penetrates into the old multi-movement symphony with the enhanced subjectivism of the new art; with its extensively developed principles

---

[23]   My thanks to Dr Marian Bizan-Prakken of the Albertina in Vienna for help in identifying and locating this drawing. The picture is numbered 233 in the catalog for the 17th Exhibition.

[24]   Julius Korngold (3029), p. 1: "In einem Winkelchen einer der letzten Ausstellungen der 'Sezession' hing eine kleine seltsame Zeichnung. Man sah ein geöffnetes Klavier, dahinter flutende Wasserwogen. Und aus diesen erhob sich, hochaufgerichtet, die Vordertatzen dräuend vor sich hingestemmt halb Sphinx halb Seeschlange, ein grauenerregendes Ungeheuer. Darüber stand 'Die Symphonie.' 'Die Mahler-Symphonie'—mag lächelnd ein sinnender Betrachter ergänzt haben. Wie solch einem rätselvollen, fratzenhaften Ungeheuer stand das musikalische Wien lange Mahlers Symphonien gegenüber. 'Symphonie, que me veux tu?'—die ratlose Frage klang weit milder nach dem letztaufgeführten Werke, Mahlers Dritter, oder sie wurde gar nicht mehr gestellt. Dieses Ungeheuer schien vom Publikum schon umgänglicher befunden worden zu sein, etwa ganz so,wie es der Prinzessin mit ihrem Ungetüm ergeht im Grimmschen Märchen. Hat doch diese dritte Symphonie auch in Deutschland den Widerspruch gegen Mahler entwaffnet. Sie ist als das 'Ereignis' des Crefelder Musikfestes des Allgemeinen deutschen Musikvereines gepriesen worden und eroberte eine Anzahl deutscher Musikstädte. Seit kurzem scheint ihr Mahlers fünfte Symphonie mit Erfolg nachzudrängen. Sollte sich das greuliche Untier eben wie in jenem Märchen, schon in den artigen Prinzen verwandeln beginnen?"

of expression; with poetic, dramatic, and speculative tendencies; with reckless realistic detail. Amid a language of forms that the great masters of the symphony had used, we hear the most audacious musical-poetic vocabulary of the "modern." That was, in the first place, what was so astonishing about Mahler—and had to astonish. The fight between the old and the new appeared to be carried out even on that consecrated ground.[25]

In other words, Mahler's problem, or difficulty, lay in his choice of the symphony as his genre, while Strauss, by choosing the symphonic poem, had, to a certain extent avoided these pitfalls. Although Bruckner is acknowledged as one of Mahler's teachers, Korngold believed that "Mahler's real ancestor is Berlioz":

> With Mahler, as with Berlioz, we find the thoughtless heaping up of representational devices, the increase in the number of symphonic movements; the union of instrumental and vocal elements; the extravagant imagination for sound, the mixture of strangeness and exaltation with the primitive; the "sulphur-yellow flashes of irony," as Heine called them; the alternating excursions heavenward and down to hell.[26]

While granting that both Mahler and Strauss were masters of orchestration, it is in Mahler's music that Korngold finds "thoughtless heaping up." Like Schoenaich, Korngold identifies this with Berlioz (again, an outsider), but where other writers

---

[25] Korngold (3029), p. 1: "Warum hat es Mahler um so viel schwerer als Richard Strauß? Man stellt beide Komponisten oft genug nebeneinander als die Spitzen der 'musikalischen Moderne.' Aber bisher war nur Strauß nicht bloß modern, sondern auch in Mode. Ist nicht auch Mahler blendender Techniker, Virtuose orchestraler Serpentinentänze, glänzender Vertreter des 'Musikalisch = Geistreichen'? Gewiß, aber er ist dies alles anders als Richard Strauß. Man kann sagen: er ist konservativer und fortschrittlicher zugleich als dieser. Strauß ist im Grunde blos der potenzierte 'neudeutsche Musiker.' Er konnte Pfade schreiten, die seit fünfzig Jahren Wagner und Liszt gangbar gemacht hatten. Die symphonische Dichtung, die ihre Form von einem außermusikalischen Inhalt erhält, war neben die klassische Symphonie getreten. Mahler bricht nicht völlig mit den alten formalistischen Stilgrundsätzen. Er dringt vielmehr mit dem gesteigerten Subjektivismus der neuen Kunst, mit ihren weitgetriebenen Ausdrucksprinzipien, mit poetischen, dramatischen und spekulativen Tendenzen, mit rücksichtslosem realistischen Detail in die alte mehrsätzige Symphonie. Wir hören inmitten einer Formensprache, deren sich die großen Meister der Symphonie bedient haben, das verwegenste musikalisch-poetische Vokabular der 'Moderne.' Das war es in erster Linie, was so befremdete bei Mahler, befremden mußte. Der Kampf zwischen Altem und Neuem schien auf den gewcihten Boden selbst getragen."

[26] Korngold (3029), p. 1: "Wie bei Berlioz finden sich bei Mahler die ungemessene Häufung der Darstellungsmittel, die Vermehrung der Symphoniesätze, die Vereinigung instrumentaler und vokaler Elemente, die ausschweifende Klangphantasie, die Mischung von Bizarrerie und Exaltation mit dem Primitiven, die 'schwefelgelben Blitze der Ironie,' wie es Heine nannte, die abwechselnden Fahrten gen Himmel und zur Hölle."

used the names of Berlioz and Liszt interchangeably, Korngold claims that, "Mahler belongs to the lineage of Berlioz, as Strauss to the line of Liszt." If one looks closely, the differences between the two becomes even clearer:

> Mahler strives visibly for broad themes, from which he seeks to spin melodic variations; Strauss works with motives and motive particles, which he plunges into convoluted polyphonic adventures. With Mahler, diatonic thinking still prevails, with Strauss the chromatic. Strauss seems to be cacophonous out of whimsical contradiction, Mahler, as it were, out of conviction. And while Strauss remains completely under the spell of the artistic, in Mahler there stirs with deeper gravity at least the longing for nature and naturalness, for the naïve and naturalness, for the naïve and the popular. The preference for simple folk song that controls this complicated artist, both as musician and occasionally as poet, turns out to be too pervasive to doubt its sincerity.[27]

While Korngold here seems sympathetic to Mahler, later in the review he would claim that Mahler's melodic invention cannot support an entire symphony, and that no program can make sense of the "potpourri of marches" that is the first movement.[28] Korngold devoted two other reviews to Strauss's works

---

[27]   Korngold (3029), p. 1: "Mahler strebt sichtlich nach breiten Themen, die er melodisch variierend auszuspinnen sucht; Strauß arbeitet mit Motiven und Motivpartikelchen, die er in verwickelte polyphone Abenteuer stürzt. Bei Mahler überwiegt immer noch das diatonische Denken, bei Strauß das chromatische. Strauß scheint aus Witz und Widerspruchsgeist kakophon, Mahler gleichsam aus Ueberzeugung. Und während Strauß ganz im Banne des Artistischen verharrt, regt sich im Mahler bei tieferem Ernste wenigstens die Sehnsucht nach Natur und Natürlichkeit, nach dem Naiven und Natürlichkeit, noch dem Naiven und Volkstümlichen. Die Vorliebe, die dieser komplizierte Künstler als Musiker wie als gelegentlicher Poet für das schlichte Volkslied betätigt, erweist sich als zu ausdauernd, um in ihre Aufrichtigkeit verdächtig zu scheinen."

[28]   Korngold (3029), p. 2: "Mahlers erster Satz ist in den größten Dimensionen gehalten; er dauert allein fast so lange wie sonst eine ganze Symphonie. Aber sein musikalischer Gehalt—nach seinem poetischen sollen wir ja nicht mehr fragen—scheint uns nicht ganz ausreichend für eine solche ganze Symphonie. Nicht als ob es an thematischem oder melodischem Material fehlte; ganz im Gegenteil. Wie bei Bruckner treten Haupt- und Gesangsthemen gleich in ganzen Gruppen auf. Nimmt man das System der melodischen Variation dazu, die bei Mahler, in einer ihm eigentümlichen Weise so oft an die Stelle der thematischen Durchführungen tritt, so gibt es sogar einen Ueberfluß an Gedankenmaterial. Aber man ist noch nicht reich, wenn man viel ausgibt. Dem Themenbestande dieses Satzes scheint uns vielfach die Eigennote zu fehlen, und zum Teile, wie der zweiten Themengruppe, auch der echte symphonische Charakter. Verführt durch seine Vorliebe für volkstümliche Weisen, hat der Komponist Tongedanken für symphoniefähig angesehen, deren banaler rhythmischer Zuschnitt Stilisierung wie symphonische Ausbeutung erschwert, wenn nicht ausschließt. Auch kein Programm vermag das Marschpotpourri zu rechtfertigen, das in den ersten Satz Mahlers geraten ist. 'Pan zieht ein'—in den Prater."

and was no kinder to him, but in neither did he again invoke Mahler's name for comparison.[29]

A short review of Schoenaich's appeared in *Die Musik* in early January and offered a summary of the previous month's musical activities in Vienna. He begins by stating that a flurry of new music had been heard in the Viennese concert halls: "The doors of our concert enterprises, once shut tight or at least difficult to open, have jumped from their hinges with the beginning of the current season and the new and newest surge forcefully into the halls. Gustav Mahler, Richard Strauss, Hans Pfitzner—the prime movers of modernity—were repeatedly represented by important works not yet heard here."[30] He was particularly impressed with *Ein Heldenleben,* "whose rich inventiveness, impetuousness and deeply felt [instrumental] parts have strengthened the belief in the musician Strauss"; he is less interested in *Don Quixote,* which he calls "clever non-music [*geistreiche Unmusik*]" and which was taken in its stride by the public.[31] He then takes up Mahler's Third, which he claims was greeted "with nearly frightening applause" and "had to be repeated within a few days." Schoenaich finds its success problematic: "If one considers that Liszt's 'Faust' symphony and B minor Sonata took over 40 years to rise to their present position in the music world, then one cannot resist skeptical impulses in the face of such quick successes. Music of the present it is in any case. Whether it is also *Zukunftsmusik,* that is the question."[32] Schoenaich implies that

---

[29] Julius Korngold, "Feuilleton. Musik. (Orchesterkonzert der 'Vereinigung schaffender Tonkünstler in Wien': Richard Strauß' 'Sinfonia domestica,'" *Neue freie Presse,* 26 Nov. 1904, pp. 1–2; J. K., "Theater- und Kunstnachrichten." *Neue freie Presse,* 19 Dec. 1904, p. 11.

[30] Gustav Schoenaich (3038), p. 154: "Die ehemals festverschlossenen oder mindestens schwer zu öffnenden Türen unserer Konzertunternehmungen sind mit Beginn der heurigen Saison aus ihren Angeln gesprungen und mit Macht dringt das Neue und Neueste in die Säle. Gustav Mahler, Richard Strauss, Hans Pfitzner, also die ersten Kräfte der Modernen, waren wiederholt durch bedeutende, hier noch nicht gehörte Werke vertreten."

[31] Schoenaich (3038), pp. 154–5: "Als Neuheit von Strauss erschienen die symphonischen Variationen 'Don Quixote.' Ferdinand Loewe brachte das schwierige Werk im Wiener Konzertverein durch Feinheit und Präzision der Ausführung zur Geltung. Diese unterhaltende und geistreiche Unmusik wurde vom Publikum, dem allzuviel Musik geboten wird, als abwechslungbietender 'Schritt vom Wege' mit bester Laune aufgenommen. Im letzten Konzert der Philharmoniker war eine glänzende Wiederholung des 'Heldenleben' unter Mottls Leitung vorangegangen, dessen erfindungsreichen, impetuosen und tief empfundenen Partien den Glauben an den Musiker Strauss gestärkt hatten."

[32] Schoenaich (3038), p. 155: "Mit schier beängstigendem Beifall wurde Gustav Mahlers dritte Symphonie im ausserordentlichen Konzert der 'Gesellschaft der Musikfreunde' aufgenommen. Sie musste innerhalb einiger Tage wiederholt werden und rief wieder ein elegantes, beifallshitziges Publikum herbei. Bedenkt man, dass Liszts 'Faustsymphonie' und h-moll Sonate über vierzig Jahre brauchten, um sich zu ihrer heutigen Stellung in der Musikwelt zu erheben, so kann man sich skeptischer Regungen solchen raschen Erfolgen

such acclamation means little in any event. While he does not elaborate on the Strauss works at all, he expends quite a bit of text on Mahler's weaknesses:

> Mahler's work certainly contains great beauties, the final Adagio appearing as the purest and most exalted of these. Even if it stands on the shoulders of Beethoven and Wagner, this fervent melody still sings itself deeply into the soul. All the more deeply here, where simple means are utilized, Mahler's highly developed sense of sound conjures up almost transfiguring effects. What is questionable is the bloated design of the whole, the monstrosity of the apparatus, and the aesthetic twilight into which the composer pushes his work, which—unmistakably born from a program—now demands to be enjoyed as absolute music. Why Beethoven, after the first three movements of the "Ninth," strikes up the Ode to Joy can be understood by anyone who has absorbed what has gone before. But why Gustav Mahler after three movements—already completely disparate in their scope—couples together the words of the antichrist Zarathustra-Nietzsche with an overly precious little Christian poem from "Des Knaben Wunderhorn"— to take this as self-explanatory is more than a bit much.[33]

It is interesting that, for Schoenaich, the place where Mahler is the most effective is the Adagio, where he restrains his natural inclination to use exorbitant means; this is also the moment most unlike Mahler himself, for it reminds Schoenaich of Beethoven and Wagner.[34] Mahler's overall project, however, lacks logic, for

---

gegenüber nicht erwehren. Gegenwartsmusik ist's jedenfalls. Ob auch Zukunftsmusik, das ist die Frage."

[33]   Schoenaich (3038), p. 155: "Mahlers Werk enthält unbedingt grosse Schönheiten, als deren lauterste und erhebendste das abschliessende Adagio erscheint. Steht es auch auf den Schultern Beethovens und Wagners, so singt sich diese inbrünstige Melodik doch tief in die Seele. Um so tiefer als Mahlers höchstentwickelter Klangsinn, hier, wo einfache Mittel zur Verwendung kommen, geradezu verklärende Wirkungen hervorzaubert. Bedenklich macht die barocke Anlage des Ganzen, die Monstruosität des Apparates und das ästhetische Zwielicht, in das der Komponist sein Werk rückt, das, unverkennbar aus einem Programm heraus geboren nun den Anspruch erhebt, absolut musikalisch genossen zu werden. Warum Beethoven nach den ersten drei Satzen der 'Neunten' den Freudenhymnus anstimmt, kann jeder verstehen, der das Vorangegangene in sich aufgenommen hat. Warum aber Gustav Mahler nach drei schon in ihrer Ausdehnung ganz disparaten Sätzen die Worte des Antichrist Zarathustra-Nietzsche mit einem überzärtelt christlichen Gedichtchen aus 'Des Knaben Wunderhorn' zusammenkoppelt—das als sich selbst erklärend hinzunehmen, ist eine starke Zumutung."

[34]   See Margaret Notley, "Late Nineteenth-century Chamber Music and the Cult of the Classical Adagio," *19th-Century Music* 23 (1999), pp. 33–61; given the status of the adagio in German culture, Schoenaich's comments are high praise, even though he tempers them by suggesting that the movement reminds him of other composers. Mahler never indicated any movement "Adagio"; the closest he came was the Adagietto of the Fifth Symphony. The "Adagio" that Schoenaich is discussing is actually titled "Langsam.

something conceived as program music cannot then be understood without the program. Unlike Beethoven's Ninth, in which the entrance of the words are made self-explanatory—Schoenaich is essentially taking Wagner's stance here—Mahler's introduction of text into his symphony is inexplicable. While Schoenaich is far from dismissive of the work, he chooses to praise Mahler in ways that expose Mahler's lack of control.[35] The remainder of Schoenaich's review is devoted to Hans Pfitzner, whose piano trio was performed by Bruno Walter, Arnold Rose, and Friedrich Buxbaum. Schoenaich calls Pfitzner "a musical thoroughbred" who creates a "clear-cut, strong musical personality that asserts itself through the whole piece." One is left with the impression that of the three, Hans Pfitzner is the least problematic, least in need of explanation, and most worthy of praise.[36]

Theodor Helm was also a supporter of the New German school, and he wrote for both the *Deutsche Zeitung* and for the *Musikalisches Wochenblatt*. On 5 January 1905 he published a long article in the latter paper, in which he compared the Strauss–Mahler quarrel to the Gluck–Piccini battle in Paris during the 1770s, his point being that "the quarrel ultimately had to remain undecided, since, after all, whoever had once sworn allegiance to a favorite master would allow himself to be convinced of the contrary opinion only with difficulty or not at all."[37] While conceding that, at least in "outer success," Mahler "won the palm," he goes on to point out that Mahler's cheering section in Vienna is "incomparably larger" than Strauss's.[38] Otherwise, Helm agrees with Schoenaich that Mahler's Third

---

Ruhevoll. Empfunden." According to Notley, it was the title "Adagio" that was important and that carried the weight, not any German or other equivalents.

[35] By spending many more lines on Mahler's piece, Schoenaich reinforces the impression that the Strauss stands on its own and needs no further elucidation from him. Mahler's Third is the piece that both demands explanation yet remains an enigma.

[36] Schoenaich (3038), p. 155: "Das durchaus eigenartige Werk rief eine Ergriffenheit der Zuhörer hervor, von der sich ein Publikum, das leider nur allzu musikgewohnt ist, nur selten erfassen lässt. Man sah sich da einem tiefen Ernst, einem Reichtum, einer musikalischen Vollblutnatur gegenüber, die wegen ihrer Seltenheit überraschend und beglückend wirken musste. Die schöne Herbheit, das Sprechende der Akzente, die überirdische Melodik des Adagio, die festumrissene, starke Persönlichkeit, die sich durch das ganze Stück geltend macht—alles wirkte zusammen, um einen nicht leicht verwischbaren Eindruck hervorzubringen."

[37] Theodor Helm (3037), p. 12: "Gustav Mahler und Richard Strauss: diese beiden Komponistennamen waren in den letzten 14 Tagen hier wieder in aller Munde. Es wurde lebhaft debattiert, wer von den beiden kühnen musikalischen Secessionisten bedeutender sei, und musste der Streit schliesslich unentschieden bleiben, da ja, wer einmal auf irgend einen Lieblingsmeister eingeschworen, sich nur schwer oder gar nicht von gegenteiliger Meinung überzeugen lässt. Anlass zu den heftigen—fast an den berühmten Gluck-Piccinni-Kampf 1777–1779 in Paris erinnernde—Kontroversen gaben zwei fast unmittelbar aufeinanderfolgende sensationelle Symphonie-Premièren."

[38] Helm (3037), p. 12: "Nun, was den äusseren Erfolg anbelangt, so errang diesmal unbestreitbar Mahler die Palme. In den seiner dritten Symphonie gespendeten

Symphony is in reality program music and makes no sense without its program. He, too, singles out the Adagio, again claiming to hear the influence of other composers, while commenting on the titles that had originally accompanied each of the six movements.[39]

After discussing Mahler's symphony and relating the gossip that Mahler might be taking over the Philharmonic from Felix Mottl, Helm turns at last to Strauss:

> The reception of Richard Strauss's "Don Quixote" in the Konzertverein turned out to be not quite as noisy as the Mahler premier in the first nonsubscription concert, but did considerable honor nonetheless to the unfortunately absent composer, especially on the second evening, since the orchestra, equal only in part to such a gigantic task, was already much more comfortable with itself and also with F. Löwe [who] directed with far greater security, as well as with pleasure and love. I confess that I personally gained a much more sympathetic and convincing impression from this exceedingly clever and amazingly polyphonic Humoresque—which drew the boldest, most unprecedented tone painting from the orchestra as mood effects— than from the demanding giant symphony of Mahler's, at which I was of course not bored for a moment, but after which I left the concert in a kind of stupor.[40]

Like Schoenaich, Helm seems more intent on criticizing Mahler than on praising Strauss, or, perhaps, is content to assume that Strauss's music can speak for itself.

---

enthusiastischen Beifall mischte sich nicht eine Stimme der Opposition, bei 'Don Quixote' und dem 'Heldenleben' aber machte sich neben der lebhaft applaudierenden Majorität doch auch eine zischende Minderheit geltend (die allerdings bezüglich 'Don Quixote' bei der Wiederholung am 19. Dezember verstummte oder vielleicht überhaupt gar nicht mehr vertreten war). Das war nun freilich alles so ziemlich vorauszusehen. Mahler und Strauss besitzen in Wien jeder eine geschlossene Verehrergemeinde, aber die Mahler's ist ungleich grösser."

[39] Helm (3037), p. 12: "Hätte nun Mahler das poetische Programm in ganzen und in allen Details aufrecht erhalten, dann würde man die überaus geistreiche und farbenprächtige, im abschliessenden Adagio sogar tief empfundene orchestrale Illustration eben als solche trotz der zahlreichen wunderlichen Grotesken willig hinnehmen."

[40] Helm (3037), p. 13: "Nicht ganz so geräuschvoll wie die Mahler-Premiere im ersten ausserordentlichen Gesellschaftskonzert, aber immerhin den leider fern gebliebenen Komponisten doch sehr ehrend, gestaltete sich die Aufnahme von Richard Strauss' 'Don Quixote' im Konzertverein, besonders am zweiten Abend, da das einer solchen Riesenaufgabe doch nur bedingt gewachsene Orchester mit derselben schon viel mehr vertraut war und auch F. Löwe mit ungleich grösserer Sicherheit, wie Lust und Liebe dirigierte. Ich gestehe, das ich persönlich von dieser überaus geistreichen und staunenswert polyphonen, die kühnsten, unerhörtesten tonmalerischen, wie Stimmungseffekte aus dem Orchester ziehenden Humoreske einen viel sympathischeren, überzeugenderen Eindruck gewann, als von der anspruchsvollen Riesensymphonie Mahler's, bei der ich mich zwar keinen Augenblick langweilte, nach welcher ich aber doch zuletzt in einer Art Betäubung das Konzert verliess."

Because Helm does not make an issue of the fact that Strauss writes program music, the reader is left to conclude that it is a worthwhile exercise when practiced without deception. Helm also praises Strauss's orchestration without suggesting that it is problematic in any way, whereas in regard to the Mahler he does make note of the difficulty for the listener of organizing so much without a program. Both Schoenaich and Helm are careful to affirm their allegiance to the New German School by not dismissing either the large orchestra or program music out of hand. However, they suggest that the difference between Mahler and Strauss is that the former is incapable of sustaining or controlling a mood and that his orchestration is a device for hiding flaws or tricking the listener into believing that something actually lies behind the brilliant façade.

As always, the most interesting critic in Vienna was Robert Hirschfeld. Writing as he did for the *Wiener Abendpost*, a supplement to the official court paper, the *Wiener Zeitung*, Hirschfeld was of course aware of his sensitive position as a Jewish critic judging the Jewish composer Mahler for an audience that was perhaps equally Jewish and non-Jewish. More than any other Jewish critic, he understood his position as being essentially compromised: like Sigmund Freud, who as Jewish physician was "both physician and prospective patient,"[41] Hirschfeld's Jewishness would have, for many of his readers, invalidated his ability to judge German culture. It is perhaps one of the reasons why his deep ambivalence to Mahler is often not recognized as such, and his profoundly ironic tone missed. Karl Kraus, one of the greatest literary voices of the day, and also a precariously situated Jewish writer, greatly admired Hirschfeld as a writer and critic, and one cannot help wondering if it was because of the constant balancing act that Hirschfeld managed with his prose. His ability to place the true meaning of his words between the lines, in addition to his rather conservative leanings, make him one of the most memorable voices in Vienna during Mahler's tenure there. And given his uncertain position vis-à-vis his public, Hirschfeld's articles following the November–December concerts of 1904 embody not only the most complicated stance regarding Strauss and Mahler but also the most revealing one.

Hirschfeld published a lengthy feuilleton on 28 December 1904, in which he summarized the events of the previous two months: he begins with the three Strauss tone poems before turning to Mahler's Third. He simply dismisses the *Sinfonia domestica*:

> The living were never so alive. Their time has come. They must complain no more. If we could live on the art of the living, that would be quite beautiful. But what was recently presented to us in Vienna could only be endured by the unmusical with blunted eyes and blunted senses, by the curious and those who need sensations, sensations no matter if delivered by art or scandal or a by a window display. Richard Strauss: "*Sinfonia domestica*," depiction of domestic scenes; uncles and aunts arrive, look at the child; the score literally reads: "Just

---

[41] Sander L. Gilman, *Freud, Race, and Gender* (Princeton, 1993), p. 12.

like the papa!" and so forth; the clock strikes; the child screams; the nursery fills; domestic quarrel. With such unmusical jokes a composer of today fills his time, and for them a technical apparatus is mobilized to which even the giant orchestras of the present day cannot provide all that is necessary. The disproportion between the monstrous means and the tiny idea is pitiful—as if household jokes could possibly belong to the realm of ideas ...[42]

Hirschfeld's comments regarding Strauss recall his comments directed at almost every Mahler symphony, that the ideas do not justify the forces required to produce them. He seems to imply, however, that the fault is not entirely Strauss's, because the audiences of today demand such productions. Likewise, in *Don Quixote*, "every bar gives a new picture" and the score "resembles a picture book for children ... everything marked in the score with explanatory words":

Violoncello (the knight) and bass clarinet (Sancho) ride out together, discern Dulcinea (violin melody with flutes and oboes), then fight with the windmills (whistling woodwind figures and harp glissandos), timpani beat on F—the knight falls, Violoncello-solo—Sancho Panza helps him up. The orchestra raises dust (tremolo violins) and the winds imitate the bleatings of the aforementioned flock of sheep so beguilingly, that the listeners cannot stop laughing and crane their necks toward the imitating instruments ... A conversation between the knight and Sancho in the third variation can be understood only if we know that Sancho demands a higher fee ("with some urgency") and the knight becomes indignant on account of it ("very violently"). Later we hear how, as Sancho Panza falls asleep and snores (contrabassoon, glissando from E flat to low D) ... For the pair's famous ride through the air, a wind machine (!) assists in the orchestra. Don Quixote and his Sancho fall off on the low D; but so that one may know that they have never really lost the earth beneath their feet, this D is heard throughout the entire ride. That is certainly a joke of a most doubtful kind ... So it continues, until solemn woodwind chords with a diminuendo in the violins

---

[42] Robert Hirschfeld (3034a), p. 1: "Die Lebenden waren noch nie so lebendig. Ihre Zeit ist gekommen. Sie müssen nicht mehr klagen. Könnten wir von der Kunst der Lebenden leben, so wäre das recht schön. Was uns in Wien aber während der letzten Zeit geboten wurde, können nur Unmusikalische mit stumpfen Ohren und stumpfen Sinne ertragen, Neugierige und solche, die Sensationen brauchen, gleichviel, ob ihnen die Kunst oder der Skandal oder ein Auslagfenster diese Sensationen liefert. Richard Strauß: '*Sinfonia domestica*,' Schilderung häuslicher Szenen; Onkel und Tanten kommen, besehen das Kind; die Partitur schreibt wörtlich vor: 'Ganz der Papa!' und so weiter; die Uhrglocke ertönt; das Kind schreit; die Kinderstube füllt sich; häuslicher Streit. Mit solchen unmusikalischen Witzen füllt ein Tonsetzer von heute seine Zeit aus, und ein technischer Apparat wird dafür aufgeboten, dem die Riesenorchester der Gegenwart gar nicht alles Nötige zubringen können. Kläglich ist das Mißverhältnis der ungeheuren Mittel und der winzigen Idee— wenn Hausspäße noch in das Reich der Ideen gehören ..."

(6 desks, 4 desks, 2 desks, finally solo) indicate to us that the noble knight has returned to his senses.[43]

The problem with all of this, according to Hirschfeld, is composers have "with their program music reached the level of absurd depiction of things which do not stir our feelings at all":

> Because this variety of music is not suited to the expression of exalted or even merely serious ideas, because it clings to petty tone painting, the symphony has gotten caught in a funny operetta-age: "Till Eulenspiegel," "Don Quixote," "Heldenleben," "Sinfonia domestica." There one certainly needs eight horns, four trumpets, three trombones, bass tuba, four saxophones, four bassoons, contrabassoon, four clarinets etc., to show small family scenes in the "Sinfonia domestica."[44]

The listing of instruments is familiar from reviews of Mahler's work, and Hirschfeld employs it here to the same *ad absurdum* effect. Even more similar is

---

[43]   Hirschfeld (3034a), p. 1: "Bald darauf '*Don Quixote*': wir sollen den edlen Ritter in den alten Büchern lesen sehen; musikalische Trugfortschreitungen weisen auf des Ritters 'Neigung zu falschen Schlüssen' (!) und jeder Takt gibt ein neues Bild; bei einem furchtbar dissonanten Akkord ist der Ritter endlich übergeschnappt—die Partitur ('Universal-Edition,' Wien) gleicht einem Bilderbuch für Kinder. Die Baßklarinette führt den Sancho Panza vor—alles in der Partitur mit erklärenden Worten bezeichnet. Violoncello (der Ritter) und Baßklarinette (Sancho) reiten selbander aus, erblicken die Dulcinea (Geigenmelodie mit Flöten und Oboen), dann Kampf mit den Windmühlen (Sausende Holzbläserfiguren und Harfen-Glissando), Paukenschlag auf F—der Ritter fällt, Violoncello-Solo—Sancho Panza hilft ihm auf. Das Orchester wirbelt Staub auf (Tremolierende Geigen) und die Bläser imitieren das Geblöcke der bewußten Schafherde so täuschend, daß die Hörer nicht aus dem Lachen kommen und die Hälse nach den imitierenden Instrumenten recken … Ein Gespräch zwischen dem Ritter und Sancho in der dritten Variation ist nur dann zu verstehen, wenn wir wissen, daß Sancho erhöhte Honorarforderungen stellt ('etwas drängend') und der Ritter darob unwillig wird ('sehr heftig'). Später vernehmen wir, wie Sancho Panza einschläft und schnarcht (Kontrafagott, glissando vom es [sic] ins tiefe D) … Bei dem berühmten Luftritte der beiden wirkt auch eine—Windmaschine im Orchester mit. Don Quixote und sein Sancho fallen auf das tiefe D herunter; damit man aber wisse, daß sie nie eigentlich die Erde unter den Füßen verloren haben, klingt dieses D schon während des ganzen Rittes durch. Das ist doch ein Witz bedenklichster Art … So geht's fort, bis feierliche Holzbläser-Akkorde mit einem Diminuendo der Geigen (6 Pulte, 4 Pulte, 2 Pulte, endlich Solo) uns anzeigen, daß der edle Ritter wieder zu Verstand kommt."

[44]   Hirschfeld (3034a), p. 1: "Weil diese Abart von Musik sich zum Ausdruck erhabener oder auch nur ernster Ideen nicht eignet, da sie an der kleinlichen Tonmalerei haften bleibt, so ist die Sinfonie in ein lustiges Operetten-Zeitalter geraten: 'Till Eulenspiegel,' 'Don Quixote,' 'Heldenleben,' 'Sinfonia domestica.' Da braucht man freilich acht Hörner, vier Trompeten, drei Posaunen, Baßtuba, vier Saxophone, vier Fagotte, Kontrafagott, vier Klarinetten u.s.w., um in der 'Sinfonia domestica' kleine Familienszenen vorzuführen."

his poking fun at all the performance directions in the score, in this case, in *Ein Heldenleben*:

> The "Heldenleben" paints the hero's female companion in a rather long violin lesson "hypocritically languishing," "frivolously," "somewhat sentimentally," "in high spirits," "with urgency," "playfully," "very sharply" and "nagging," and however else the instructions in the score read. The symphonic poem then shows the hero in battle with the opponents that are one minute "very sharp and pointed," the next "rasping" and after the large battle, which, with a hellish array of noise and dissonances lies already far beyond all musical perception, it also delivers the hero's "works of peace," namely, approximately two dozen themes from the earlier works of Richard Strauss compressed onto several pages of score.[45]

Hirschfeld does not blame German critics for assuming that the entire thing was not meant all that seriously, since it does not appear that Strauss had a deeper meaning. Before he turns to Mahler, however, he summarizes his opinion of Richard Strauss and his musical project:

> Richard Strauss is really clever, though; he has, with a technique that he himself created, led program music to its last consequences, reached the outermost limits in his own peculiar polyphony, tested all possibilities in the utilization of the instrumentation. The musical sense can scarcely follow him beyond that. His method to set music on its head is nonetheless unified and has its specifically Straussian quality; he shows despite many very beautiful inspirations, an iron and in some sense logical perseverance to kill music.[46]

---

[45]   Hirschfeld (3034a), p. 1: "Das 'Heldenleben' malt die Gefährtin des Helden in einer längeren Violinlektion 'heuchlerisch schmachtend,' 'leichtfertig,' 'etwas sentimental,' 'übermütig,' 'drängend,' 'spielend,' 'sehr scharf und keifend,' und wie die Vorschriften der Partitur sonst lauten. Die sinfonische Dichtung zeigt dann den Helden mit den bald 'sehr scharfen und spitzigen,' halb auch 'schnarrenden' Widersachern im Kampfe und bringt nach der großen Schlacht, die mit einem Höllenaufgebot von Lärm und Mißklängen bereits jenseits aller musikalischen Wahrnehmung liegt, auch die 'Friedenswerke' des Helden, nämlich ungefähr zwei Dutzend Themen aus den früheren Werken von Richard Strauß auf einige Partiturseiten zusammengedrängt." The program, which included *Don Quixote*, performed with Löwe on 17 December, was repeated in its entirety on Monday, 19 December.

[46]   Hirschfeld (3034a), pp. 1–2: "Es ist nichts so absurd, daß deutsche Kritiker nicht einen tiefen Sinn dahinter suchten. Richard Strauß ist aber wirklich geistreich; er hat mit einer Technik, die er sich selbst geschaffen [hat?], die Programmusik bis zu den letzten Konsquenzen geführt, in der ihm eigentümlichen Polyphonie die äußersten Grenzen erreicht, in der Verwendung der Instrumentation alle Möglichkeiten ausprobiert. Der musikalische Sinn kann ihm dahin kaum mehr folgen. Seine Methode, die Musik auf den Kopf zu stellen, ist jedoch einheitlich und hat ihre spezifisch Straußsche Eigentümlichkeit;

While this may seem damning on its surface, it needs to be read within the context of what immediately follows it:

Gustav Mahler lacks continuity and uniformity in the same pursuits. One minute he wants to grapple with Beethovenian pathos in the clouds, the next he pours music from a dainty little dish into a little folk song; one minute he tears chasms in the ground, then his music hops with the flirtatious grace of an old dance master; he has no emotional tone and wants to appear full of feeling; he strives toward naïveté by means of the most artificial, ingenious refinements; eight bars triviality, sixteen bars titanic obstinacy, then again longing for the banal and again a bit of Prometheus; if his music becomes sad, it seems inwardly to laugh; if it becomes cheerful, it betrays a bit of inner pain; it wants to appear purely spiritual but is composed only of sound effects, which it changes with amazing suddenness or else prolongs; it is a self-satisfied music, which assumes poses as if before a mirror and keeps changing the pose: now grandeur, now passion, now escapism, now contrition. Gustav Mahler has the technique of Bernard Shaw: one is never sure if he treats himself or only others with irony—what is left is the same distorting play with funeral marches as with love melodies.[47]

In Hirschfeld's prose, it becomes clear why the labels "favorable" or "unfavorable" will not suffice: while he cares for neither composer, he does grant Strauss a sense of autonomy and free will that he denies Mahler. Hirschfeld may not appreciate what Strauss is doing, but he does believe that Strauss has a plan, a "method"; that Hirschfeld thinks it is madness does not take away Strauss's agency. Mahler,

---

er zeigt trotz mancher wunderschöner Eingebungen eine in seinem Sinne folgerichtige und eiserne Beharrlichkeit, die Musik umzubringen." Likewise, Hirschfeld reviews *Zarathustra* in 1897, claiming that although there are "certainly sparks of genius … it awakens horror, for we are at the end of music" (*Neue musikalische Presse* 13 [27 March 1897], trans. Susan Gillespie in *Richard Strauss and His World*, pp. 323–4; quote is p. 323).

[47]   Hirschfeld (3034a), p. 2: "Gustav Mahler läßt in dem gleichen Streben die Stetigkeit und Einheitlichkeit vermissen. Bald will er mit Beethovenschem Pathos in die Wolken greifen, bald gießt er aus einem kleinen zierlichen Näpfchen Musik in ein Volksliedchen; bald reißt er Schlünde in die Erde, bald hüpft seine Musik mit der koketten Grazie eines alten Tanzmeisters; er hat keinen Gemütston und will sich gemütvoll zeigen; er strebt auf dem Wege des künstlichsten, eines ausgeklügelten Raffinements zur Naivetät; acht Takte Trivialität, sechzehn Takte Titanentrotz, dann wieder Sehnsucht nach dem Banalen und wieder ein Stückchen Prometheus; wird seine Musik traurig, so scheint sie innerlich zu lachen; wird sie heiter, so verrät sie ein bißchen inneren Schmerz; sie will rein geistig erscheinen und setzt sich nur aus Klangeffekten zusammen, die sie mit verblüffender Plötzlichkeit wechselt oder zum Verweilen bestimmt; es ist eine selbstgefällige Musik, die wie vor dem Spiegel Posen annimmt und verändert die Pose der Erhabenheit, der Leidenschaft, der Weltflucht oder der Zerknirschung. Gustav Mahler hat die Technik des Bernard Shaw; man ist keinen Augenblick sicher, ob er sich selbst oder die anderen ironisiert; es bleibt dasselbe Vexierspiel bei Trauermärschen wie bei Liebesmelodien."

on the other hand, wants to do a lot but can accomplish nothing—the desire is there, but the result is muddled, lacking any unifying plan or goal. Strauss goes forth to set music on its head; Mahler can only flail around, producing nonsense or juxtaposing incommensurate details. Hirschfeld implies that Strauss does have what Mahler lacks, an emotional tone and the control to exercise it. Mahler's music, Hirschfeld seems to say, like the Jews themselves, can only "pose." They are the great actors of the day since they lack any self, and it is easy to take on but one more mask.

The difference in their use of the orchestra follows from this: Strauss uses an enormous orchestra in an attempt to "kill music," to take program music "to its ultimate consequences." While Hirschfeld may be appalled at the goal, he has no doubt that Strauss can and will achieve it. Mahler, on the other hand, is not in control of his "sound effects," and because of this they "alternate with startling suddenness." Mahler's orchestration is only one more aspect of his musical pose, one that cannot create a lasting impact because, in the end, it only serves to hide a lack. While Hirschfeld indicates that he does not approve of either composer's pursuits, Strauss knows what he is doing and does it while Mahler, attempting similar things, "lacks continuity and coherence." What Mahler creates is what Wagner claims that Jewish composers create: an "intolerably jumbled blabber," and Hirschfeld seems to confirm Wagner's claim that "when we hear this Jewish talk, our attention dwells involuntarily on its repulsive *how*, rather than on any meaning of its intrinsic *what*."[48] Strauss, the German composer, can master and thus control his heritage while for Mahler, as for all Jews, "European art and civilization ... have remained ... a foreign tongue." The Jew, standing outside the community and denied its essence, has no access to the source of art.[49]

Mahler's use of the orchestra differs from Strauss's in that it is often described as harsh or ugly. Not only does orchestration cover up Mahler's lack of ideas, but those ideas themselves are, if not ugly to begin with, then are made to sound ugly by Mahler's manipulation of the orchestra. It is worth recalling some of Hirschfeld's comments on Mahler's First Symphony: "The parodistic treatment of the instruments in the D major Symphony seeks to take the individual instruments through unfamiliar registers and manipulations of all types of their natural sounds; the violins (col legno) must rattle, the trumpets [must] flute, the horn may not sound like a horn, nor the cello like a cello."[50] The means not only overpower the

---

[48]   Richard Wagner, "Judentum in der Musik," *Richard Wagner's Prose Works*, trans. William Ashton Ellis (8 vols, New York and London, 1966; rpt 1894), vol. 4, p. 85; orig. italics.

[49]   Wagner, *Judentum*, p. 84.

[50]   Robert Hirschfeld (2800), p. 2: "Die parodistische Behandlung der Instrumente in der D-dur-Symphonie geht darauf aus, den einzelnen Instrumenten durch ungewohnte Lage und Manipulationen aller Art ihren natürlichen Klang zu nehmen, die Geigen (col legno) müssen klappern, die Trompeten flöten, das Horn darf nicht wie Horn, das Cello nicht wie Cello klingen."

ideas, but the results are not even pleasant: "[In the opening of the first movement] [t]he whole string orchestra, with the cellos and contrabasses themselves triply divided, must hold an A harmonic in all achievable octaves for 50 bars, ultimately in order to achieve the effect of a creaking door."[51] Nowhere does Hirschfeld imply that Strauss's ideas are unaesthetic, that they do not work, or that he is not in complete control of them. Hirschfeld may not agree that the ideas are worth such opulent means, but Strauss's control ensures that the results are at least worth consideration.

Hirschfeld published a longer and less restrained comparison of the two composers in the *Österreichische Rundschau*. He begins his article, titled "Mahler und Strauss in Wien," by speculating on the relationship of the artistic personality to the artistic result. Bruckner, for example, has suffered because "biographers and the laymen in the public" have applied their perception of his comic mannerisms to his works. This is backwards, according to Hirschfeld: the works must be understood alone. The problem is similar with Mahler, who, if not for his personality, would be dismissed:

> It is my innermost conviction: if Gustav Mahler were a corpulent gentleman with a reddish stubbly beard, by whom no Orlik could be excited, so we would not have the whole symphony to-do. Cross my heart! Who has ever been truly uplifted by a symphony by Gustav Mahler, been led beyond the world, allowed to feel the unsayable?[52]

Hirschfeld's use of the noun "Unsagbare" here could echo Wagner's own language in the *Judentum* essay where he juxtaposed Beethoven's ability to strive "for the clearest, certainest Expression of an unsayable Content [*unsäglichen Inhalt*]" to Mendelssohn's own reduction of these to "vague, fantastic shadow-forms."[53] It is

---

[51] Hirschfeld (2800), p. 2: "Das ganze Streichorchester muß mit je dreifach getheilten Celli und Contrabässen über fünfzig Takte ein Flageolet-A durch alle erreichbaren Octaven halten, um schließlich den Effect einer knarrenden Thür zu erzielen."

[52] Hirschfeld, "Mahler und Strauss in Wien," *Österreichische Rundschau* 9 (1904), pp. 535–40, at p. 536: "Es ist meine innerste Überzeugung: Wäre Gustav Mahler ein beleibter Herr mit einem rötlichen Stoppelbart, der keinen Orlik reizen könnte, so hätten wir den ganzen Sinfonierummel nicht. Hand aufs Herz! Wen hat denn eine Sinfonie von Gustav Mahler wahrhaft erhoben, hinter die Welt geführt, das Unsagbare empfinden lassen?" Hirschfeld implies that it is the otherness, or strangeness of Mahler's body that inspires the painter Orlik to produce his portraits; "ein beleibter Herr," on the other hand, cannot interest a painter precisely because his body is "normal." Emil Orlik created a famous charcoal drawing of Mahler in 1902; it is reproduced in many Mahler biographies and in my "Hypermoderner Dirigent." Orlik exhibited works with the Wiener Secession, but was not considered a member, although he did help to establish the movement in Berlin. He was born in Prague in 1870 and is perhaps best known as an innovative printmaker.

[53] Wagner, *Judentum*, p. 96; as Ellis points out in his note, the phrase "eines unsäglichen Inhaltes" did not appear in the original pseudonymous 1850 version of the essay, only the

Mahler's physiognomy—not just his body but his *different* body, and all the traits implied thereby—that is seductive, not his music; unfortunately, no one, according to Hirschfeld, can see past the physical person to the music. The sentiment is typically double-edged: no one would complain if such a corpulent man wrote symphonies, but those are nevertheless incapable of transporting a listener. Hirschfeld refuses to give in to Mahler's supporters—"the immature, the women, the compromise men"—he will make a judgment: "The Mahlerian symphony is not progress but rather a setback."[54]

Then, he invokes the specter of Meyerbeer, making explicit the veiled references of the preceding paragraphs:

> In [the Mahler symphony] Meyerbeer lives again. Except Meyerbeer's music testifies to rich, robust invention. The sound sense should be excited again; the instrument, the means has again become an end in itself; the Effect is again canonized. Meyerbeer is there: a hundred styles; the sudden, unmediated sound contrasts; the over-indulgence in the "solo"; magnificent, heartfelt, truly beautiful passages next to all kinds of banalities, embarrassments, misfortunes; the Flügelhorn in the forest immediately followed by the barracks, after the barracks a moment of Nietzsche (naturally misunderstood), and after Nietzsche, the naïve *Des Knaben Wunderhorn*.[55]

Of course, the description of Meyerbeer's (and thus Mahler's) style echoes Wagner's descriptions of Jewish music: "the Jew musician [hurls] together the diverse forms and styles of every age and every master. Packed side by side, we find the formal idiosyncrasies of all the schools, in motleyest chaos."[56] Mahler has

---

later version, republished under Wagner's own name in 1869.

[54]   Hirschfeld, "Mahler/Strauss", p. 537: "Wollen wir feige sein? Den Unreifen, den Frauen, den Kompromißmenschen nachgeben? Wir müssen uns ein Urteil zutrauen. Die Mahlersche Sinfonie ist kein Fortschritt, sondern ein Rückschlag."

[55]   Ibid., pp. 537–8: "In ihr lebt Meyerbeer wieder auf. Nur zeugt Meyerbeers Musik von reicher, starker Erfindung. Der Klangsinn soll wieder gereizt werden; das Instrument, das Mittel ist wieder Selbstzweck geworden; der Effekt wird wieder heilig gesprochen. Meyerbeer ist da: hundert Stile; die plötzlichen, unvermittelten Klangkontraste; das Schwelgen im 'Solo'; neben herrlichen, innigen, wahrhaft schönen Stellen gleich Banalitäten, Peinlichkeiten, Widrigkeiten aller Art; nach dem Flügelhorn im Walde sofort die Kaserne, nach der Kaserne augenblicklich Nietzsche (natürlich mißverstanden) und nach Nietzsche des naiven Knaben Wunderhorn." *Des Knaben Wunderhorn* ("The Boy's Magic Horn"), published between 1805 and 1808, is a compilation of "folk poetry," assembled by Achim von Arnim and Clemens Brentano. While the poetry was idealized (and edited) by Arnim and Brentano, it was hailed at the time as an important source of nationalistic pride and a force for stabilization of the language by none other than Goethe. Many composers, other than Mahler, set the poems to music, including Zemlinsky, Mendelssohn, Brahms, Schumann, and Loewe.

[56]   Wagner, *Judentum*, pp. 92.

fewer ideas even than Meyerbeer and cannot understand the texts (Nietzsche, *Des Knaben Wunderhorn*) that he uses. Yet Hirschfeld is not content merely to imply Wagner's presence, he evokes it outright:

> In the Mahler symphony—this can be proven in countless cases—even the counterpoint is chiefly *Effekt*, according to Wagner's eternally true definition: effect [*Wirkung*] without cause, effect that is not driven by internal necessity. The counterpoint does not germinate here; it is simply *made to happen*. The changing sound color remains then the main thing, the instrumental surprises from bar to bar. That is music for the unmusical. They believe themselves to be dealing with art and have only the outward appearance. It is characteristic that the Secession-gang, who find nothing to do with [Joseph] Olbrich[57] anymore, occupy the boxes at Mahler rehearsals and performances. At Brahms and Bruckner [performances] they were never to be seen. It is the surest criterion: Wherever you are *not*—there is the true, deep, pure art.[58]

With the mention of Meyerbeer and Wagner's definition of "Effekt," Hirschfeld clearly lays his cards on the table. There would have been no doubt in anyone's mind that he was referring to Mahler's Jewishness as the thing that debarred him from composing true music. True, he does not cite *Judentum in der Musik*, but rather *Oper und Drama*. And, as we have seen in Chapter 3, Wagner does not mince any words: "As a Jew, [Meyerbeer] owned no mother-tongue, no speech inextricably entwined among the sinews of his inmost being: he spoke with precisely the same interest in any modern tongue you chose, and set it to music with no further sympathy for its idiosyncrasies."[59] As if to reinforce the Jewish inability in art, Hirschfeld purposefully misquotes Georg Philipp Schmidt von Lübeck's "Der Wanderer," whose final stanza ends "'Dort, wo du nicht bist, dort ist dein Glück'" ["'There, where you are not, there is your

---

[57]   Joseph Maria Olbrich (1867–1908) was one of the founding members of the Vienna Secession; he was primarily an architect, most famous for the design of the Secession building itself. His name, therefore, after Gustav Klimt's, would have been one of the most immediately recognizable in Vienna as "Secessionist" and "modernist."

[58]   Hirschfeld, "Mahler/Strauss," p. 538: "In der Mahlerschen Sinfonie—das ließe sich an unzähligen Fällen nachweisen—ist auch der Kontrapunkt zumeist Effekt, nach Wagners ewig wahrer Definition: Wirkung ohne Ursache, Wirkung, die nicht aus innerer Notwendigkeit hervorgetrieben ist. Der Kontrapunkt keimt hier nicht, sondern er wird eben *effektuiert*. Die wechselnde Klangfarbe bleibt da die Hauptsache, die instrumentalen Überraschungen von Takt zu Takt. Das ist Musik für Unmusikalische. Sie glauben bei der Kunst zu sein und haben nur den äußeren Schein. Es ist bezeichnend, daß die Sezessionsmeute, die bei Olbrichs jetzt keine Beschäftigung mehr findet, in Mahlerschen Proben und Aufführungen die Logen besetzt. Bei Brahms und Bruckner waren sie nie zu sehen. Es ist das sicherste Kriterium: dort wo du *nicht* bist—da ist die wahre, tiefe, reine Kunst …"

[59]   Wagner, *Opera and Drama*, *Wagner's Prose Works*, vol. 2, p. 87 and p. 95.

happiness'"].[60] Hirschfeld's message is that it is only the absence of the 'Secession-Gang' (read: the Jewish modernists) that denotes the presences of true art.

Hirschfeld is writing here for a very different audience from that of the *Wiener Abendpost*, and therefore just as his criticism of Mahler is more explicit, so is his treatment of Strauss more equivocal. In a six-page article, almost four and a half pages are devoted to Mahler while only a single paragraph addresses Strauss. Like Schoenaich, Hirschfeld puts criticism of Mahler in place of praise for Strauss. Some of the statements echo the article in the *Wiener Abendpost*:

> More sincere are the symphonic jokes of Richard Strauss; for them he has a characteristic style, a characteristic thematic invention, a characteristic polyphony at his disposal; they are authenticated by the title, in the scores and by official commentaries. One knows exactly where the gallows for Till Eulenspiegel stands; one knows the chord at which Don Quixote loses his mind; the bleating sheep flock is so lifelike, that one believes he can smell mutton: and the wind machine leaves no doubt of Don Quixote's and Sancho's ride through the air. We notice how in the pizzicato the drops fall from the clothes of the soaked men; the two bassoons make us think of the two little priests; it is clear that with the quiet woodwind harmony the noble knight's reason returns. In "Heldenleben" explicit designations in the score state that the "opponents" come; some "very sharply and pointed," the others "rasping." The changing moods of the "female companion," who is apparently taking a violin lesson, are faithfully shown; it is written next to the measures in question, if the companion is "tender and loving" or "merry" or "cunning" or also "hypocritically languishing," even "fast and nagging." While Gustav Mahler includes in his scores brief treatises on specifically musical matters, for example the idea of the Wiener-ism "rattling" (which he recommends should be imitated with a tremolo), Richard Strauss, in the *Sinfonia domestica* tells us explicitly where the uncles and where the aunts visit the baby, and next to a certain phrase the uncle's remark is clearly readable: "Just like the mama!," next to the aunt's "Just like the papa!" One knows exactly where and how.[61]

---

[60]   Translation © Paul Hindemith; set by Franz Schubert as "Der Wanderer," D. 493.

[61]   Hirschfeld, "Mahler/Strauss," pp. 539–40: "Ehrlicher sind die sinfonischen Scherze von Richard Strauß; er hat für sie einen eigenen Stil, eine eigene Thematik, eine eigene Polyphonie zur Verfügung; sie werden durch die Überschrift, in den Partituren und durch offizielle Kommentare beglaubigt. Man weiß genau, wo der Galgen für Till Eulenspiegel steht; man kennt den Akkord, bei dem Don Quichotte den Verstand verliert; die blöckende Schafherde ist so naturgetreu dargestellt, daß man die Hammeln zu riechen glaubt, und die Windmaschine läßt an dem Lufttritt des Don Quichotte und des Sancho nicht zweifeln; wir merken, wie im Pizzicato die Tropfen der Durchnäßten von den Kleidern fallen; die beiden Fagotte lassen an die zwei Pfäfflein denken; es ist klar, daß mit den ruhigen Holzblasharmonien der Verstand des edlen Ritters wiederkehrt. Im 'Heldenleben' sagen es ausdrückliche Bezeichnungen der Partitur, daß die 'Widersacher' kommen, 'sehr

Strauss writes program music and does not, like Mahler, try to hide that fact. That is one reason that he is "more genuine [*ehrlicher*]." Another is that he has a true style of his own—something that is explicitly denied to Mahler. As in his essay in the *Wiener Abendpost*, Hirschfeld does not accept this without reservation: he acknowledges that Strauss "has the lead" in symphonic music, but that while "the jokes are executed with wit," "that is precisely what is shameful." He then goes on to criticize Strauss's overall project:

> Have we come so wonderfully far, after the heights of German art, that the spirit of our leading composers concerns itself now solely with such jokes? And for the jokes one needs giant orchestras, which are admittedly no longer orchestras in Straussian tone poems, but rather slews of instruments, which are driven beyond their nature. If at all costs several voices must sound together, then hideous dissonance may result. The cello is taken into the violin range and a horn part looks exactly like a viola part, then one can hardly speak of a *technique*, which, after all, can only be a *natural* and *economic* appropriation of artistic means.[62]

Unlike his assessment of Mahler, Hirschfeld does not imply that Strauss does not have ideas, nor that Strauss's ideas are "effects without causes"—Strauss is talented, but misguided. Hirschfeld believes that Strauss is making the wrong artistic choices,

---

scharf und spitzig' die einen, 'schnarrend' die anderen. Die wechselnden Stimmungen der 'Gefährtin,' die anscheinend Violinunterricht nimmt, sind getreulich angegeben; es steht bei den betreffenden Takten geschrieben, wenn die Gefährtin 'zart und liebevoll' oder 'lustig' oder 'listig' oder auch 'heuchlerisch schmachtend,' sogar 'schnell und keifend' wird. Während Gustav Mahler in seiner Partitur kleine Abhandlungen über spezifisch musikalische Angelegenheiten, so über den Begriff des wienerischen 'Scheppern' einträgt, das er bei einem Tremolo nachzumachen empfiehlt, sagt uns Richard Strauß in der Sinfonia domestica ausdrücklich, wo die Onkels und wo die Tanten das Kindlein besuchen, und bei einer bestimmten Tonphrase steht die Bemerkung der Onkels: 'Ganz die Mama!', bei einer anderen die Bemerkung der Tanten 'Ganz der Papa!' deutlich zu lesen. Man weiß doch, wo und wie."

[62] Hirschfeld, "Mahler/Strauss," p. 540: "Das ist die Blüte der heutigen sinfonischen Musik; Richard Strauß hat die Führung; die deutsche Kunst ist nie witziger gewesen. Daß diese Witze mit Geist ausgeführt sind, wird man zugeben. Aber das gerade ist beschämend. Haben wir es so herrlich weit gebracht nach den Erhebungen der deutschen Kunst, daß ,der Geist unserer Führenden sich nun lediglich mit solchen Späßen beschäftigt? Und für die Späße braucht man Riesenorchester, die freilich in Straußschen Tondichtungen keine Orchester mehr sind, sondern Zerstreuungen von Instrumenten, die über ihre Natur hinausgetrieben werden. Wenn unter allen Umständen mehrere Stimmen zusammenklingen müssen, mag auch der greuliche Mißklang entstehen. Wenn das Cello in die Geigenregion geführt wird und eine Hornstimme genau so aussieht wie eine Bratschenstimme, so läßt sich von einer *Technik* kaum sprechen, die doch nur eine *naturgemäße* und *ökonomische* Verwendung der Kunstmittel sein darf."

and they are wrong because they—consciously or unconsciously—place him in the same camp as Mahler. Strauss has the ability to choose to do something else, while Mahler does not. Strauss errs in not taking the whole enterprise seriously enough, by using his genius simply to create games and jokes. Hirschfeld can be taken to mean that Strauss's choices are problematic because they make his music sound "Jewish." Perhaps this is why Hirschfeld asks several times in the essay, "Wollen wir feige sein?"—"Do we want to be cowards?" The message is masked, but stronger than in the *Wiener Abendpost* essay. By invoking Meyerbeer and Wagner when discussing Mahler, and then using the terms "Zerstreuung" and "ökonomisch" when discussing Strauss, Hirschfeld overtly and then subtly links his language to the image of the Jew. The difference between Strauss and Mahler, however, is that Strauss can change but Mahler cannot.

Hirschfeld believes that the current path is a dead end and despairs of it. At the end of his article, he makes reference to a "Tongemälde" by Ludwig Gruber, a "serious, sincere, and well-meant homage for the monarch." He discusses the work, describing how various effects are achieved, for example "the ringing of bells (system Gustav Mahler) should remind us of the 'Dedication of the Votivkirche.'" After invoking Mahler's name three times in relation to this work, Hirschfeld summarizes:

> The upright composer [Gruber] stands precisely on the aesthetic ground upon which our most distinguished musical spirits have trod; he places himself ethically higher, because for him it is not about jokes. He takes the matter seriously; for him it is a heartfelt need, to express himself musically. What he produced springs from a truly *naïve* soul. That too is an advantage. Mr Strauss and Mr Mahler will say: "As if he had any of our masterly technique!" … He thus lacks only the technique.[63]

In other words, the only difference between the hack Gruber and the "distinguished musical spirits" is a lack of talent. All are engaged in the same dead-end project of program music, and while Strauss and Mahler have a greater grasp of the means by which to create "Tongemälde," the project remains flawed. Hirschfeld values Gruber because "for him it is not about jokes." Gruber may not be a great composer, but his are honest deficiencies. Neither are Strauss and Mahler great composers, but for less honorable reasons: Strauss refuses to take things seriously, but Mahler, worst of all, lacks "internal necessity."

Written in 1902, Hans Liebstöckl's comparison can still serve as a summary:

---

[63]   Hirschfeld, "Mahler/Strauss," p. 540: "Der biedere Komponist steht genau auf dem ästhetischen Boden, der unsere vornehmsten musikalischen Geister betreten haben; er stellt sich ethisch höher, da es ihm nicht um Spässe zu tun ist. Er nimmt die Sache ernst; es ist ihm Herzensbedürfnis, sich musikalisch auszusprechen. Was er vorbrachte, entspringt einem wirklich naiven Gemüte. Auch das ist ein Vorzug. Die Herren Strauß und Mahler werden sagen: 'Wo hat denn der unsere Meistertechnik!'… Er hat also nur die Technik nicht."

It is already quite advisable to ascertain what differences there are between Strauss and Mahler, and therefore to prepare the material for a time that will, no doubt, attempt to answer the question some day: who of the two was the lesser. To us contemporaries, they fortunately still appear equally large, Richard somewhat more philosopher, Gustav somewhat more "of the theater," both have an outstanding capacity for orchestration, both inseparable friends of refinement, only Richard is just a little more "Will and Representation," while Gustav is somewhat more the dreamer of the Middle Ages, pre-Raphaelite, ready at any moment to sound the Knaben Wunderhorn and march into paradise.[64]

This comparison comes from a review of Mahler's Fourth Symphony, and it is not difficult to map the ideas of philosophy and theater on to the image of depth versus surface. By linking Strauss to Schopenhauer, Liebstöckl explicitly legitimizes him as the heir to German ideas—and, through Wagner, German music. Jews, of course, were thought to be great actors—"of the theater" by their very nature— because they had no self, and to be a "dreamer of the Middle Ages" was to be stylistically rootless and ahistorical, or perhaps distanced from the Will itself, what Schopenhauer identified as the source of all creativity. The stinger at the end, that Mahler is somehow hoping through his dreamy naïveté to find redemption, serves only to make sure that the reader understands who is, in fact, "der kleinere."

Contemporary Cartoons

Orchestral size was occasionally a subject for cartoons. Figure 5.1 shows Strauss atop a huge pile of instruments, animals, artillery, and other miscellaneous noisemakers—a huge saw, factories, all manner of bells (it is supposed to represent the orchestra for his opera *Elektra*, so dates from around 1909) (Figure 5.1). The whole is quite well organized (note the pigs—with strings attached to their tails— lined up by size, the various tiers divided by activity); even the bottom of the pile, the most chaotic scene, is nevertheless centered around the elephant and lion. The picture is characterized by symmetry and balance, and Strauss is in control of the entire enterprise. He stands above all the musicians, his head in the clouds, and he conducts with an expansive gesture. He seems calm in relation to what goes on

---

[64] Hans Liebstöckl (3135), p. 1: "Es ist überhaupt jetzt schon gerathen, festzustellen, welche Unterschiede zwischen Strauß und Mahler bestehen, und so das Material für eine Zeit vorzubereiten, die zweifellos einmal an die Lösung der Frage herantreten wird, wer von Beiden der kleinere war. Uns Zeitgenossen scheinen sie glücklicherweise noch gleich groß, Richard etwas mehr Philosoph, Gustav etwas mehr 'vom Theater,' Beide außerordentliche Orchestercapacitäten, Beide unzertrennliche Freunde des Raffinements, Richard nur etwas mehr 'Wille und Vorstellung,' Gustav etwas mehr Träumer vom Mittelalter, Präraphaelit, jeden Augenblick bereit, in des Knaben Wunderhorn zu stoßen und in das Paradies einzuziehen."

Figure 5.1   Strauss's Elektra orchestra, 1910, *Lustige Blätter.* Source: Kurt
              Wilhelm, *Richard Strauss persönlich: Eine Bildbiographie*
              (Munich: Kindler Verlag, 1984), p. 177.

around him, his body is relaxed, and he seems imperturbable. There is order here,
in spite of the sheer numbers and odd collection of "instruments." Compare now
the caricature of Mahler drawn after the premiere of the First Symphony in Vienna:
here all is chaotic and out of control (Figure 5.2). Mahler himself is not quite
centered and seems to be falling off the drum on which he is sitting. His coattail is
flying, his tie is askew, and his "hair" is disheveled. Drops of sweat come from his
brow—Strauss, on the other hand, is certainly not sweating and indeed gives the
impression of never having done so. (Max Graf recounts hearing Strauss conduct
Tristan "in a most thrilling way" and afterwards having a conversation with
Strauss: "'Feel me here!' Strauss said to me and placed my hand on his armpit.

Figure 5.2   Mahler's First Symphony, Theo Zasch, 1900. Source: Collection
Kaplan Foundation, New York, Kaplan, plate 285.

'Absolutely dry! I can't stand conductors who perspire!'"[65]) Although there are
fewer "instruments" in the Mahler cartoon, the effect is much more jumbled:
things overlap, they are at odd angles, and Mahler does not appear to be the master
even though he is clearly working very hard. Images from the critics' reactions to
the symphony appear here also, including "Brother Martin" of the nursery rhyme
who is sleeping (or dead? The text next makes fun of the original words, asking
instead, "Bruder Martin, lebst du noch?" [Brother Martin, do you still live?]), and
the "Kuckuck" calls in its interval of a fourth (the "Überkuckuck" Helm had called
it, because cuckoos had previously always been represented by the interval of a
minor third). Instruments are shown broken, in pieces, and the drums have holes
in them, presumably because the demands of the music have destroyed them; it
has clearly destroyed several listeners as well, who litter the bottom of the scene,
as do some "broken" notes. Whereas the Strauss scene gives the impression of

---

[65]   Max Graf, *Legend of a Musical City* (New York, 1956), p. 201; after the 1st act.

Die „Elektrische" Hinrichtung
durch den musikalischen Scharfrichter.

Figure 5.3   "The 'Elektric' Execution, by the musical executioner."[66] F. Jüttner,
1909, *Lustige Blätter.* Source: *Der zerflückte Richard Strauss:
Richard Strauss Karikaturen in Bild und Wort,* Verlag der "Lustigen
Blätter" (Berlin: Dr. Eysler & Co., G.m.b.H., 1910), p. 19.

controlled megalomania, the Mahler cartoon is sheer bedlam, and Mahler himself
seems demonic: lightning comes from his left hand which looks like a claw; he
scowls; his face drawn into a tense line (there is also a skull and crossbones on
the bell next to his head). The effect of the entire scene is threatening, even the

66   "Die 'Elektrische' Hinrichtung durch den musikalischen Scharfrichter."

instruments seemingly serving as "artillery." (Strauss, of course, has more actual artillery and it is better organized.) While the first cartoonist may not have approved of Strauss's massive orchestras, Strauss is presented as successfully pulling it together. Mahler, on the other hand, struggles and seems to fail.

A similar—if more ominous—presentation of Strauss as a megalomaniac in control of it all is shown in another cartoon spoofing *Elektra* (Figure 5.3). Here is a man being executed, his "elektric" chair made from a drum and the strings of a harp. Strauss, holding a score of his opera, is himself the executioner, blowing a trumpet onto the man's head. Lines of music spill forth, with much chromaticism and ledger lines, clearly meant to be the "elektric" shocks. Strauss again looks quite complacent and is clearly not exerting himself—he is just as calm as the condemned man is tortured. The execution is a public one, witnessed by lines of soldiers, all of whom look as calm as Strauss, the exception being one rather astonished-looking civilian. A judge holds a document, perhaps the orders for the execution. Strauss alone is responsible for the death, although he clearly receives support from the soldiers. No one threatens his authority and he is dressed quite smartly, appearing to have awards or medals on his coat. The pun on "Elektra/Elektrisch" serves to place musical modernism on the same level as technological advances—it was also during this time that electric shocks were proposed as cures for neurasthenia and other nervous diseases.[67] Strauss himself, of course, does not need this treatment but only dispenses it to the unwilling public. Whereas Strauss's "elektricity" is directed, even meant to kill, Mahler's lightening in Figure 5.2 simply goes astray, zooming about harum-scarum, thus potentially more dangerous.

A third cartoon about *Elektra* is titled "Ein furchtbares Paar" [A Scary Pair] (Figure 5.4). Both Hugo von Hofmannstahl (the librettist for *Elektra*) and Strauss are shown beating up Sophocles, whose original play becomes the basis for their opera. Sophocles is clearly getting the better of Hofmannstahl, but Strauss has the upper hand and is ready to beat him over the head with a drumstick. Strauss dominates both the scene and Sophocles—one foot is on Sophocles's back and the other steps on the tragedian's toga, pinning him down. Hofmannstahl appears to be losing the battle and is listing to one side (Sophocles is biting his hand as well). Again, like his role as executioner in the previous cartoon, Strauss is the aggressor, he alone seems to be inflicting harm. He is also simultaneously thumping Sophocles on the head while manipulating the drum and cymbals—a one-man band of pain.

---

[67] Richard von Krafft-Ebing, *Text-Book of Insanity, Based on Clinical Observations: For Practitioners and Students of Medicine*, trans. Charles Gilbert Chaddock, M.D. (Philadelphia, 1905; orig. German edn 1879), p. 451: "Among physical remedies the most important place is to be given to fresh air (sojourn in the mountains), hydrotherapy, rubbings, half-baths, river and sea bathing, and electricity (general faradization, electric baths)." See also Tom Lutz, *American Nervousness, 1903: An Anecdotal History* (Ithaca, 1991), pp. 47–8 on the use of electricity as a cure in the American context.

Ein furchtbares Paar.

Wen der erste — „bearbeitet" hat, den „vertont"
sofort der zweite!

Figure 5.4   "A Scary Pair. Once the first has—'*adapted,*' then immediately the
second '*sets to music!*'"[68] 1910, Stein, *Lustige Blätter*. Source: *Der
zerflückte Richard Strauss*, p. 18.

   In a final cartoon, both Strauss and Mahler—in addition to Arnold Rosé
and Arnold Schoenberg—are represented, and, at first glance, it seems to indict
everyone with equal malice (Figure 5.5). The scene is chaotic, similar to Figure
5.2, with the obligatory animals, weapons, bells, an anvil, and even a pair of
dancing Indians—certainly a comment on the "savagery" or "primitivism" of the
supposed "music." Three people struggle to play an enormous harp, and Rosé

---

   [68]   "Ein furchtbares Paar. Wen der erste—'*bearbeitet*' hat, den '*vertont*' sofort der
zweite!"

Figure 5.5   Strauss, Mahler, Schoenberg, and Rosé, *Illustrirtes Wiener Extrablatt*, 21 March 1907. Source: Collection Kaplan Foundation, New York, Kaplan, plate 295.

(the concertmaster of the Hofoper orchestra and the Philharmonic) plays a double violin with two bows. A train chugs along in the background, a cat tweeks the tail of a pig as cows, a dog, and an elephant all contribute to the clamor. Both Rosé and Schoenberg are sweating, although Schoenberg is shown "playing" the sewing machine, a feminizing gesture emphasized by Schoenberg's wary glance at the singing dog. Schoenberg's exertion and discomfort seem out of proportion to his actions—can playing the sewing machine really be that stressful? The dog, it seems, ignores him completely. (The man "playing" the elephant seems to have a more legitimate reason to sweat profusely.) Mahler, in fact, is the only one *not* sweating in this picture. Mahler is in the position of conductor, and he twirls a ratchet above his head while simultaneously lighting a large bomb upon which he is sitting. He is the only one in the picture who is performing an overtly self-destructive act, albeit, one could argue, potentially detrimental for the entire ensemble. Mahler may be as the conductor, but he cannot be said to be leading the ensemble in any meaningful way—he does not even have the correct tool with which to control the cacophony before him. Mahler does not work hard and he is making poor choices, choices that will affect everyone. Strauss, on the other hand, pounds the "public" with a pile driver. As in Figures 5.3 and 5.4, Strauss is the aggressor, which, when placed against Mahler's suicidal gesture, gives the impression that Strauss can make choices and act on them while never harming himself in any way. (In both, we saw that Strauss is not above harming others.)

However, unlike the cool, collected Strauss shown in Figure 5.3, here Strauss does sweat—but then again, unlike Mahler, Schoenberg, or Rosé, Strauss is the only one who is doing "real" work.

In these cartoons, unlike the cartoons of Mahler discussed here and in Chapter 4, Strauss is in control. Like the critics who despise his means but grant him autonomy, the cartoonists simultaneously praise and berate Strauss. In all the cartoons, Strauss makes the decisions, has a method, carries out a plan. The cartoons celebrate Strauss's perceived megalomania, implying that he could make different choices while bemoaning the fact that he does not.

Bruckner in Vienna

By focusing on reviews that specifically compared Strauss to Mahler, I have tried to show that, within that dichotomy, Strauss had to be saved from the taint of Jewishness. Those musical choices that seemed to evoke Wagner's categories were defensively explained away. Yet the situation in Vienna was complicated by the overlay of political ideas with musical criticism. As we have seen, critics such as Helm or Hirschfeld could write very differently depending on their audience. Therefore, one cannot assume that any given review necessarily reveals the proclivities of the critic. The musical split of absolute vs. program music was another complicating factor, since it did not easily map itself onto the political—or musical–political—situation in Vienna. The strong presence of Hanslick for so many years and the central position that his treatise *Vom Musikalisch-Schönen* [On the Musically Beautiful] holds historically and aesthetically even today has tended to obscure the other fault lines that ran through Vienna and divided critics.[69] Context therefore becomes all the more important when attempting interpret any given review, for in Vienna, the most musical of cities, critics were pulled in many directions, not all of them musical.

The problem, particularly in Vienna, was exacerbated by the rise of Anton Bruckner during the late 1880s and early 1890s: in many ways it is the figure of Bruckner who explains the inconsistencies and problems in Strauss reception, at least in the Habsburg capital. While Bruckner remained largely unknown outside Vienna during this time, in the city itself he had many ardent followers who actively

---

[69] On the Viennese political situation, see, for example, Carl E. Schorske, *Fin-de-siècle Vienna: Politics and Culture* (New York, 1981); John W. Boyer, *Culture and Political Crisis in Vienna: Christian Socialism in Power, 1897–1918* (Chicago, 1995); William J. McGrath, *Dionysian Art and Populist Politics in Austria* (New Haven and London, 1974); Margaret Notley, "Brahms as Liberal: Genre, Style, and Politics in Late Nineteenth-century Vienna," *19th-Century Music* 17 (1993), pp. 107–23; Brigitte Hamann, *Hitler's Vienna: A Dictator's Apprenticeship* (New York and Oxford, 1999); and Ryan R. Kangas, "Remembering Mahler: Music and Memory in Mahler's Early Symphonies," PhD diss., University of Texas at Austin, 2009, esp. pp. 21–7.

worked to program his music and to advance his cause. The Wiener Akademische Wagner-Verein was formed in 1872 to promote the works of Richard Wagner, but also those of Hugo Wolf and Anton Bruckner.[70] The brothers Josef and Franz Schalk, along with Ferdinand Löwe and the friends and pupils of the composer, sought, particularly after Wagner's death, to promote Bruckner as the rightful heir to the German mantle and to emphasize the many ties between the two.[71] Josef Schalk in particular was influential in forging this connection, in part by fabricating anecdotes to show that Wagner not only recognized Bruckner's genius but wanted to help him.[72]

As can be seen from Table 5.3 below, Bruckner's works also had a tortured beginning in Vienna, taking more than 30 years to receive their first performances in the Habsburg capital. Bruckner's position at the Vienna University, however, guaranteed him a small but loyal following of students, many of whom actively worked to promote his music. August Göllerich, for example, claimed to have converted Theodor Helm to Bruckner's cause in 1883, although it may have been a performance of the String Quintet that secured Helm's advocacy.[73] In 1886 Helm contributed a biographical article on Bruckner to the *Musikalisches Wochenblatt*. Commenting on the fact that Bruckner was now at work on his Eighth Symphony, Helm wrote: "This unbroken and tireless freshness in creation, this ceaseless devotion to an artistic genre chosen as a favorite form, with such relatively little outward recognition, speaks for the inner necessity of the composer, for his true calling." Helm went on to compare Bruckner to the deaf Beethoven and to quote Wagner's *Beethoven* essay; Wagner himself was mentioned with regard to the "inner necessity" of creating the *Ring* without hope of performance.[74] When Helm's Strauss criticism is viewed in light of his championing of Bruckner, his 1892 dismissal of Strauss as "a musical Makart of the first rank" can be seen not as a rejection of program music or the New German school—or as evidence that Helm was a Hanslickian in disguise—but rather as an indication that, in

---

[70] Andrea Harrandt, "Students and Friends as 'Prophets' and 'Promoters': The Reception of Bruckner's Works in the Wiener Akademische Wagner-Verein," in *Perspectives on Anton Bruckner*, ed. Crawford Howie, Paul Hawkshaw, and Timothy Jackson (Aldershot, 2001), pp. 317–27.

[71] Thomas Leibnitz, "Anton Bruckner and 'German' Music': Josef Schalk and the Establishment of Bruckner as a National Composer," in *Perspectives on Anton Bruckner*, pp. 328–40.

[72] Margaret Notley, "Bruckner and Viennese Wagnerism," in *Bruckner Studies*, ed. Timothy L. Jackson and Paul Hawkshaw (Cambridge, 1997), pp. 54–71, at p. 56.

[73] Helm wrote a review of the String Quintet in the *Musikalisches Wochenblatt* 15 (1884), pp. 296–7; cited in Notley, "Bruckner and Viennese Wagnerism," p. 63. It is worth pointing out that Helm's conversion experience with the quintet is similar to Wagner's conversion to late Beethoven following a performance of Op. 131 by the Chevelliard Quartet in 1853.

[74] Notley, "Bruckner and Viennese Wagnerism," pp. 63–4.

Table 5.3   Viennese Premieres of Bruckner's Symphonies (orchestral versions)

Work	Conductor	Viennese premiere[a]	Comments
Symphony no. 1	Richter	13 Dec. 1891	Wiener Fassung; Musikvereinsaal, Vienna Philharmonic
Symphony no. 2	Bruckner	26 Oct. 1873	1872 version; Vienna Philharmonic
	Bruckner	20 Feb. 1876	1876 version; Musikvereinsaal, Gesellschaftskonzert (revised 1877)
	Richter	25 Nov. 1894	Print version; Musikvereinsaal, Vienna Philharmonic
Symphony no. 3	Bruckner	16 Dec. 1877	2nd version; Musikvereinsaal, Gesellschafts-Orchester
	Richter	21 Dec. 1890	1889 version; Vienna Philharmonic
Symphony no. 4	Richter	20 Feb. 1881[b]	2nd version; Musikvereinsaal, Vienna Philharmonic
	Richter	22 Feb. 1888	3rd version; Musikvereinsaal, Vienna Philharmonic
Symphony no. 5	Mahler	24 Feb. 1901	Vienna Philharmonic
Symphony no. 6	Mahler	26 Feb. 1899	Vienna Philharmonic (w/cuts)
	Jahn	11 Feb. 1883	2nd and 3rd mvts only, Musikvereinsaal, Vienna Philharmonic
Symphony no. 7	Richter	21 Mar. 1886	Vienna Philharmonic (?)
Symphony no. 8	Richter	18 Dec. 1892	2nd version; Musikvereinsaal, Vienna Philharmonic
Symphony no. 9	Löwe	11 Feb. 1903	Löwe version; Musikvereinsaal, Wiener Konzertvereinsorchester

Source: *Anton Bruckner: Ein Handbuch*, ed. Uwe Harten et al. (Salzburg and Vienna, 1996).

[a]   Order of Viennese premieres: 2, 3, 4, 7, 1, 8, 6, 5, 9.
[b]   10 Dec. 1881, first performance of a Bruckner symphony in Germany (Felix Mottl in Karlsruhe, Fourth Symphony).

Vienna at least, there was a "third way." Once Mahler came to Vienna and began performing his own symphonies, Helm's advocacy of Strauss became more pronounced, albeit never uncritical.

Part of the attraction of Bruckner and his music was his perseverance in the face of obstacles. Josef Schalk, in an article from 1885, asked, "how is it possible that in our musically blessed age that an artist of such significance could remain unrecognized into his sixties?" Ultimately, Schalk thought he could answer this question:

> It may, after all, have been an impediment to the appreciation of Bruckner that his music is more German than anything else that we have had until now in purely instrumental music. To be sure, not more German than Bach or Beethoven in so far as their basic character and that of their work is concerned, but more German in the form of expression ... To be German means, as our Master [Wagner] splendidly explained: to do a thing for its own sake.[75]

The co-opting of Bruckner by the German nationalists was the product of many factors: the association of the Liberal party in Vienna with the Jewish bourgeoisie; the strong ties between Brahms and the Liberals; the subsequent decline of the Liberals after the institution of universal (male) suffrage; the appeal that Bruckner's humble background—real or imagined—had for the new socialist parties; the "resurgence of Catholicism" as a political and cultural force in Vienna; and the rise of Georg von Schönerer and his Pan-German party on their platform of antisemitism. Bruckner thus appealed at once to the political left and right. "Bruckner emerged repeatedly from the Wagnerites' interpretation as the quintessential 'German' composer," and in Vienna, with its ethnic and linguistic mix of an enormous empire, the problem of defining "Was ist deutsch?" took on new meaning. "Bruckner's background and personality, as described by most commentators, perfectly matched Wagner's 'German' archetype": he was from the country not the city; he exhibited the depth of feeling and creativity required; his Catholic spirituality emphasized morality over intellect.[76] Bruckner also appeared to uphold one of Wagner's most important tenets: in "On German Music," an earlier essay written in Paris, Wagner had written, "The German is capable of writing music merely for himself and friend, uncaring if it will ever be executed for a public."[77] Bruckner seemed, at least on the outside, to persevere in writing music despite every possible obstacle. Bruckner made even Beethoven seem self-serving. Bruckner was a thus perfect figurehead because his lack of personal influence or important contacts meant that his music and actions could be interpreted by others, while his own desperation for getting

---

[75] Ibid., p. 65.

[76] Ibid., p. 62.

[77] Wagner, "On German Music," *Richard Wagner's Prose Works*, vol. 7, p. 85; the article, "De la musique allemande" was originally published in the *Gazette Musicale* on 12 and 26 July 1840. Ellis identifies this as Wagner's earliest contribution to the journal.

his music performed—neatly ignored by those choosing to promote his music for political ends—meant that he was willing to follow where others led, regardless of his own personal feelings toward their politics.

There has been a tendency to assume that absolute vs. program music was an inviolate pair, stable and interpretable in musical terms as conservative vs. progressive. The ascendance of Bruckner and the claims made for the "Germanness" of his music meant that the Hanslickian dichotomy of absolute vs. program music no longer signified a certain type of musical and political allegiance. Therefore, before 1900 in Vienna, Strauss's early tone poems were viewed through the lens not of the New German school and its ideologies—which would have typically seen them as a continuation of the Liszt–Wagner line—but rather through the lens of the absolute music of Bruckner. Max Graf wrote in 1946 that, "Strauss entered Viennese musical life when the great Brahms and Bruckner epoch had come to an end ... and with [the deaths of] these two symphonists, classical music itself terminated."[78] The situation changed when Mahler, himself identified as a student of Bruckner, arrived on the scene and began to produce his own symphonies and to champion performances of Bruckner's.[79] The problem was not just the choices that Strauss made, but Mahler's as well. Arthur Schnitzler summed up the situation very nicely in around 1904 in a passage that, I would argue, only makes sense if we recognize the invisible presence of Bruckner:

> If you didn't know which, Mahler or Richard Strauss, was the Jew, you would certainly think that the erotic exuberant sensuality, the unbridled oriental imagination, the taste for extraneous effect and ... the skill [Strauss] applies to the economic exploitation of his talent were properly Semitic characteristics. In contrast one takes Mahler, a man of mystic ruminations ... the chaste Wunderhorn singer ... the folk-based composer ... idealistic ... the perfect type of German artist.[80]

In other words, had Mahler chosen to designate his works as symphonic poems or even to write in another genre entirely, the music of Strauss would not have been perceived to be nearly as problematic. If both composers wrote program music, then Strauss could simply be shown to be the better. The size of his orchestras; the attempt to depict realistically and in great detail his stories, high or low; the apparent inconsistency between his ideas and the means—none of these would have mattered. But Mahler wrote symphonies and Strauss wrote "Jewish" music— and Bruckner was the one who made any simple binary opposition impossible.

---

[78] Graf, *Legend of a Musical City*, p. 203.

[79] See my "'Polemik im Conzertsaal': Mahler, Beethoven, and the Viennese Critics," *19th-Century Music* 29 (2006), pp. 289–321 for a discussion of Mahler's performances of Bruckner with the Philharmonic.

[80] Norman Lebrecht, *Mahler Remembered* (New York, 1987), p. xxii.

Strauss after Mahler

For the first fifty years of his long life Richard Strauss enjoyed success on a scale that has been granted to few composers in their youth and middle years. In 1885, at the age of only twenty-one, he was engaged as assistant at Meiningen to the greatest conductor of the day, Hans von Bülow, and from that auspicious start he seemed to float from one favored position to another with a nonchalance that was to desert him only in Germany's hour of reckoning in 1945. In 1886 he was appointed junior *Kapellmeister* at the Opera of his native city, Munich. By the age of twenty-five he had already conducted at Bayreuth and become a protégé of Cosima Wagner. By 1897 he had appeared with triumphant success in most of the capitals of Western Europe, and in the following year he was appointed Royal Prussian Court Conductor in Berlin, a position he held until the collapse of the Hohenzollern monarchy in 1918. Measured by standards such as these, the careers of Herbert von Karajan and Leonard Bernstein are tortoise-like.

But Strauss's early development as a composer was even more phenomenal. By the time he was thirty, three symphonic poems, *"Don Juan," "Tod und Verklärung"* and *"Till Eulenspiegel,"* had brought him world-wide fame, and *"Don Quixote," "Also Sprach Zarathustra"* and *"Ein Heldenleben"* followed in quick succession before the turn of the century. Indeed by 1898 the Dutch, a stolid people not given to snap judgments, had erased the name of poor Gounod from the roll of honour on the pillars of the Amsterdam Concertgebouw and, in its place, alongside the names of Wagner and Liszt, had inscribed that of Strauss. By the turn of the century Strauss was established as the most recent member of that long illustrious line of composers that reached back to Haydn and Mozart and had for well over a century maintained Austro-German hegemony over the musical world.[81]

Any discussion of the reception of Strauss's works has to take into account not just the composer's meteoric rise but also his catastrophic fall, and one will assume that I am referring here either to his retreat from modernism or to his support of the Nazi regime. Yet, although those events have received quite a bit of attention, the truth is that Strauss was a profound disappointment to many long before he wrote *Der Rosenkavalier*. Perhaps it was inevitable: who could have possibly lived up to, let alone continued, such spectacular early progress? Yet Strauss presented a different kind of problem for critics, not just in the genres he chose (he was after all composing program music), but in his musical style and manner as well. Whereas when he first appeared on the scene, he seemed to be the shining example of the future, he consistently made choices that foiled the expectations of the critics. He also made no attempt to hide his desire for money or to deny that

---

[81]   Peter Heyworth, "The Rise & Fall of Richard Strauss," *Encounter* 31/2 (Aug. 1968), pp. 49–53; quote is p. 49.

monetary gain was his primary concern—a concern that in and of itself may have seemed "Jewish."[82] This problem was summed up by Richard Eichenauer, in his book of 1932, *Music and Race*, where he remarked that: "Strauss typifies how difficult it is in our modern times to equate the physical appearance of a composer with his music. According to this, [Strauss] is predominantly Nordic, but who is brave enough to claim this with regard to his music?"[83] Whether this statement indicates that Strauss was believed to have fallen victim to modern times, to have followed the wrong path, or simply to have been a profound disappointment, it demonstrates that musically and aesthetically he was somehow considered a failure, despite outward success. I suggest that certain musical characteristics were viewed negatively because of their resonance with the language of Wagner's essay, and that Strauss's music was too close to *Judentum* for critical comfort.

However disappointing Strauss may have been during Mahler's lifetime, his greatest sins were yet to come. As John Deathridge has recently written, using Strauss's own words against him:

> In order to assuage real fears about the provocative modernity of *Salome*, Strauss is said to have jocularly described it to skeptical orchestral musicians shortly before its first performance in 1905 as a "scherzo with a fatal conclusion." Over forty years later, the remark could have applied to Strauss himself, though hardly in a jocular sprit.[84]

While Deathridge is, of course, hinting at Strauss's collaboration with the Nazis, one could certainly call the entire last 40 years of Strauss's life a "fatal conclusion." Indeed, Deathridge marvels at "the idea that Strauss, who before the First World War was once modern, could be accepted by the *new* Nazi order precisely because he had sidestepped the disruptive modernity of the 1920s by bringing, in the name of an *old*, good and supposedly healthy modernity, a phase of musical history to culmination, and with it a steady state of continuing cultural solidarity."[85] Many have attempted to explain—or explain away—Strauss's turn from modernism after *Salome* and *Elektra*, a move that is startling not least because those operas had been so successful. Indeed, when Kaiser Wilhelm II remarked that *Salome* (which he had never heard) would be harmful to Strauss, Strauss answered: "The

---

[82]   See, for example, the information provided in Scott Allan Warfield, "The Genesis of Richard Strauss's *Macbeth*," PhD diss., The University of North Carolina at Chapel Hill, 1995.

[83]   Cited in Erik Levy, *Music in the Third Reich* (London, 1994), p. 223.

[84]   John Deathridge, "Richard Strauss and the Broken Dream of Modernity," in *Richard Strauss und die Moderne: Bericht über das Internationale Symposium München, 21. bis 23 July 1999*, ed. Bernd Edelmann et al. (Berlin, 2001), pp. 79–92; quote is p. 81.

[85]   Ibid., p. 84.

harm it did me enabled me to build my villa in Garmisch."[86] Why would he, a man always in it for the money, turn away from something so financially successful?

While there have been many attempts to explain Strauss's musical choices after *Salome* and *Elektra*, Sander Gilman's reading of this moment in Strauss's career is particularly pertinent in the context of the present discussion. Gilman is interested in how the opera *Salome* involves overlapping stereotypes of homosexuality and eastern Jews:

> In choosing to set Oscar Wilde's play, Strauss draws on a fundamental ambiguity in German-Jewish self-understanding during the *fin-de-siècle*. He clearly plays on the increased popularity of Wilde's work, a popularity fostered by Wilde's iconic role among the German avant-garde. But he also echoes the association between the Jews, as defenders of homosexual emancipation, and the "perverted" text of *Salome*. The association of degeneration in Jews and homosexuals creates a category that Strauss's idealized "liberal" (read: Jewish) audience could have understood as the biological result of social prejudice. But they would also have distanced anti-Semitic charges concerning their own perverted nature by projecting these charges onto a subgroup, the Eastern Jews, just as [Karl] Kraus read Wilde's representation of the "Jews" as a discussion of the "Pharisees"... The conflation of "Oriental" and "Eastern" was one that acculturated Western Jews of the *fin-de-siècle* made easily ... it was the Jews from the East, the embodiment of the anti-Semitic caricatures that haunted the dreams of the assimilated Jews.[87]

Gilman contends that Strauss chose his libretto in a very calculating way, taking into account not just the popularity of Wilde's play in Germany but the possibilities of the work as a "Judenoper," an opera that would be read as Jewish not just because of its subject matter but also because of its treatment by Strauss. By manipulating the "self-hating model of Jewish identity with its pathological image of the Eastern Jew," Strauss creates an opera that "fulfills all the necessary categories for acceptance by this idealized, self-hating audience." Indeed, Strauss himself claimed that his interest in *Salome* came from his belief that "operas based on oriental and Jewish subjects lacked true oriental colour and scorching sun," something that he presumably believed that he could bring to the topic.[88]

Strauss's turn away from modernism, according to Gilman, was a direct result of his success in creating a "Judenoper." By appealing to the ambiguous, self-hating position of the Jewish avant-garde, he guaranteed not just financial success

_____

    [86]   Michael Kennedy, *Richard Strauss: Man, Musician, Enigma* (Cambridge, 1999), p. 150.

    [87]   Sander L. Gilman, "Strauss and the Pervert," in *Reading Opera*, ed. Arthur Groos and Roger Parker (Princeton, 1988), pp. 306–27; quote is p. 325.

    [88]   Richard Strauss, *Recollections and Reflections*, ed. Willi Schuh, trans. L.J. Lawrence (London et al., 1953), p. 150.

but a position for himself as the leader of that avant-garde. His success was thus not only beyond "his wildest expectations," but also not without costs:

> Strauss, the arch-manipulator of audiences, had been overtaken by events: he had become, against his will, a "Jewish" composer, a "pervert." The financial and artistic breakthrough of *Salome* was achieved with a double-edged sword. He had conquered the avant-garde; but in doing so he had engendered a "perverted" creation from which—protest as he might—he could not distance himself.[89]

As testimony to just how well Strauss was able to manipulate "Jewish" tropes, Günther's treatise on the "racial anthropology" of the Jews uses none other than the Jews' quintet from *Salome* as its example of "the musical representation of the Mauscheln of excited Jews."[90]

Whether one accepts Gillman's argument or not, it must be conceded that it explains Strauss's bizarre actions quite well—Strauss not only turned his back on the high modernist style but abandoned it completely. Igor Stravinsky, a fellow modernist, had called "the infinity of possibilities" presented by modernism "the abyss of freedom." Strauss, with *Elektra* and *Salome*, had looked into the abyss, but then he walked away: he preferred not "to drown in the infinite."[91] He never again was to write anything that could be taken either as modernist—or "oriental" or "Jewish." Yet even if Strauss's own actions remain a mystery, there seems to be no doubt that critics were ambivalent at best, and, at worst, seemed to believe that Strauss's choices were wrong precisely because they were "un-German." The power of Wagner's language had always been its lack of specificity; that it could be turned against the composer who began his career as Wagner's heir-apparent is but one of the many ironies of fin-de-siècle antisemitism.

---

[89] Gilman, "Strauss," p. 327.

[90] Hans F.K. Günther, *Rassenkunde des jüdischen Volkes*, 2nd edn (Munich, 1930; 1st edn 1922), p. 255: "Richard Strauß hat in seiner 'Salome' im Streitgespräche der fünf Juden versucht, das Mauscheln erregter Juden tonkünstlerische darzustellen."

[91] William W. Austin, *Music in the 20th Century: From Debussy through Stravinsky* (New York, 1966), pp. 38, 33, and 139. Austin uses Stravinsky's metaphor (from *Poétique musicale*, 1942; trans. as *Poetics of Music*) throughout his book as a way to discuss various composers' reactions to modernism.

Chapter 6
Eine musikalische Physiognomik

An Uncomfortable Journey

Recently, I flew from one major US city to another and happened to be seated in the first exit row—always nice for a little extra legroom. Of course, the best part is that the seats in front of you cannot recline, so that you will not have your tray table pressed against your face at some point during the flight. As the plane filled, a clearly frazzled couple with two child seats and a toddler sat in the row in front of me. The husband, with one car seat, sat on the A/B side of the plane, while the wife, with the other seat and the toddler, sat on the D/E/F side of the MD-80.

A flight attendant soon came forward: "Oh, I am so sorry, but child seats cannot be used in [the row in front of the exit row]. Let me see if I can find you other seats."

The exhausted couple looked at each other, then at the flight attendant, and, with effort, made ready to move. The flight attendant went to the row directly in front of them. "Can this whole row move back one row? We need a row that can accommodate car seats."

Most of the row began to gather their belongings, but an older man in seat D refused: "No. I will be further from my wife," he stated, flatly refusing to budge; his wife, apparently, was in the seat in front of him. Sheesh, I was thinking, what's the difference if you are one or two seats behind her? It is hardly a transcontinental— or transatlantic—flight! (I never saw Seat D speak a single word to his wife during the entire trip.)

The now clearly harassed flight attendant eventually found a row willing to move: two friends or perhaps new acquaintances traveling together with three young boys between them. They looked to be in their late 30s. As the great migration began to take place, Seat D looked smugly up at the flight attendant: "It's because they always travel with so much luggage." The flight attendant made some vague comment about "the rules." Seat D nodded, watching with apparent distaste.

The transfer achieved, the 30-something men made comments throughout the flight, comments that, sitting a row behind and a seat to the left, I found easy to hear. What particularly bothered them was one man who kept leaving his seat to come and visit the couple. "This guy thinks he's in charge, huh?" was a typical comment. The man was certainly not the only one who, from several rows up, would come back to chat with the couple, who, with newborn babies, could hardly move themselves. One young woman I took to be an older daughter. Others seemed to be relatives or friends. It became clear that this was a family and friends group, traveling together to some function important to all of them.

Interestingly, despite the almost constant commentary on the couple, the group in general, and the one man in particular, one incident did impress the two 30-something guys: the husband's speed and efficiency with which he changed one of the baby's diapers. This event caused them to reminisce about their own diaper changing days and about the seeming impossibility of doing so in an airplane bathroom.

It should be clear, occurring as it does at the end of book on antisemitism, that the group was Jewish, probably modern orthodox. Many of the men wore no beards, although all wore regular black suits and some form of head covering. In one or two cases, the fringes of the prayer shawl were visible below the tail of the coat, but this was not the rule. One young man even had quite long hair and wore a green yarmulke, perhaps with the Israeli Army anagram on it. The wife had her hair covered, but this was not a startling group of Hassidim whose dress would have stood out starkly from the rest of the passengers. Only the men's head coverings, I believe, "gave them away."

For me, the two-and-a-half-hour flight was excruciating. Several things struck me during that awful time. First, that the Jew is still recognizable, and subject to the same ridicule that they have endured for centuries. Yet if this had been an obvious—say, in matching T-shirts—church or athletic group traveling in such a manner, it would hardly have caused a comment (except perhaps pride). Second, how is it possible, in an age when cultural difference is front-page news, that such language is not only accepted, but even encouraged? Had the flight attendant really missed Seat D's slur, or was she ideologically on his side? Third, I find it remarkable that the same Jewish canards (obsession with moveable goods, acquisition of wealth, clannishness, haughtiness) are not only still common currency but also recognized and unchanged.

The image that bothered me the most, however, involved the ire caused by the one man who visited the couple most frequently. I finally realized that the 30-somethings' fear was really fear of Jewish control. Although almost every flight has one or two people who will get up and walk around (or must walk around, due to medical conditions), in this case, he was seen to be "checking in" on everyone. While I cannot know either the dynamics of the Jewish group or what was really going through the minds of the 30-somethings, it seemed that they wanted to say, "Who does he think he is?" or "Minorities should know their place—and sit down!" Oddly, their own moment of bonding with the husband revolved around the changing of a diaper: surely a feminizing act if there ever was one.

Mahler Today

In Marc Weiner's brilliant book, *Richard Wagner and the Anti-Semitic Imagination*, he closes his introduction with two interlocking and disconcerting questions: "What if the meaning behind those corporeal icons has not completely vanished over time? That is, do today's scholars and audiences *continue* to respond to the nineteenth-century ideology associated with these images, even as they refuse to acknowledge their implications?"[1] Similarly, the question haunting *this* book is the extent to which we have allowed our own reactions to Mahler and his music to be controlled by the discourse of his earliest critics, a discourse that was antisemitic in the sense that it was framed by a community that simply expected Mahler to look, act, conduct, and compose differently from a German composer.

My question, therefore, is whether we have thought enough about the way in which the language we use to talk about Mahler's music shapes what we hear in it? Do we understand where this vocabulary comes from? Are we willing to continue to use it, despite its origins? Would we be willing to start over, rethink the categories, and approach his music from a new angle? Are we willing, in the end, to address the question of the difference between what "hearing" Mahler meant in Vienna in 1900 and what it means today?

Henry-Louis de La Grange seems to be pondering a similar idea:

> If music critics could consign to oblivion music they considered unworthy of survival, Mahler's music would have been finally forgotten long ago, for the "infernal judges" of his time were almost unanimous in finding him guilty of unforgivable faults. Their verdict was delivered in tones ranging from the most sarcastic irony to violent indignation, but the substance was always the same: such "Kapellmeistermusik," consisting exclusively of "banalities" and "reminiscences" of the past, was clearly fated to be soon forgotten, since its author revealed in it nothing so much as a total lack of melodic imagination. The severest judges went so far as to call Mahler's symphonies "gigantic pot-pourris."[2]

While de La Grange is here referring to critics from the earlier part of the century, one can find these same characteristics mentioned in more modern scholarly works. With the exception of his orchestration, every aspect of Mahler's style seems to make critics uncomfortable, demanding that they explain it away or at least attempt to contextualize it. For example, in a small book intended as an overview of Mahler's works, Deryck Cooke calls Mahler "a composer *sui generis*," and singles out his orchestration as "his most admired feature [which] ... speaks for itself."[3] Nevertheless:

---

[1]   Marc Wiener, *Richard Wagner and the Anti-Semitic Imagination* (Lincoln and London), p. 30.

[2]   Henry-Louis de La Grange, "Music about Music in Mahler: Reminiscences, Allusions, or Quotations?" in *Mahler Studies*, ed. Stephen E. Hefling (Cambridge, 1997), pp. 122–68; quote is p. 122.

[3]   Deryck Cooke, *Gustav Mahler: An Introduction to IIis Music*, 2nd edn (Cambridge, 1988), pp. 10 and 14. Cooke is perhaps best known for put together a performing edition of movements one and three of Mahler's Tenth Symphony, a work which was incomplete at Mahler's death in 1911. He is thus regarded as one of the most important Mahler scholars and the one most familiar with his style.

His adoption of many different styles to suit his expressive purpose ... led early critics to declare that he had no style of his own at all. But he redeemed any borrowings by imprinting his personality vividly on practically every note. In any case, most of his material is the undeniable product of his own fantastic invention ... there is the Austrian folk style, ingrained from childhood, and also derived through Schubert and Bruckner. Then there is the Faustian element, the yearning for fullness of being: an individual modification of Wagner's soaring melody and chromatic harmony. Next, discouragement, 'the spirit that denies,' tormented despair, and the terror of death: here the quintessential Mahler appears, throwing grisly shadows across the music of life's joy, distorting it, disintegrating it with hideous chromaticisms and grotesque orchestration ...

Above all, there is the astounding originality of the purely Mahlerian elements: the aforesaid 'distortion' music; the elemental voices of nature, mysterious and lonely, or brutally ferocious; the cosmic power of the funeral march; the sheer horror of some of the scherzos; the bounding ebullience of some of the Ländler; the exultant stride of the triumphal marches; the ecstatic outbursts of jubilation. These unique conceptions stamp Mahler as a highly original genius.[4]

The problem is threefold: Mahler borrows melodic material from other composers, he composes in many different styles, and he attempts to weld all this together by sheer force of personality. Cooke clearly believes that these quirks can only be understood in terms of Mahler's biography, that the problem emerges from a "struggle with fate," his "inner conflict,"[5] but regardless of where it originates, a biographical explanation is clearly necessary. And anyway, if he did borrow, he imprinted the material with his own original style, and even so, he really did not borrow that much!

Perhaps it will be argued that I am "picking" on Cooke. I am not. I chose Cooke for the respect that he demands and his stature in the field of Mahler studies. Yet I could choose almost anyone to "pick" on, and it would be equally unfair: all scholars writing about Mahler are writing as they have been trained. One cannot be criticized for that.

One might legitimately ask, with de La Grange, why it is that we cling to the language of the early critics, language that was seeped in a culture that is no longer our own and where each critic attempted to score "political points" with their constituency by "calling out" Mahler's race and thus his deficiencies. As discussed in Chapter 1, listening is not a neutral experience, but a learned one. If Mahler's melodies are described as "eclectic" universally by these critics, then *some*thing has to be going on, right? Wrong. Reception history only tangentially concerns the music and, in the case of Mahler, was often concerned with finding

---

4   Ibid., pp. 13–14.
5   Ibid., pp. 14 and 9.

signs of his "race." But how did *that* language become *the* language with which to discuss Mahler?

I suspect that it would require another study, perhaps another book, to answer that question. Certainly some of the critics (Max Graf, for example) emigrated to the United States. Others, teachers, musicians, scholars, also left, fleeing Hitler or the coming war. Books were written; positions in colleges and universities were found—it is not hard to imagine how ideas born in Vienna could eventually reappear and become current in America. Yet I am only speculating. It would require far more knowledge than I currently possess to track down the careers and endeavors of those influential in Mahler's life and criticism to the United States after his death.

I do agree, however, that the work of the philosopher and music critic Theodor W. Adorno has had a profound effect on Mahler scholarship. In his monograph on Mahler, and in an essay written slightly later, Adorno attempts to explain the elements of Mahler's style as a commentary on the social situation at the end of the nineteenth century. Adorno sees music as a manifestation of society and reads into it a history of social progress or regress. According to Adorno, Mahler's inability to synthesize diverse materials becomes evidence that Mahler was in fact responding to his surroundings. Adorno states quite boldly that Mahler's music cannot be judged in terms of its "originality," at least as that term had been defined since the early nineteenth century.[6] Mahler's themes "are frequently borrowed or else open to the accusation of banality." Mahler's music rebels against the "norms of a fastidious musical culture," and therein lies the problem for the critics:

> Mahler's music shakes the foundations of a self-assured aesthetic order in which an infinity is enclosed within a finite totality. It knows moments of breakthrough, of collapse, of episodes which make themselves autonomous, and finally, of disintegration into centrifugal complexes. In its attitude toward form it is recklessly advanced, despite a harmonic, melodic and colouristic stock-in-trade which seems downright conservative when set beside Strauss or Reger.[7]

Yet, for Adorno, these "failures" are precisely what makes Mahler's music great:

> But what the apostles of authenticity really hold against Mahler, namely his thoroughgoing discontinuity, the musical non-identity with whatever stands behind it, emerges now as a necessary development. *Weltschmerz*, the disharmony between the aesthetic subject and reality, had been the posture of the musical spirit ever since Schubert. But this had not led composers to modify the formal language of music. That was Mahler's achievement. The soul thrown back on itself

---

[6]   Theodor W. Adorno, "Mahler," in *Quasi una Fantasia: Essays on Modern Music*, trans. Rodney Livingstone (London and New York, 1992; orig. German edn 1963), p. 84.

[7]   Adorno, "Mahler," p. 84.

no longer feels at home in its traditional idiom. It feels distraught; its language is no longer able to accommodate the direct violence of its suffering ...

Instead, by attributing to the traditional words and syntax of music intentions which they no longer possessed, [Mahler] signaled his recognition of the rupture. The inauthenticity of the language of music becomes the expression of its substance. Mahler's tonal chords, plain and unadorned, are the explosive expressions of the pain felt by the individual subject imprisoned in an alienated society.[8]

Rather than a mistake or a liability, Mahler's discontinuity in Adorno's view is the only moral answer to the situation. Mahler's music does not lie, it does not pretend a unity that does not exist; rather, it exposes disunity for what it is. Mahler's achievement is not musical so much as ethical—the realization that the musical language can no longer express the subject's position in society.

Adorno states it slightly differently in his book-length study:

> The emerging antagonism between music and its language reveals a rift within society. The irreconcilability of the inward and the outward can no longer be harmonized spiritually, as in the classical age. This induces in Mahler's music the unhappy consciousness that that age believed overcome. The historical hour no longer allows it to see human destiny as reconcilable in the existing conditions with the institutional powers that force human beings, if they would earn their livings, into conditions contrary to them in which they can nowhere find themselves.[9]

Mahler's music signifies the death of the Enlightenment mentality that had everything figured out, revealing the impossibility of the Enlightenment view. Likewise, Adorno sees in the banality of Mahler's material a striking comment on the class conflict:

> Mahler inferred the revolt against bourgeois music from that very music ... ill-dressed, unmannerly people romp in a ceremonial chamber, the absolutistic imago of which bourgeois music continues to delineate. With the consolidation of the bourgeoisie the plebeian element had been gradually toned down to a folkloristic charm. In Mahler, in a phase when the crushing reality could no longer be placated through metaphor by the aesthetic sensorium, that unruly noise grows shrill. What bourgeois taste had earlier savored as red blood cells for its own regeneration now threatens its life.[10]

---

[8]   Ibid., p. 85.

[9]   Theodor W. Adorno, *Mahler: A Musical Physiognomy*, trans. Edmund Jephcott (Chicago and London, 1992; orig. pub. in German as *Mahler: Eine musikalische Physiognomik*, 1971), p. 16.

[10]   Adorno, *Physiognomy*, p. 37.

Mahler's social comment comes not just from simply including the banal in a "high" art form, but from the manner in which the two cultures collide:

> [Mahler's] symphonies shamelessly flaunt what rang in all ears, scraps of melody from great music, shallow popular songs, street ballads, hits ... Sometimes he lets these collide without transition, showing solidarity with Schoenberg's later criticism of mediation as something ornamental, superfluous. The potpourri satisfies more than one of Mahler's desiderata. It does not dictate to the composer what is to follow what; it demands no repeats, does not de-temporize time by a prescribed order of contents. It assists the decayed themes it accumulates to an afterlife in the second language of music. This Mahler prepares artificially. In his works the potpourri form, through the subterranean communication of its scattered elements, takes on a kind of instinctive, independent logic. Jacobinically the lower music irrupts into the higher.[11]

Mahler's music is a revolt against society—represented here as form: the artificial structure which forces individuals to conform to its nature. Adorno sees in Mahler's formal "problems" an indication of intention on the part of the composer. Adorno readily admits that each of Mahler's forms "enters the zone of potential miscarriage,"[12] but nevertheless implies that this is the price an individual at war with society must pay. He even sees signs of this war in respect to Mahler's orchestrational technique—an area usually reserved for praise: "the lack of expertise is remarkable in a conductor of his experience."[13] Mahler's rejection of the "New German school's luxuriation in color," is read as a criticism of "the ideal of euphony that encourages the sound to puff itself up around the music," or in a sense, to appear as more than it really is.[14]

Implicit also in Adorno's critique is the Holocaust. Like *Dialectic of Enlightenment*, the thesis is driven by the inability to explain fascism and Hitler, and the despair that such a failure brings about. While remaining within the general paradigm suggested by German culture, Adorno nevertheless tries to critique that same culture. Mahler therefore becomes a voice in the wilderness who "scented Fascism decades ahead": "If Mahler's music identifies itself with the masses, at the same time it fears them. The extreme points of its collective urge, as in the first movement of the Sixth Symphony, are the moments when the blind and violent march of the many irrupts: moments of trampling."[15] Ultimately, for Adorno, Mahler's music is about despair, the inability to understand, the inability of a single person to change the course of events. This is the ultimate failure, the one that can

---

[11]   Ibid., p. 35.

[12]   Ibid., p. 136.

[13]   Ibid., p. 116.

[14]   Ibid., pp. 116–17; the "New German" quote is from Paul Bekker, *Gustav Mahlers Sinfonien* (Berlin, 1921), p. 28.

[15]   Adorno, *Physiognomy*, p. 34.

never be forgiven or forgotten, and it is this that Adorno hears in the music. At the end of his book, Adorno again addresses the issues of banality, disruption, and lack of mediation:

> Music admits that the fate of the world no longer depends on the individual, but it also knows that this individual is capable of no content except his own, however fragmented and impotent. Hence [Mahler's] fractures are the script of truth. In them the social movement appears negatively, as in its victims. Even the marches in these symphonies are heard and reflected by those whom they drag away.[16]

Clearly, it is difficult to do justice to Adorno's complex argument about Mahler, but even the short excerpts given here indicate Adorno's interest in what he sees as Mahler's morality, or "truth": the ability to admit that "human beings want to be redeemed and are not."[17] Therefore any of Mahler's "failures" are simply read as his recognition that unity, or freedom, or redemption are no longer possibilities, as they perhaps were still for other Romantic or late nineteenth-century composers. Adorno's analyses of late Beethoven are implicit here, because whereas Beethoven had signaled—with his "absent subject"—the failure of utopia, that understanding had been ignored by later composers until Mahler. Therefore, Adorno never questions the existence of "problems" in Mahler's music that must be explained away, but rather erects a complex sociological platform that then redefines (or justifies) those "problems" as being in fact "solutions."

Adorno's writings, particularly the *Physiognomy* that was translated into English in 1992, have been particularly influential, perhaps because they seem to abandon a tone of apology. It must be stressed, however, that Adorno is working within the same framework as the early critics: the categories of banality, melodic eclecticism, problematical form, orchestration. He discusses all of these, but inverts their traditional meaning, giving Mahler control and turning the flaws into features. Adorno asserts that it was only in the Fourth Symphony that Mahler "acquired full control of the compositional means available to him."[18] On the other hand, Mahler is not the master orchestrator but rather "inept": "Nowhere is Mahler's music inspired primarily by a sense for sound ... The lack of expertise is remarkable in a conductor of his experience."[19] Perhaps Adorno, writing after the Second World War, felt that he could defend Mahler only within the cultural context that already existed, that he had to use the extant vocabulary to defend Mahler, for to invent a new vocabulary would be to imply that Mahler was, as the Nazis had insisted, not "German." It is even possible that Adorno had internalized both the vocabulary and image of Mahler, and his genius was to determine how to work within that restrictive environment. Nevertheless, to stand a duality on its

---

[16]   Ibid., p. 166.
[17]   Ibid., p. 129.
[18]   Adorno, "Mahler," p. 90.
[19]   Adorno, *Physiognomy*, p. 116.

head is not to challenge its efficacy or value. The unease with orchestration as a category might well betray Adorno's inability to get beyond his own cultural binary oppositions.

In a similar vein, Adorno's writings on Mahler cannot be separated from his writings on Strauss: Strauss becomes the neurotic, nervous composer, whereas Mahler is the strong, far-sighted and more meaningful musician:

> The difference between Strauss's high-bourgeois, vitalistic musical gratification and the transcendent concerns of Mahler is not, however, merely one of what is expressed, but of what in musical terms is composed. In Mahler the form forgets itself. In Strauss it remains the mise-en-scène of a subjective consciousness that never breaks free of itself, which, for all its concentration on externals, never externalizes itself in the musical object. Strauss never advanced beyond the immediacy of talent and, ossifying himself within it, was obliged to copy himself, to write *Joseph-Legende* and the Alpine Symphony, not to mention the desolate late works like *Capriccio*.[20]

Strauss, the self-centered egotist, cannot compose transcendent music—for all that he is supposedly Wagner's heir—because he is too blinded by himself. He may have the talent, but he does not, in the end, have the will: "Strauss controls his materials with such nonchalant assurance just because he is little concerned where the music is seeking to go by its own inner logic."[21] Strauss cannot hear the music over his own subjective consciousness.[22] Strauss sees and hears only himself. Thus Adorno simply inverts yet another opposition: Strauss, the great "German" composer, is the one who, in the end, fails to write great music; Mahler, on the other hand, according to Adorno's new taxonomy, is the one who can see into the future and write music with lasting significance.

The image of Mahler the Jew (as opposed to Mahler the composer) lies just under the surface in the writing of Theodor W. Adorno. He seems to believe that Mahler, as one of the "victims," may have insights that are unavailable to others. It is perhaps not stretching a point to read Adorno's attempts to reinstate Mahler into the canon as the ultimate act of subversion against the regime that attempted to eradicate every trace of Jewish music from the history books. As a German refugee writing in the wake of the Holocaust, Adorno felt the double bind of the love of his heritage and the realization of what it had done. Needless to say, his "reevaluation" of Mahler is rather an attempt to turn the bad into the good. Adorno was incapable of breaking the dichotomies he had inherited; he could

---

[20]   Adorno, *Physiognomy*, p. 133.

[21]   Ibid.

[22]   See also Adorno, "Richard Strauss" and "Richard Strauss, Part II," trans. Samuel and Shierry Weber, *Perspectives of New Music* 4 (1965), pp. 14–32 and 113–29; and Richard Wattenbarger, "A 'Very German Process': The Contexts of Adorno's Strauss Critique," *19th-Century Music* 25 (2002), pp. 313–36.

only work within them. Therefore he does not so much eradicate Mahler's Jewishness as apologize for it.

Adorno seems to offer hope, but fails to solve the problem. We are still working within the binary oppositions set up by Wagner, yet in Adorno's case, he has simply made banality and surface good, the inability to create depth a sign of genius. How could the problem be solved? If we accept that listening is a learned experience, if we accept that Mahler's music does not have to be that way, then we are free to reject the categories and look for new ones. For example, how does timbre function in the music of Mahler? What is the role of dynamics? Can we, as Ryan Kangas has done, allow the programs for the early symphonies to exist without relying on them or allowing them to control the way we hear the music?[23] Here I offer not criticism but only suggestions.

It is my hope that, after we examine (and, where appropriate, clear away) the critical detritus that currently obscures and constructs our impressions, the possibility will exist for a reevaluation of Mahler's musical style. While this project has been by its very nature interdisciplinary, I hope that it will be particularly liberating for music historians and allow commentators to take a fresh look at Mahler and his music. It is certainly not my claim that these reviews, cartoons, and reminiscences can be read only in the light of antisemitism; nor that antisemitism accounts for everything within them; nor that every single one of Mahler's reviewers was an antisemite. But if there is even the slightest possibility that we have taken over a way of thinking about Mahler and his music from a culture that could not deal with his Jewishness—and whose criticism and perceptions therefore reflect their own unease rather than "objective" reactions to his music—then we owe it to ourselves to rethink what makes Mahler's music unique, thought-provoking, and valuable.

---

[23]   Ryan R. Kangas, "Remembering Mahler: Music and Memory in Mahler's Early Symphonies," PhD diss., The University of Texas at Austin, 2009.

Appendix I
Mahler Reviews Consulted

Numbers refer to *Gustav Mahler Dokumentation: Sammlung Eleonore Vondenhoff, Materialien zu Leben und Werk*, ed. Bruno and Eleonore Vondenhoff (Tutzing, 1978) and *Zweiter Ergänzungsband zur Gustav Mahler Dokumentation, Sammlung Eleonore Vondenhoff : Materialien zu Leben und Werk*, ed. Veronika Freytag (Tutzing, 1997).

Reviews not numbered do not appear in the Vondenhoff catalog but are included here for ease of reference.

Table columns include Vondenhoff number (if applicable); newspaper or journal title; volume number (if applicable); author or signature (if given); date of issue or volume number (abbreviated H. [*Heft*], if issue number already given); and page numbers. In some cases, a title replaces the author entry for an anonymous article.

I. Mahler Symphony Premieres in Vienna, Symphonies nos. 1–6

For order of premieres, see Chapter 4, Table 4.1

First Symphony: 18 November 1900 (2nd Philharmonic Concert, 3rd Season)

2799	*Neue freie Presse*		Eduard Hanslick	20 Nov. 1900	7–8
2800	*Wiener Abendpost*		Robert Hirschfeld	20 Nov. 1900	1–2
2801	*Neues Wiener Tagblatt*		Max Kalbeck	20 Nov. 1900	1–3
2802	*Deutsche Zeitung*		Theodor Helm	20 Nov. 1900	7
2803	*Wiener Rundschau*	IV	Max Graf	1 Dec. 1900	415–16
2804	*Musikalisches Wochenblatt*	32	Theodor Helm	4 Apr. 1901	204–5
	Die Zeit		Richard Wallaschek	24 Nov. 1900	125
	Neue musikalische Presse	9	Hans Geisler	25 Nov. 1900	351–2

Second Symphony: 9 April 1899 (Nicolai-Konzert, 1st Season)

2880	*Neue freie Presse*	Richard Heuberger	10 Apr. 1899	1
2880b	*Deutsche Zeitung*	"Die Inszenierung ..."	8 Apr. 1899	7

2880c	*Deutsche Zeitung*		Maximillian Muntz	10 Apr. 1899	3
2880d	*Deutsche Zeitung*		Maximillian Muntz	11 Apr. 1899	1–3
2881	*Wiener Abendpost*		g.	10 Apr. 1899	6 (?)
2882	*Neues Wiener Tagblatt*		Ludwig Karpath	10 Apr. 1899	1–2
2882a	*Arbeiter-Zeitung*		Josef Scheu	12 Apr. 1899	5–6
2882b	*Die Zeit*		Richard Wallaschek	15 Apr. 1899	45
2883	*Neue musikalische Presse*	8	Hans Geisler	16 Apr. 1899	5–6
2884	*Wiener Rundschau*	III	Max Graf	1899	315–18
2885	*Die Reichswehr*		Hans Liebstöckl	10 & 12 Apr. 1899	4 & 5
2886	*Musikalisches Wochenblatt*	30	Theodor Helm	11 May 1899	287–8
2887a	*Wiener Son- und Montags-Zeitung*		H. Wörz	17 Apr. 1899	3

Third Symphony: 14 December 1904 (Außerordentliches Gesellschafts-Konzert; rep. 22 Dec.)

3028	*Neue freie Presse*		"Vorbericht" (J.K.)	15 Dec. 1904	9
3029	*Neue freie Presse*		Julius Korngold	17 Dec. 1904	1–3
3032	*Neues Wiener Journal*		"Vorbericht" (M.G.)	15 Dec. 1904	7
3033	*Neues Wiener Journal*		Max Graf	20 Dec. 1904	5–6
3033a	*Arbeiter-Zeitung*		D.J. Bach	20 Dec. 1904	1–2
3034	*Wiener Abendpost*		"Vorbericht" (R.H.)	15 Dec. 1904	3
3034a	*Wiener Abendpost*		Robert Hirschfeld	28 Dec. 1904	1–2
3035	*Neue musikalische Presse*	13	Max Vancsa	24 Dec. 1904	376–7
3036	*Die Zeit*		Richard Wallaschek	20 Dec. 1904	3
3037	*Musikalisches Wochenblatt*	36	Theodor Helm	5 Jan. 1905	12–13
3038	*Die Musik*	4	Gustav Schoenaich	H. 8 (1904/05)	154–5

Fourth Symphony: 12 January 1902 (5th Philharmonic Concert, dir. Mahler)

3130	*Neue freie Presse*	R. (Richard Heuberger)	13 Jan. 1902	4
3131	*Neues Wiener Journal*	Max Graf	13 Jan. 1902	1–2
3132	*Wiener Abendpost*	Robert Hirschfeld	14 Jan. 1902	1–2
3134	*Neues Wiener Tagblatt*	Max Kalbeck	16 Jan. 1902	1–2
3134b	*Fremden-Blatt*	Albert Kauders	13 Jan. 1902	7
3135	*Die Reichswehr*	Hans Liebstöckl	14 Jan. 1902	1–2

3136	*Musikalisches Wochenblatt*	33	Theodor Helm	23 Jan. 1902	69
3137	*Die Musik*	1	Max Graf	H. 9 (1901/02)	845–6
	Die Zeit		Richard Wallaschek	18 Jan. 1902	45
	Neue musikalische Presse	11	Hans Geisler	19 Jan. 1902	37–8

Fifth Symphony: 7 December 1905 (Gesellschaft der Musikfreunde, dir. Mahler)

3226	*Neue freie Presse*			8 Dec. 1905	15
3227	*Neue freie Presse*		Julius Korngold	12 Dec. 1905	1–3
3228	*Neues Wiener Journal*		Max Graf	15 Dec. 1905	9
3229	*Wiener Abendpost*		Robert Hirschfeld	14 Dec. 1905	1–2
3231	*Signale für die musikalischen Welt*	64	Ludwig Karpath	3 Jan. 1906	14
3232	*Musikalisches Wochenblatt*	37	Theodor Helm	11 Jan. 1906	34–5
3233	*Der Kunstwart*	19	Max Vancsa	H. 17 (1906)	266
	Fremden-Blatt		Albert Kauders	8 Dec. 1905	17–18
	Deutsche Zeitung		Maximillian Muntz	14 Dec. 1905	1–2

Sixth Symphony: 4 January 1907 (Außerordentlisches Konzert [Novitäten-Konzert] Wiener Konzertverein, dir. Mahler)

3313	*Neue freie Presse*		Julius Korngold	5 Jan. 1907	12
3314	*Neue freie Presse*		Julius Korngold	8 Jan. 1907	1–3
3315	*Neues Wiener Journal*		H. Reinhardt	5 Jan. 1907	8
3316	*Wiener Abendpost*		Robert Hirschfeld	5 Jan. 1907	3
3317	*Wiener Abendpost*		Robert Hirschfeld	10 Jan. 1907	1–3
3318	*Neues Wiener Tagblatt*		Max Kalbeck	7 Jan. 1907	1–2
3319	*Fremden-Blatt*		Albert Kauders	5 Jan. 1907	17–18
3320	*Illustrirtes Wiener Extrablatt*		Hans Liebstöckl	5 Jan. 1907	8
3321	*Die Wage*	10	Max Vancsa	Nr. 2 (1907)	37–8
3323	*Musikalisches Wochenblatt*	38	Theodor Helm	17 Jan. 1907	56
3324	*Die Musik*	6	Julius Korngold	H. 11 (1906/07)	326–7
	Die Reichspost		G. v. B.	6 Jan. 1907	11

II. Mahler Premieres, 1907–1912

Seventh Symphony, Premiere, Prague, 19 September 1908 (Philharmonic Concert in the Konzerthalle der Jubiläumsausstellung, dir. Mahler)

3369	*Neue freie Presse*		Richard Specht	20 Sept. 1908	
3371	*Neues Wiener Tagblatt*			21 Sept. 1908	
3372	*Fremden-Blatt*		Richard Batka	20 Sept. 1908	13
3373	*Die Wage*	11, bd. 2	Victor Joß	1908, nr. 39	883–4
3374	*Erdgeist. Illustrirtes Wiener Extrablatt*	3	Paul Stefan	H. 8, 10 Oct. 1908	801

Seventh Symphony, Viennese Premiere, 3 November 1909 (Konzert-Verein, dir. Ferdinand Löwe)

3384	*Neue freie Presse*		Julius Korngold	4 & 6 Nov. 1909	
3385	*Neues Wiener Journal*		Elsa Bienenfeld	10 Nov. 1909	8
3386	*Wiener Abendpost*		Robert Hirschfeld	5 Nov. 1909	
3387	*Musikalisches Wochenblatt*	40	Theodor Helm	18 Nov. 1909	486–7
3388	*Die Musik*	9	Richard Specht	H. 5 (1909/1910)	323

8th Symphony, Premiere, Munich, 12 September 1910 (Neue Musik-Festhalle der Austellung, dir. Mahler)

3457	*Neue freie Presse*		Generalprobe	11 Sept. 1910	
3458	*Neue freie Presse*		Julius Korngold	12 Sept. 1910	
3460	*Neue freie Presse*		Julius Korngold	14 Sept. 1910	
3461	*Neues Wiener Journal*			10 Sept. 1910	
3462	*Neues Wiener Journal*		Elsa Bienenfeld	13 Sept. 1910	
3463	*Arbeiterzeitung*		D.J. Bach	Sept. 1910	
3464	*Wiener Mode*	24	D.J. Bach	H. 2 (Sept. 1910)	
3471	*Neue Musik Zeitung (Stuttgart)*	32	Robert Holtzmann	H. 8, 1911	169–75

***Das Lied von der Erde*, Premiere, Munich, 20 Nov.ember 1911 (Gedenkfeier für Gustav Mahler, dir. Bruno Walter; with Second Symphony)**

3587	*Die Musik*	11	Rudolf Louis	H. 6 (1911/1912)	382

3592	*Der Kunstwart*	25	Richard Specht	H. 6, 1911	440–42
	(Munich)				
3593	*Neue freie Presse*		"Vorbesprechung"	21 Nov. 1911	
3594	*Neue freie Presse*		Richard Specht	4 Dec. 1911	
3595	*Wiener Abendpost*			22 Nov. 1911	
3596	*Der Merker*	2		1911	
3597	*Der Merker*	2	Richard Specht	Nr. 29 (1911)	1169–74

Ninth Symphony, Premiere, Vienna, 26 June 1912 (Musikfestwoche 1912, dir. Bruno Walter)

3668	*Neue freie Presse*		Julius Korngold	27 June 1912	
3669	*Wiener Abendpost*		Robert Hirschfeld	27 June 1912	
3670			Max Graf		
3671	*Der Merker*	3	Richard Specht	July (1912)	552–3
3672	*Der Kunstwart*	25	Richard Batka	H. 21 (1912)	193–5
	(Munich)				
3673	*Wiener Mode*	25	Th. Isnenghi	H. 21 (1912)	1261–2
	Wiener Allgemeine		Moriz Scheyer	27 June 1912	2
	Zeitung				
	Neues Wiener Tagblatt		Max Kalbeck	27 June 1912	15
	Wiener Mittags-		–k.	27 June 1912	3
	Zeitung				
	Illustrirtes Wiener		Richard Specht	27 June 1912	10
	Extrablatt				
	Arbeiter-Zeitung		D.J. Bach	4 July 1912	1
	Neues Wiener Journal		Elsa Bienenfeld	27 June 1912	4
	Reichspost		M.S.	27 June 1912	7
	Wiener Sonn- und			1 July 1912	1
	Montags-Zeitung				
	Ostdeutsche		D.	27 June 1912	7
	Rundschau				
	Deutsches Volksblatt		H.	27 June 1912	7
	Fremden-Blatt		K.	27 June 1912	14
	Österreichische		Er.	27 June 1912	6
	Volkszeitung				
	Montags Revue			1 July 1912	5
	Illustrierte Kronen			28 June 1912	9
	Zeitung				
	Der Morgen			8 July 1912	6

Appendix II
Strauss Reviews Consulted

Numbers refer to Gustav *Mahler Dokumentation: Sammlung Eleonore Vondenhoff, Materialien zu Leben und Werk*, ed. Bruno and Eleonore Vondenhoff (Tutzing, 1978) and *Zweiter Ergänzungsband zur Gustav Mahler Dokumentation, Sammlung Eleonore Vondenhoff: Materialien zu Leben und Werk*, ed. Veronika Freytag (Tutzing, 1997).

Table columns include Vondenhoff number (if applicable); newspaper or journal title; volume number (if applicable); author or signature (if given); date of issue or volume number (abbreviated H. [*Heft*], if issue number already given); and page numbers. In some cases, a title replaces the author entry for an anonymous article.

Strauss Viennese Premieres

Don Juan, 10 January 1892, Vienna Philharmonic, Hans Richter conducting

Neue Freie Presse	Julius Korngold	15 Jan. 1893	
Deutsche Zeitung	Theodor Helm	16 Jan. 1893	1–3
Wiener Abendpost	dr. h. p.		
For Hanslick, see below			

Tod und Verklärung, 15 Jan.uary 1893, Vienna Philharmonic, H. Richter conducting

Wiener Abendpost	dr. h. p.	20 Feb. 1893	1–2
For Hanlsick, see below			

Also sprach Zarathustra, 21 March 1897, Vienna Philarmonic, H. Richter conducting

Deutsche Zeitung	Theodor Helm	27 Mar. 1897	1–2
Neues Wiener Journal	Albert Kauders	28 Mar. 1897	6
Wiener Abendpost	Robert Hirschfeld	3 Apr. 1897	1–2

Aus Italien, 19 November 1899, Vienna Philharmonic, Gustav Mahler conducting (Second season, 2nd Concert)

Neues Wiener Journal	(a. k.)	21 Nov. 1899	5

Reichspost		G. v. B.	22 Nov. 1899	4
Neue musikalische Presse	8	Hans Geisler	26 Nov. 1899	6
Wiener Abendpost		Robert Hirschfeld	7 Dec. 1899	5–6

Ein Heldenleben, 23 Jan 1901, Richard Strauss conducting

Neue musikalische Presse	Max Vancsa	1899	52–4

Sinfonia domestica (with Don Quixote and Ein Heldenleben), 23 November 1904, G. Mahler (see Chapter 5, Table 5.2)

	Neue freie Presse	Julius Korngold	26 Nov. 1904	1–2
	Reichspost	G. v. B.	26 Nov. 1904	10
	Deutsche Zeitung	Maximillian Muntz	2 Dec. 1904	1–2
3028	*Neue freie Presse*	"Vorbericht" (J.K.)	15 Dec. 1904	9
3029	*Neue freie Presse*	Julius Korngold	17 Dec. 1904	1–3
3032	*Neues Wiener Journal*	"Vorbericht" (M.G.)	15 Dec. 1904	7
	Neue freie Presse	"Kunstnachrichten"	19 Dec. 1904	11
3033	*Neues Wiener Journal*	Max Graf	20 Dec. 1904	5–6
3033a	*Arbeiter-Zeitung*	D.J. Bach	20 Dec. 1904	1–2
3034	*Wiener Abendpost*	"Vorbericht" (R.H.)	15 Dec. 1904	3
	Neue freie Presse	Julius Korngold	19 Dec. 1904	11
3034a	*Wiener Abendpost*	Robert Hirschfeld	28 Dec. 1904	1–2
3035	*Neue musikalische Presse* 13	Max Vancsa	24 Dec. 1904	376–7
3036	*Die Zeit*	Richard Wallaschek	20 Dec. 1904	3
3037	*Musikalisches Wochenblatt* 36	Theodor Helm	5 Jan. 1905	12–13
3038	*Die Musik* 4	Gustav Schoenaich	H. 8 (1904/05)	154–5
	Österreichische Rundschau 9	Robert Hirschfeld	1904	535–40

Eduard Hanslick's reviews in *Vienna's Golden Years of Music, 1850–1900*, trans. Henry Pleasants III (New York, 1950); *Am Ende des Jahrhunderts [1895-1899]. Der Modernen Oper VIII. Musikalische Kritiken und Schilderungen*, 2nd edn (Berlin, 1899); *Aus neuer und neuester Zeit. Der Modernen Oper IX Teil. Musikalische Kritiken und Schilderungen*, 2nd edn (Berlin, 1900).

Bibliography

Adorno, Theodor W., *Mahler: A Musical Physiognomy*, trans. Edmund Jephcott (Chicago and London: University of Chicago Press, 1992); orig. German pub., *Mahler: Eine musikalische Physiognomik* (1971).

Adorno, Theodor W., *Quasi una fantasia* (New York and London: Verso, 1992; orig. German pub. by Suhrkamp Verlag, 1963).

Adorno, Theodor W., "Richard Strauss," trans. Samuel and Shierry Weber, *Perspectives of New Music* 4 (1965), pp. 14–32 and 113–29.

Adorno, Theodor W., "Spätstil Beethovens (1934)," *Moments musicaux* (Frankfurt am Main: Suhrkamp, 1964), pp. 13–17; trans. as "Text 3: Beethoven's Late Style" in Theodor W. Adorno, *Beethoven: The Philosophy of Music*, ed. Rolf Tiedemann, trans. Edmund Jephcott (Stanford: Stanford University Press, 1998), pp. 123–6.

Adorno, Theodor W. and Max Horkheimer, *Dialectic of Enlightenment* (New York: Continuum, 1991; orig. Eng. edn 1972).

Almog, Shmuel, "What's in a Hyphen?" *SICSA Report: Newsletter of the Vidal Sassoon International Center for the Study of Antisemitism* (Summer 1989); archived: http://sicsa.huji.ac.il/hyphen.htm

Anderson, Mark M., *Kafka's Clothes: Ornament and Aestheticism in the Habsburg Fin de Siècle* (Oxford: Clarendon Press, 1992).

Applegate, Celia and Pamela Potter, eds, *Music and National Identity* (Chicago: The University of Chicago Press, 2002).

Aschheim, Steven E., *Brothers and Strangers: The East European Jew in German and German Jewish Consciousness, 1800–1923* (Madison: University of Wisconsin Press, 1982).

Austin, William W., *Music in the 20th Century: From Debussy through Stravinsky* (New York: W.W. Norton & Co., 1996).

Barham, Jeremy, ed., *The Cambridge Companion to Mahler* (Cambridge and New York, et al.: Cambridge University Press, 2007).

Bauman, Zygmunt, "Allosemitism: Premodern, Modern, Postmodern," in *Modernity, Culture and "The Jew,"* ed. Bryan Cheyette and Laura Marcus (Stanford: Stanford University Press, 1998), pp. 143–56.

Beard, George M., *American Nervousness: Its Causes and Consequences* (G.P. Putnam's Sons, 1881).

Bekker, Paul, *Gustav Mahlers Sinfonien* (Berlin: Schuster and Loeffler, 1921).

Beller, Stephen, *Vienna and the Jews, 1867–1938: A Cultural History* (Cambridge: Cambridge University Press, 1989).

Bernstein, Herman, *The Truth about "The Protocols of Zion": A Complete Exposure* (New York: Ktav Publishing House, Inc., 1971).

Bittner, Julius, "Instrumentations-Retouchen bei Beethoven," *Der Merker* 11 (1920), pp. 567–70.

Blaukopf, Kurt, *Gustav Mahler*, trans. Inge Goodwin (London: Futura Publications, 1974).

Blaukopf, Kurt and Herta, *Mahler: His Life, Work, and World*, trans. Paul Baker et al. (London: Thames & Hudson, 1991); enlarged edn of *Mahler: A Documentary Study* (London: Thames & Hudson, 1976).

Botstein, Leon, "Music and Its Public: Habits of Listening and the Crisis of Musical Modernism in Vienna, 1870–1914," PhD diss., Harvard University, 1985.

Botstein, Leon, *Judentum und Modernität: Essays zur Rolle der Juden in der deutschen und österreichischen Kultur, 1848 bis 1938* (Vienna: Bohlau, 1991).

Botstein, Leon, "Analysis and Criticism," *Musical Quarterly* 85 (2001), pp. 225–31.

Botstein, Leon, "Whose Gustav Mahler? Reception, Interpretation, and History," in *Mahler and His World*, ed. Karen Painter (Princeton: Princeton University Press, 2002).

Botstein, Leon and Linda Weintraub, eds, *Pre-Modern Art of Vienna, 1848–1898* (Annendale-on-Hudson: Edith C. Blum Art Institute, 1987).

Boyer, John W., *Culture and Political Crisis in Vienna: Christian Socialism in Power, 1897–1911* (Chicago and London: The University of Chicago Press, 1995).

Brown, Peter D.G., *Oskar Panizza: His Life and Works* (Bern: P. Lang, 1983).

Burnham, Scott *Beethoven Hero* (Princeton: Princeton University Press, 1995).

Burton, Robert, *The Anatomy of Melancholy, What It Is. With All the Kindes, Causes, Symptomes, Prognostickes, and Severall Cures of It* (Oxford: John Lichfield and James Short, for Henry Cripps, 1621).

Carner, Mosco, "Mahler's Re-scoring of the Schumann Symphonies," *The Music Review* 2 (1941), pp. 97–110.

Castagne, André, Michel Chalon, and Patrick Florençon, eds, *Gustav Mahler et l'ironie dans la culture viennoise au tournant du siècle: Actes du colloque de Montpellier 16–18 juillet 1996* (Paris: Climats, 2001).

Chandak Sengoopta, *Otto Weininger: Sex, Science, and Self in Imperial Vienna* (Chicago: The University of Chicago Press, 2000).

Chua, Daniel K.L., *Absolute Music and the Construction of Meaning* (Cambridge: Cambridge University Press, 1999).

Cohn, Norman, *Warrant for Genocide: The Myth of the Jewish World Conspiracy and the Protocols of the Elders of Zion* (London: Serif, 1996).

Comini, Alessandra, *The Changing Image of Beethoven: A Study in Mythmaking* (New York: Rizzoli, 1987).

Cone, Edward T., ed., *Hector Berlioz, Fantastic Symphony: An Authoritative Score, Historical Background, Analysis, Views and Comments* (New York: W.W. Norton & Company, Inc., 1971).

Cooke, Deryck, *Gustav Mahler: An Introduction to his Music*, 2nd edn (Cambridge: Cambridge University Press, 1988).

Crist, Elizabeth Bergman, "Critical Politics: The Reception History of Aaron Copland's Third Symphony," *Musical Quarterly* 85 (2001), pp. 232–63.

Crittenden, Camille, *Johann Strauss and Vienna: Operetta and the Politics of Popular Culture* (Cambridge and New York: Cambridge University Press, 2000).

Crocker, Richard L., *A History of Musical Style* (New York: Dover Publications, 1986; rpt 1966 McGraw-Hill).

Dahlaus, Carl, *Nineteenth-century Music*, trans. J. Bradford Robinson (Berkeley and London: University of California Press, 1989).

Dahlaus, Carl, *The Idea of Absolute Music*, trans. Roger Lustig (Chicago and London: University of Chicago Press, 1989).

Damrosch, Walter, "Hans von Bülow and the Ninth Symphony," *Musical Quarterly* 13 (1927), pp. 280–93.

Deathridge, John, "Richard Strauss and the Broken Dream of Modernity," in *Richard Strauss und die Moderne: Bericht über das Internationale Symposium München, 21. bis 23 July 1999*, ed. Bernd Edelmann et al. (Berlin: Henschel Verlag, 2001), pp. 79–92.

Decsey, Ernst, "Stunden mit Mahler," *Die Musik* 18 & 21 (1911), pp. 352–6 and 143–53.

Deleuze, Gilles and Félix Guattari, *A Thousand Plateaus: Capitalism and Schizophrenia*, trans. and foreword Brian Massumi (Minneapolis: University of Minnesota Press, 1987).

Draughton, Francesca, "Mahler and the Music of Fin-de-Siècle Identity," PhD diss., University of California at Los Angeles, 2002.

Dundes, Alan, ed., *The Blood Libel Legend: a Casebook in Anti-Semitic Folklore* (Madison: University of Wisconsin Press, 1991).

Eckstein, Friedrich, *"Alte unnennbare Tage!" Erinnerungen aus siebzig Lehr- und Wanderjahren* (Vienna et al.: Herbert Reichner, 1936).

Eichhorn, Andreas, *Beethovens Neunte Symphonie: Die Geschichte ihrer Aufführung und Rezeption* (Kassel: Bärenreiter, 1993).

Elon, Amos, *The Pity of It All: A portrait of the German–Jewish Epoch, 1743–1933* (New York: Picador, 2002).

Endler, Franz, "Julius Korngold und die Neue Freie Presse," PhD diss., Vienna University, 1981.

Engländer, Martin, *Die auffallend häufigen Krankheitserscheinungen der jüdische Rasse* (Vienna: J.L. Pollak, 1902).

Esau, Erika, "Artists' Biographies Vienna 1848–1898," in *Pre-Modern Art of Vienna, 1848–1898*, ed. Leon Botstein and Linda Weintraub (Annendale-on-Hudson: Edith C. Blum Art Institute, 1987).

Feder, Stuart, *Gustav Mahler: A Life in Crisis* (New Haven and London: Yale University Press, 2004).

Filler, Susan M., *Gustav and Alma Mahler: A Guide to Research* (New York: Garland Publishing, Inc., 1989).

Filler, Susan, "Mahler as a Jew in the Literature," in Theodore Albrecht, ed., *Dika Caecilia: Essays for Dika Newlin November 22, 1988* (Kansas City, Mo.: Dept. of Music, Park College, 1988).

Fischer, Jens Malte, *Richard Wagners "Das Judentum in der Musik": Eine kritische Dokumentation als Beitrag zur Geschichte des Antisemitismus* (Frankfurt am Main and Leipzig: Insel Verlag, 2000).

Fischer, Jens Malte, *Gustav Mahler: Der fremde Vertraute, Biographie* (Vienna: Paul Zsolnay Verlag, 2003).

Fischer, Klaus P., *The History of an Obsession: German Judeophobia and the Holocaust* (New York: Continuum, 1998).

Fishberg, Maurice and Joseph Jacobs, "Types, Anthropological," in *The Jewish Encyclopedia: A Descriptive Record of the History, Religion, Literature, and Customs of the Jewish People from the Earliest Times to the Present Day* (12 vols, New York and London: Funk and Wagnalls Co., 1901–06).

Forchert, Arno, "Mahler und Schumann," in *Mahler-Interpretation: Aspekte zum Werk und Wirken von Gustav Mahler*, ed. Rudolf Stephan (Mainz: Schott's Söhne, 1985), pp. 29–44 and 45–53.

Fox, Richard Wightman and T.J. Lears, eds, *Culture of Consumption: Critical Essays in American History, 1900–1980* (New York: Pantheon Books, 1983).

Freud, Sigmund, *The Standard Edition of the Complete Psychological Works of Sigmund Freud* (24 vols, London: Hogarth Press and the Institute of Psycho-Analysis, 1953–74).

Frisch, Walter, *German Modernism: Music and the Arts* (Berkeley, Los Angeles, and London: University of California Press, 2005).

Franklin, Peter, *The Life of Mahler* (Cambridge, New York, and Melbourne: Cambridge University Press, 1997).

Fritsch, Theodor, *Handbuch der Judenfrage* (Leipzig: Hammer Verlag, 1935).

Fuchs, Eduard, *Die Juden in der Karikatur* (Munich: Albert Langen, 1921).

Gay, Peter, *Freud, Jews, and Other Germans: Masters and Victims in Modernist Culture* (New York: Oxford University Press, 1978).

Gay, Peter, *Schnitzler's Century: The Making of Middle-class Culture, 1815–1914* (New York: W.W. Norton & Co., 2002).

Gilliam, Bryan, "Strauss, Richard (Georg)," in *The New Grove Dictionary of Music and Musicians*, ed. John Tyrell, 2nd edn (29 vols, New York and London: MacMillan and Co., 2001).

Gilliam, Bryan, ed., *Richard Strauss: New Perspectives on the Composer and His Work* (Durham and London: Duke University Press, 1992).

Gilliam, Bryan, ed., *Richard Strauss and His World* (Princeton, Princeton University Press, 1992).

Gilman, Sander L., *The Case of Sigmund Freud: Medicine and Identity at the Fin de Siècle* (Baltimore and London: The Johns Hopkins University Press, 1993).

Gilman, Sander L., *Difference and Pathology: Stereotypes of Sexuality, Race and Madness* (Ithaca and London: Cornell University Press, 1985).

Gilman, Sander L., *Franz Kafka: The Jewish Patient* (New York and London: Routledge, 1995).

Gilman, Sander L., *Freud, Race, and Gender* (Princeton: Princeton University Press, 1993).

Gilman, Sander L., "The Image of the Hysteric," in Gilman et al., *Hysteria Beyond Freud* (Berkeley and London: University of California Press, 1993), pp. 345–454.

Gilman, Sander L., *Jewish Self-hatred: Anti-Semitism and the Hidden Language of the Jews* (Baltimore and London: The Johns Hopkins University Press, 1986).

Gilman, Sander L., *The Jew's Body* (New York: Routledge, 1991).

Gilman, Sander L., *Love + Marriage = Death: And Other Essays on Representing Difference* (Stanford: Stanford University Press, 1998).

Gilman, Sander L., *Making the Body Beautiful: A Cultural History of Aesthetic Surgery* (Princeton: Princeton University Press, 1999).

Gilman, Sander L., *Smart Jews: The Construction of the Image of Jewish Superior Intelligence* (Lincoln and London: University of Nebraska Press, 1996).

Gilman, Sander L., "Strauss and the Pervert," in *Reading Opera*, ed. Arthur Groos and Roger Parker (Princeton: Princeton University Press, 1988), pp. 306–27.

Goehr, Lydia, *The Imaginary Museum of Musical Works: An Essay in the Philosophy of Music* (Oxford: Clarendon Press, 1992).

Goldstein, Jan, "The Wandering Jew and the Problem of Psychiatric Antisemitism in Fin-de-Siècle France," *Journal of Contemporary History* 20 (1985), pp. 521–52.

Graf, Max, *Legend of a Musical City* (New York: Philosophical Library, 1946).

Graf, Max, *Wagner-Probleme und andere Studien* (Vienna: Wiener Verlag, 1900).

Grey, Thomas, "Bodies of Evidence," *Cambridge Opera Journal* 8 (1995), pp. 185–97.

Grunsky, Peter, "Epigone oder gescheiterter Reformer? Richard Heuberger in historischer Sicht," in *Brahms-Kongress Wien 1983* (Tutzing: Schneider, 1988), pp. 187–98.

Günther, Hans F.K., *Rassenkunde des jüdischen Volkes*, 2nd edn (Munich: J.F. Lehmanns Verlag, 1930; 1st edn 1922).

Hallman, Diane R., *Opera, Liberalism, and Antisemitism in Nineteenth-century France: The Politics of Halévy's* La Juive (Cambridge: Cambridge University Press, 2002).

Hamann, Brigitte, *Hitler's Vienna: A Dictator's Apprenticeship* (Oxford and New York: Oxford University Press, 1999).

Hanslick, Eduard, *Am Ende des Jahrhunderts [1895–1899]. Der Modernen Oper VIII. Musikalische Kritiken und Schilderungen*, 2nd edn (Berlin: Allgemeiner Verein für Deutsche Literatur, 1899).

Hanslick, Eduard, *Aus neuer und neuester Zeit. Der Modernen Oper IX Teil. Musikalische Kritiken und Schilderungen*, 2nd edn (Berlin: Allgemeiner Verein für Deutsche Literatur, 1900).

Hanslick, Eduard, *On the Musically Beautiful: A Contribution Towards the Revision of the Aesthetics of Music*, trans. and ed. Geoffrey Payzand from the 8th edn (1891) (Indianapolis: Hackett Publishing Company, 1986).

Hanslick, Eduard, *Vienna's Golden Years of Music, 1850–1900*, trans. Henry Pleasants III (New York: Simon and Schuster, 1950).

Harrandt, Andrea, "Gustav Schonaich: Ein Wiener Falstaff, Musikkritiker und Bohemien," *Musicologica austriaca* 13 (1995), pp. 77–125.

Harrandt, Andrea, "Gustav Schonaich: Ein Wiener Musikkritiker aus dem Bruckner-Kreis," *Mitteilungen der Österreichischen Gesellschaft für Musikwissenschaft* 20 (July 1989), pp. 28–31.

Harrandt, Andrea, "Students and Friends as 'Prophets' and 'Promoters': The Reception of Bruckner's Works in the Wiener Akademische Wagner-Verein," in *Perspectives on Anton Bruckner*, ed. Crawford Howie, Paul Hawkshaw, and Timothy Jackson, (Aldershot et al.: Ashgate, 2001), pp. 317–27.

Harrowitz, Nancy, *Antisemitism, Misogyny and the Logic of Cultural Difference: Cesare Lombroso and Matilde Serao* (Lincoln and London: University of Nebraska Press, 1994).

Harrowitz, Nancy A. and Barbara Hyams, eds, *Jews and Gender: Responses to Otto Weininger* (Philadelphia: Temple University Press, 1995).

Hellsberg, Clemens, *Demokratie der Könige* (Schweizer Verlagshaus, Kremayr & Scheriau, & Musikverlag Schott, 1992).

Helm, Theodor, *Beethovens Streichquartette: Versuch einer technischen Analyse* (Leipzig: E.W. Fritzsch, 1885).

Herf, Jeffrey, *Reactionary Modernism: Technology, Culture, and Politics in Weimar and the Third Reich* (Cambridge: Cambridge University Press, 1984).

Heyworth, Peter (1968), "The Rise & Fall of Richard Strauss," *Encounter* 31/2 (1968), pp. 49–53.

Hilmar, Ernst, "'Schade, aber es muss(te) sein': Zu Gustav Mahlers Strichen und Retuschen insbesondere am Beispiel der V. Symphonie Anton Bruckners," in *Bruckner-Studien: Festgabe der Österreichischen Akademie der Wissenschaften zum 150. Geburtstag von Anton Bruckner*, ed. Othmar Wessely (Vienna: Verlag der Österreichischen Akademie der Wissenschaften, 1975), pp. 187–201.

Hitler, Adolf, *Mein Kampf*, trans. Ralph Manheim (Boston: Houghton Mifflin Co., 1943).

Hsia, R. Po-chia, *The Myth of Ritual Murder: Jews and Magic in Reformation Germany* (New Haven: Yale University Press, 1988).

Janik, Allan and Stephen Toulmin, *Wittgenstein's Vienna* (New York: Simon and Schuster, 1973).

Jarman, Douglas, "Secret Programs," in *The Cambridge Companion to Berg*, ed. Anthony Pople (Cambridge: Cambridge University Press, 1997), pp. 167–79.

Jones, Ernest, *The Life and Work of Sigmund Freud* (3 vols, New York: Basic Books, 1953–57).

Jung, Carl G., *Collected Works*, ed. Herbert Read et al., trans. R.F.C. Hull (20 vols in 21, London: Pantheon Books, 1953–79).

Kähler, Willibald, *150 Jahre Musikalische Akademie des National theater-Orchesters Mannheim 1779–1929* (Mannheim: J. Bensheimer, 1929).

Kalisch, Volker, "Zu Mahlers Instrumentationsretuschen in den Sinfonien Beethovens," *Schweizerische Musikzeitung/Revue musicale Suisse* 121 (1981), pp. 17–22.

Kangas, Ryan R. "Remembering Mahler: Music and Memory in Mahler's Early Symphonies," PhD diss., The University of Texas at Austin, 2009.

Kaplan, Gilbert, ed., *The Mahler Album* (New York: The Kaplan Foundation, 1995).

Karbuskicky, Vladimír, "Gustav Mahlers musikalisches Judentum," *Hambuburg Jahrbuch für Musikwissenschaft* 16 (1999), pp. 179–207; trans. and ed. Jeremy Barnum as "Gustav Mahler's Musical Jewishness," in his *Perspectives on Gustav Mahler* (Aldershot: Ashgate, 2005), pp. 195–216.

Karpath, Ludwig, *Begegnung mit dem Genius: denkwürdige Erlebnisse mit Johannes Brahms—Gustav Mahler—Hans Richter, und vielen anderen bedeutenden Menschen* (Vienna and Leipzig: Fiba Verlag, 1934).

Katz, Jacob, *The Darker Side of Genius: Richard Wagner's Anti-Semitism* (Hanover and London: University Press of New England, 1986).

Kennedy, Michael, *Mahler* (New York: Schirmer Books, 1991).

Kennedy, Michael, *Richard Strauss: Man, Musician, Enigma* (Cambridge: Cambridge University Press, 1999).

Kienzl, Wilhelm, *Meine Lebenswanderung, Erlebtes und Erlauschtes* (Stuttgart: J. Engelhorns Nachf, 1926).

Klein, Herman, *The Golden Age of Opera* (New York: G. Routledge & Sons, Ltd, 1933).

Knapp, Raymond and Francesca Draughton, "Gustav Mahler and the Crisis of Jewish Identity, *Echo* 3 (2001); available at www.echo.ucla.edu.

Knittel, K.M., "'Ein hypermoderner Dirigent': Mahler and Anti-Semitism in *Fin-de-Siècle* Vienna," *19th-Century Music* 18 (1995), pp. 257–76.

Knittel, K.M. "'Polemik im Concertsaal': Mahler, Beethoven, and the Viennese Critics," *19th-Century Music* 29 (2006), pp. 289–321.

Knittel, K.M., "Wagner, Deafness, and Beethoven's Late Style," *Journal of the American Musicological Society* 51 (1998), pp. 49–82.

Korngold, Julius, *Die Korngolds in Wien* (Zürich and St. Gallen: M&T Verlag AG, 1991).

Krafft-Ebing, Richard von, *Nervosität und Neurasthenische Zustände* (Vienna: Alfred Hölder, 1895).

Krafft-Ebing, Richard von, *Text-Book of Insanity, Based on Clinical Observations: For Practitioners and Students of Medicine*, trans. Charles Gilbert Chaddock, M.D. (Philadelphia: F.A. Davis Co., 1905), orig. German edn, *Lehrbuch der*

Psychiatrie auf klinischer Grundlage für practische Ärzte und Studirende (3 vols in 1, Stuttgart: F. Enke, 1879–80).

Kraus, Karl, *Heine und die Folgen* (Munich: A. Langen, 1910).

Kravitt, Edward F., *The Lied: Mirror of Late Romanticism* (New Haven and London: Yale University Press, 1996).

Kravitt, Edward F. "Mahler, Victim of the 'New' Anti-Semitism," *Journal of the Royal Musical Association* 127 (2002), pp. 72–94.

La Grange, Henry-Louis de, *Gustav Mahler: chronique d'une vie* (3 vols, Paris: Fayard, 1979–84; Volume 1 trans. as *Mahler, Volume One* [Garden City, New York: Doubleday & Co., Inc., 1973]; Volume 2 trans. as *Gustav Mahler, Vienna: The Years of Challenge (1897–1904)* [Oxford and New York: Oxford University Press, 1995]; Volume 3 trans. as *Gustav Mahler, Vienna: Triumph and Disillusion (1904–1907)* [Oxford and New York: Oxford University Press, 1999]; Volume 4 trans. as *Gustav Mahler: A New Life Cut Short (1907–1911)* [Oxford and New York: Oxford, 2008]).

La Grange, Henry-Louis de, "Mahler in New York: The Truth Behind the Legend," paper presented at the Carnegie Hall symposium entitled "Mahler in America: 1907–1911," 19–20 Nov. 1994.

La Grange, Henry-Louis de, "Music about Music in Mahler: Reminiscences, Allusions, or Quotations?" in *Mahler Studies*, Stephen E. Hefling, ed. (Cambridge University Press, 1997), pp. 122–68.

Lawson, Colin, "Beethoven and the Development of Wind Instruments," in *Performing Beethoven*, Robin Stowell, ed. (Cambridge University Press, 1994), pp. 70–88.

Lawton, Mary, *Schumann-Heink, the Last of the Titans* (New York: Macmillan, 1928).

Lebrecht, Norman, *Mahler Remembered* (New York: W.W. Norton & Co., 1987).

Leibnitz, Thomas, "Anton Bruckner and 'German' Music': Josef Schalk and the Establishment of Bruckner as a National Composer," in *Perspectives on Anton Bruckner*, ed. Crawford Howie, Paul Hawkshaw, and Timothy Jackson (Aldershot: Ashgate, 2001), pp. 328–40.

Leroy-Beaulieu, Anatole, *Israel among the Nations: A Study of Jews and Antisemitism*, trans. Frances Hellman (New York: G.P. Putnam's Sons, 1895); orig. pub., *Juifs et l'antisémitisme: Israél chez les nations* (Paris: Lévy, 1893).

Lessing, Theodor, *Der jüdische Selbsthass* (Berlin: Jüdischer Verlag, 1930).

Levy, Erik, *Music in the Third Reich* (London: Macmillan, 1994).

Louis, Rudolf, *Die deutsche Musik der Gegenwart*, rev. edn (Leipzig and Munich: Georg Müller, 1912).

Lowenthal, David, *The Past Is a Foreign Country* (Cambridge and New York: Cambridge University Press, 1985).

Lutz, Tom, *American Nervousness, 1903: An Anecdotal History* (Ithaca: Cornell University Press, 1991).

Mahler, Alma, *Gustav Mahler: Memories and Letters*, trans. Basil Creighton, ed. Donald Mitchell and Knud Martner, 4th edn (London: Cardinal, 1990); orig.

German pub., *Gustav Mahler: Erinnerungen und Briefe* (Amsterdam: Allert de Lange, 1940); orig. Eng. trans. by Basil Creighton as *Gustav Mahler: Memories and Letters* (London: J. Murray, 1946).

Mahler-Werfel, Alma, *Tagebuch-Suiten, 1898–1902*, Antony Beaumont and Susanne Rode-Breymann, eds (Frankfurt am Main: S. Fischer Verlag, 1997; selections trans. as *Alma Mahler-Werfel Diaries, 1898–1902*, selected and trans. Antony Beaumont [London: Faber and Faber, 1998]).

Mann, Thomas, *Death in Venice and Other Stories*, trans. H.T. Lowe-Porter (New York: Vintage International, 1989).

Marx, Karl, "On the Jewish Question," in *Karl Marx: Early Writings*, trans. Rodney Livingstone and Gregor Benton (New York: Vintage Books, 1975).

McCaldin, Denis, "Mahler and Beethoven's Ninth Symphony," *Proceedings of the Royal Musical Association* 108 (1981), pp. 101–9.

McColl, Sandra, "Max Kalbeck and Gustav Mahler," *19th-Century Music* 20 (1996), pp. 167–84.

McColl, Sandra, *Music Criticism in Vienna, 1896–1897: Critically Moving Forms* (Oxford: Oxford University Press, 1996).

McGrath, William J., *Dionysian Art and Populist Politics in Austria* (New Haven: Yale University Press, 1974).

Millington, Barry, "Nuremburg Trial: Is There Anti-Semitism in *Die Meistersinger*?" *Cambridge Opera Journal* 3 (1991), pp. 247–60.

Mitchell, Donald (1995), *Gustav Mahler, Volume II: The Wunderhorn Years* (Berkeley and London: University of California Press, 1995; rpt London: Faber and Faber, 1975).

Morrison, Julie Dorn, "Gustav Mahler at the Wiener Hofoper: A Study of Critical Reception in the Viennese Press (1897–1907), PhD diss., Northwestern University, 1996.

Mosse, George, *Germans and Jews: The Right, The Left, and the Search for a "Third Force" in Pre-Nazi Germany* (New York: H. Fertig, 1970).

Mynona [Salomo Friedlaender], "Der operirte Goj: ein Seitenstück zu Panizzas operirtem Jud'," trans. Jack Zipes in his *The Operated Jew: Two Tales of Antisemitism* (New York: Routledge, 1991), pp. 75–86.

Nietzsche, Friedrich, *Ecce Homo: How One Becomes What One Is*, trans. R.J. Hollingdale (New York: Penguin Books, 1992).

Nordau, Max, *Degeneration*, trans. from 2nd German edn, no trans. given; intro. George L. Mosse (Lincoln and London: University of Nebraska Press, 1993, orig. 1968); 1st German edn, *Entartung* (1892).

Notley, Margaret, "Bruckner and Viennese Wagnerism," in *Bruckner Studies*, ed. Timothy L. Jackson and Paul Hawkshaw (Cambridge: Cambridge University Press, 1997), pp. 54–71.

Notley, Margaret, "Brahms as Liberal: Genre, Style, and Politics in Late Nineteenth Century Vienna," *19th-Century Music* 17 (1993), pp. 107–23.

Notley, Margaret, "Late Nineteenth-century Chamber Music and the Cult of the Classical Adagio," *19th-Century Music* 23 (1999), pp. 33–61.

Notley, Margaret, "Musical Culture in Vienna at the Turn of the Twentieth Century," in *Schoenberg, Berg, and Webern: A Companion to the Second Viennese School*, ed. Bryan R. Simms (Westport, CT: Greenwood Press, 1999), pp. 37–71.

Painter, Karen Lindsley, "The Aesthetics of the Listener: New Conceptions of Musical Meaning, Timbre, and Form in the Early Reception of Mahler's Symphonies 5–7," PhD diss., Columbia University, 1996.

Painter, Karen, "Contested Counterpoint: 'Jewish' Appropriation and Polyphonic Liberation," *Archiv für Musikwissenschaft* 58 (2001), pp. 201–30.

Painter, Karen, ed., *Mahler and his World* (Princeton: Princeton University Press, 2002).

Panizza, Oskar, "Der Operirte Jud'," trans. Jack Zipes in his *The Operated Jew: Two Tales of Anti-Semitism* (New York: Routledge, 1991), pp. 47–74; original story published in Panizza, *Visionen. Skizzen und Erzählungen* (Leipzig: W. Friedrich, 1893).

Paupié, Kurt, *Handbuch der Österreichischen Pressegeschichte 1848–1959* (2 vols, Vienna and Stuttgart: Wilhelm Braumüller, 1960).

Pederson, Sanna, "A.B. Marx, Berlin Concert Life, and German National Identity," *19th-Century Music* 18 (1994), pp. 87–107.

Pederson, Sanna "On the Task of the Music Historian: The Myth of the Symphony after Beethoven," *repercussions*, 2/2 (1993), pp. 5–30.

Perry, Marvin and Fredrick M. Schweitzer, *Antisemitism: Myth and Hate from Antiquity to the Present* (New York et al.: Palgrave Macmillan, 2002).

Perry, Marvin and Frederick M. Schweitzer, *Antisemitic Myths: A Historical and Contemporary Anthology* (Bloomington: Indiana University Press, 2008).

Pfitzner, Hans, *Werk und Wiedergabe,* 2nd edn (Augsberg: Hans Schneider, 1969).

Pickett, David, "A Comparative Survey of Rescorings in Beethoven's Symphonies," *Performing Beethoven*, ed. Robin Stowell (Cambridge: Cambridge University Press, 1994), pp. 205–27.

Pickett, David Anniss, "Gustav Mahler as an Interpreter: A Study of His Textual Alterations and Performance Practice in the Symphonic Repertoire," 3 vols, PhD diss., University of Surrey, 1988.

Pilcz, Alexander, *Beitrag zur Verschiedenen Rassen Psychiatrie* (Leipzig: F. Deuticke, 1906).

Plantinga, Leon, *Schumann as a Critic* (New Haven: Yale University Press, 1967).

Potter, Pamela, "Anti-Semitism in German Musicology, 1900–1945: Theory and Practice," paper read at the 60th Annual Meeting of the American Musicological Society, 28 October 1994, Minneapolis, MN; unpaginated typescript.

Potter, Pamela, *Most German of the Arts: Musicology and Society from the Weimar Republic to the End of Hitler's Reich* (New Haven: Yale University Press, 1998).

Rathenau, Walter, "Höre Israel!" in *Schriften*, 2nd edn (Berlin: Berlin Verlag, 1981), pp. 89–93.

Ritter, William, "Souvenirs sur Gustav Mahler," *Revue Musicale Suisse* 101/1 (Jan.–Feb. 1961), pp. 29–39.

Riz, Elizabeth et al., *Biographische Beiträge zum Musikleben Wiens im 19. und frühen 20. Jahrhundert* (Vienna: VWGÖ, 1992).

Rolland, Romain, "Musique française et musique allemande," in *Musiciens d'aujourd'hui*, 3rd edn (Paris: Hachette et cie, 1908).

Roller, Alfred, *Die Bildnisse von Gustav Mahler* (Leipzig and Vienna: E.P. Tal & Co., 1922).

Rose, Paul Lawrence, *German Question/Jewish Question: Revolutionary Antisemitism from Kant to Wagner* (Princeton: Princeton University Press, 1990).

Rose, Paul Lawrence, *Wagner: Race and Revolution* (New Haven and London: Yale University Press, 1992).

Rosen, Charles, "Influence: Plagiarism and Inspiration," *19th-Century Music* 4 (1980), pp. 87–100.

Schonberg, Harold C., *The Great Conductors* (New York: Simon and Schuster, 1967).

Schorske, Carl E., *Fin-de-Siècle Vienna: Politics and Culture* (New York: Vintage Books, 1981).

Schulze, Hagen, *Der Weg zum Nationalstaat: die deutsche Nationalbewegung vom 18. Jahrhundert bis zur Reichsgründung* (Munich: Deutsche Taschenbuch Verlag, 1985); trans. Sara Hanbury-Tenison as *The Course of German Nationalism: From Fredrick the Great to Bismarck, 1763–1867* (Cambridge: Cambridge University Press, 1991).

Segel, Binjamin W., *A Lie and a Libel: The History of the Protocols of the Elders of Zion*, ed. and trans. Richard S. Levy (Lincoln and Nebraska: University of Nebraska Press, 1995, orig. 1926).

Seligmann, S., *Der Böse Blick und Verwandtes: Ein Beitrag zur Geschichte des Aberglaubens aller Zeiten und Völker* (2 vols, Berlin: H. Barsdorf, 1910–11).

Shain, Milton, *Antisemitism* (London: Bowerdean Publishing Company Limited, 1988).

Showalter, Elaine, *Sexual Anarchy: Gender and Culture at the Fin de Siècle* (New York: Penguin Books, 1990).

Sombart, Werner, *The Jews and Modern Capitalism*, trans. M. Epstein (New York: Franklin, 1969, rpt 1913); orig. German edn, *Die Juden und das Wirtschaftsleben* (Leipzig: Duncker & Humblot, 1911).

Sposato, Jeffrey S., "Creative Writing: The [Self-] Identification of Mendelssohn as Jew," *The Musical Quarterly* 82 (1998), pp. 190–209.

Stefan, Paul, *Das Grab in Wien: eine Chronik 1903–1911* (Berlin: E. Reiss Verlag, 1913).

Stein, Erwin, "Mahler's Re-scorings," in *Orpheus in New Guises* (London: Rockliff, 1953), pp. 25–30.

Strauss, Richard, "Anmerkungen zu Aufführung von Beethovens Symphonien," *Neue Zeitschrift für Musik* 125 (1964), pp. 250–60.

Strauss, Richard, *Recollections and Reflections*, ed. Willi Schuh, trans. L.J. Lawrence (London et al.: Boosey & Hawkes, Ltd., 1953).

Subotnik, Rose Rosengard, "Adorno's Diagnosis of Beethoven's Late Style: Early Symptom of a Fatal Condition," *Journal of the American Musicological Society* 29 (1976), pp. 242–75.

Trachtenberg, Joshua, *The Devil and the Jews: The Medieval Conception of the Jew and its Relation to Modern Anti-Semitism*, 2nd paperback edn (Philadelphia and Jerusalem: Jewish Publication Society, 1983).

Vaget, Hans Rudolf, "*Sang réservé* in Deutschland: Zur Rezeption von Thomas Manns Wälsungenblut," *German Quarterly* 57 (1984), pp. 367–75.

Vergo, Peter, *Art in Vienna, 1898–1918: Klimt, Kokoschka, Schiele, and Their Contemporaries*, 2nd edn (Oxford: Phaidon Press Limited, 1981).

Wagner, Manfred, *Alfred Roller in seiner Zeit* (Salzburg: Rezidenz, 1996).

Wagner, Richard, *Richard Wagner's Prose Works*, trans. William Ashton Ellis (8 vols, New York and London: Broude Bros., 1966, rpt 1894).

Wagner, Richard, *Wagner on Conducting*, trans. Edward Dannreuther (New York: Dover Publications, 1989, rpt 1887).

Walter, Bruno, *Gustav Mahler*, trans. James Galston (London: K. Paul, Trench, Trubner & Co., 1937).

Walter, Marie, "Concerning the Affair Wälsungenblut," *Book Collector* 13 (1964), pp. 463–72.

Warfield, Scott Allan, "The Genesis of Richard Strauss's *Macbeth*," PhD diss., The University of North Carolina at Chapel Hill, 1995.

Was Wir Umbringen: "Die Fakel" von Karl Kraus, ed. Heinz Lunzer et al. (Vienna: Mandelbaum Verlag, 1999).

Wattenbarger, Richard, "A 'Very German Process': The Contexts of Adorno's Strauss Critique," *19th-Century Music* 25 (2002), pp. 313–36.

Weiner, Marc A., *Richard Wagner and the Anti-Semitic Imagination* (Lincoln and London: University of Nebraska Press, 1995).

Weingartner, Felix, *Ratschläge für Aufführungen der Symphonien Beethovens* (Leipzig: Breitkopf & Härtel, 1906).

Weininger, Otto, *Geschlecht und Charakter: Eine prinzipielle Untersuchung* (Vienna: W. Braumüller, 1903; anon. Eng. trans., *Sex and Character* [London: William Heinemann, 1906]).

Werner, Eric, *Mendelssohn: A New Image of the Composer and His Age*, trans. Dika Newlin (New York: Free Press of Glencoe, 1963).

Wilhelm, Kurt, *Richard Strauss Persönlich: Eine Bildbiographie* (Berlin: Henschel, 1999).

Willnauer, Franz, *Gustav Mahler und die Wiener Philharmoniker* (Vienna: Löcker Verlag, 1993).

Wistrich, Robert S., *The Jews of Vienna in the Age of Franz Joseph* (New York and Oxford: Oxford University Press, 1989).

Wyn Jones, David, *Beethoven: Pastoral Symphony* (Cambridge: Cambridge University Press, 1995).

Zweig, Stefan, *The World of Yesterday*, no trans. given (Lincoln: University of Nebraska Press, 1964; orig. New York: Viking Press, 1943).

Index